WITHDRAWN
UTSA LIBRARIES

The Political Economy of State–Business Relations in Europe

The delegation of policy-competencies to the European Union has changed the context in which national actors form their interests and represent them. Shaping European markets and societies, EU regulation has important effects in the member states. This book analyses how business interest organizations respond to this challenge and what strategies they develop to cope with European integration. Starting from the idea that institutional contexts, resource dependencies and organizational characteristics explain, to a considerable degree, how interest groups adapt to EU policy-making, this study delivers important insights into EU governance. The empirical analysis draws on a comprehensive data set of German, British, French and EU business associations and large firms. Divided into three parts, it moves from the study of domestic contexts to the analysis of multilevel governance in the EU before finally scrutinizing in greater detail the factors that shape the access of interest groups to the EU institutions.

Making an important contribution to the development of institutional and organizational accounts of interest groups in the European Union, this book will be of interest to political scientists, economists and sociologists working in the areas of European integration, comparative European politics, political economy, interest groups and civil society.

Rainer Eising is Professor of Comparative Politics at the Ruhr-University Bochum, Germany. He has published widely on EU policy-making, interest intermediation and European governance including most recently *The Politics of Interests in Europe: Lessons from EU Studies and Comparative Politics* and *The Transformation of Governance in the European Union* (also published by Routledge).

Routledge / UACES Contemporary European Studies

Edited by Tanja Börzel, Free University of Berlin, Michelle Cini, University of Bristol and Roger Scully, University of Wales, Aberystwyth, on behalf of the University Association for Contemporary European Studies.

Editorial Board: Grainne De Búrca, European University Institute and Columbia University; Andreas Føllesdal, Norwegian Centre for Human Rights, University of Oslo; Peter Holmes, University of Sussex; Liesbet Hooghe, University of North Carolina at Chapel Hill and Vrije Universiteit Amsterdam; David Phinnemore, Queen's University Belfast; Mark Pollack, Temple University; Ben Rosamond, University of Warwick; Vivien Ann Schmidt, University of Boston; Jo Shaw, University of Edinburgh; Mike Smith, University of Loughborough and Loukas Tsoukalis, ELIAMEP, University of Athens and European University Institute.

The primary objective of the new Contemporary European Studies series is to provide a research outlet for scholars of European Studies from all disciplines. The series publishes important scholarly works and aims to forge for itself an international reputation.

1. **The EU and Conflict Resolution**
   Promoting peace in the backyard
   Nathalie Tocci

2. **Central Banking Governance in the European Union**
   A comparative analysis
   Lucia Quaglia

3. **New Security Issues in Northern Europe**
   The Nordic and Baltic states and the ESDP
   Edited by Clive Archer

4. **The European Union and International Development**
   The politics of foreign aid
   Maurizio Carbone

5. **The End of European Integration**
   Anti-Europeanism examined
   Paul Taylor

6. **The European Union and the Asia-Pacific**
   Media, public and elite perceptions of the EU
   Edited by Natalia Chaban and Martin Holland

7. **The History of the European Union**
   Origins of a trans- and supranational polity 1950–72
   Edited by Wolfram Kaiser, Brigitte Leucht and Morten Rasmussen

8. **International Actors, Democratization and the Rule of Law**
   Anchoring democracy?
   Edited by Amichai Magen and Leonardo Morlino

9. **Minority Nationalist Parties and European Integration**
   A comparative study
   Anwen Elias

10. **European Union Intergovernmental Conferences**
    Domestic preference formation, trans-governmental networks and the dynamics of compromise
    Paul W. Thurner and Franz Urban Pappi

11. **The Political Economy of State–Business Relations in Europe**
    Interest mediation, capitalism and EU policy-making
    Rainer Eising

The Political Economy of State–Business Relations in Europe

Interest mediation, capitalism and EU policy-making

Rainer Eising

LONDON AND NEW YORK

First published 2009
by Routledge
2 Park Square, Milton Park, Abingdon, Oxon OX14 4RN

Simultaneously published in the USA and Canada
by Routledge
270 Madison Ave, New York, NY 10016

Routledge is an imprint of the Taylor & Francis Group, an informa business

© 2009 Rainer Eising

Typeset in Times New Roman by
Book Now Ltd, London
Printed in Great Britain by the
MPG Books Group, Bodmin and King's Lynn

All rights reserved. No part of this book may be reprinted or reproduced or utilized in any form or by any electronic, mechanical, or other means, now known or hereafter invented, including photocopying and recording, or in any information storage or retrieval system, without permission in writing from the publishers.

British Library Cataloguing in Publication Data
A catalogue record for this book is available from the British Library

Library of Congress Cataloging in Publication Data
Eising, Rainer, 1964–
The political economy of state–business relations in Europe: interest mediation, capitalism and EU policy making/Rainer Eising—1st ed.
    p. cm.—(Routledge/UACES contemporary European studies)
Includes bibliographical references and index.
1. Industrial policy—European Union countries. 2. Europe—Economic integration. 3. European Union countries—Economic policy. 4. Business and politics—European Union countries. I. Title.
HD3616.E853E57 2009
338.094—dc22   2008047309

ISBN10: 0–415–46507–9 (hbk)
ISBN10: 0–203–87823–X (ebk)

ISBN13: 978–0–415–46507–6 (hbk)
ISBN13: 978–0–203–87823–1 (ebk)

Contents

List of figures vii
List of tables ix
Preface and acknowledgements xi
List of abbreviations xv

PART I
The theoretical and empirical study of state–business relations in Europe 1

1 Introduction 3

2 Studying interest groups in the European Union: the theoretical terrain 14

3 State–business relations in the EU member states 31

PART II
Multilevel governance and the Europeanization of domestic interest group systems 59

4 The evolution of the EU interest group system: to join or not to join? 61

5 Multilevel governance and business interests in the European Union 86

6 The Europeanization of interest groups and interest intermediation 103

PART III
The access of business interests to the EU institutions   127

7   The politics of access in the European Union I:
     towards elite pluralism?   129

8   The politics of access in the European Union II:
     towards a theory of interest group access   156

9   Conclusion   182

     Appendix: Questionnaire   188
     Notes   203
     References   210
     Index   228

Figures

4.1	European associations according to domain and year of foundation from 1843 to 2001	63
4.2	How important are the following interest organizations on the EU level?	71
4.3	The financial resources of EU associations	81
5.1	Theories of integration: presumed evolution of national and EU interaction patterns with the advance of European integration	89
5.2	Change in the importance of EU institutions and national institutions for the representation of interests since the mid-1980s	93
6.1	Congruence and discongruence – consequences for national interest intermediation	105
6.2	Domestic contacts among state and business	111
6.3	Access to information from domestic political institutions	113
6.4	Timing of interest representation at the domestic level	115
6.5	Contact initiatives at the domestic level	116
6.6	Functions of national associations by cluster	122
6.7	Budget size of associations by cluster	123
7.1	European Union contacts between state and business	147
7.2	Access to information from EU institutions	149
7.3	Timing of interest representation at EU level	151
7.4	Contact initiatives at EU level	153
8.1	Contact probabilities with selected EU institutions	167
8.2	Contact probabilities with European Commission working level, contingent upon budget, political relevance and policy information	170

Tables

1.1	Rate of return of the survey	9
3.1	Modes of interest intermediation and varieties of capitalism in France, Germany and the United Kingdom	32
3.2	Sectoral domain of national business associations	43
3.3	Type of members in national associations	43
3.4	Domain size by associational system and type of organization	44
3.5	Membership density of national associations	45
3.6	Do you cooperate with other organizations to represent your interests?	47
3.7	Cooperation of trade associations with other organizations	48
3.8	Usefulness of organizational cooperation	50
3.9	Financial resources of national associations	52
3.10	Revenue sources of national associations	53
3.11	Functions of national business associations	55
4.1	Membership in EU associations by country	76
4.2	Membership of national interest groups in EU associations – regression analyses	79
4.3	Impact of selective and collective material incentives of EU associations on membership density	83
A4.1	Correlation matrix of variables included in the regression analyses	85
5.1	Test criteria for theories of European integration	92
5.2	Share of business associations and firms maintaining contacts with national and EU institutions	94
5.3	Clusters of interest organizations in the EU multilevel system	96
5.4	Cluster membership of firms, national associations and EU associations	96
5.5	Lobbying cooperation with private organizations by cluster	100

A5.1	Cluster statistics	101
A5.2	Number of contacts with political institutions, level of activity during the policy cycle and access to information by clusters	101
6.1	Cluster membership of large firms and associations by political system	121
6.2	National interest groups by clusters: a) offices in Brussels and b) federation or mixed-membership association	125
7.1	Usefulness of lobbying instruments and importance of criteria for selecting contact partners in the EU	134
7.2	Strategies of interest representation in the EU	136
7.3	Factor scores by form of organization	136
7.4	Expected and empirical ranking of interest organization contacts with EU institutions and national governments	145
8.1	Summary of hypotheses and definitions of variables	163
8.2	Access of business associations to EU institutions	164
8.3	Ordered logit regressions	166
8.4	Impact of independent variables on the probability of having weekly contacts with EU Institutions	169
A8.1	Access to EU institutions by country	178
A8.2	Descriptive statistics by country	179
A8.3	Rank correlations among national and EU-level contacts	180
A8.4	Frequency of contact initiatives between EU institutions and business associations	181
A8.5	Contact initiatives with interest organizations by EU institutions: ordered logit regressions	181

Preface and acknowledgements

'Let's do a survey on interest groups in the EU!' This innocuous proposal was the beginning of this book. It seemed like a really good idea when Beate Kohler-Koch and I discussed it in 1998. I did not know then that this project would accompany me for the decade to come. We had just put *The transformation of governance in the European Union* together, and I was about to complete my PhD-dissertation on the liberalization of the EU energy markets. Doing a survey on interest groups that focused on the transformation of interest representation in European governance seemed like a nice little project on the side. We decided to go ahead and Christine Quittkat joined our plans at the Mannheim Centre for European Social Research. With the support of our research assistants, we completed the mailing of the survey and the data entry in early 1999. After having completed my PhD in Mannheim, I moved to the Martin-Luther-University Halle-Wittenberg where Arthur Benz had offered me a position as Assistant Professor. I am very grateful that he also encouraged my plans to spend the academic year 1999/2000 as a Jean-Monnet-Fellow at the European University Institute in Florence.

Returning to Germany in the following summer, I joined Arthur Benz and his new team at the FernUniversity in Hagen to teach German Politics and Governance. In the meantime, I had taken some inroads into the survey data and found that they had more to offer than distraction. Despite our experiences in various summer schools on quantitative methods, Christine Quittkat based her PhD-dissertation on this survey, focusing on its Franco-German dimension, and I decided to write my habilitation thesis on the basis of these data. Hagen proved to be a very collegial and stimulating scientific environment for this endeavour, and the Faculty of Cultural and Social Sciences accepted the habilitation thesis in September 2006. Thereafter, I took on a position as Associate Professor for European Politics at the Friedrich-Schiller-University Jena. From there, I moved to the Ruhr-University-Bochum accepting the Chair for Comparative Politics and Policy Analysis in October 2007.

Hence, this book has had a long gestation period and it presents a substantially revised version of my habilitation. I could never have written this study without the help of many people and the support of several institutions. My greatest personal and professional debt is to Beate Kohler-Koch whose suggestions and comments have been invaluable in shaping the direction of my research, and to Arthur

Benz who provided generous guidance when I worked on this project. In the past years, I have benefited greatly from the friendly intellectual exchange with Jan Beyers and William Maloney in our joint work on interest group politics in the European Union (and elsewhere). I am also very grateful to the advisors and reviewers of my habilitation thesis: apart from Arthur Benz, Susanne Lütz and Gary Marks provided much support and helpful criticism. Finally, I am obliged for the financial support of the project to the European Centre for Public Affairs and to the University of Mannheim.

I profited greatly from presenting parts of this book in faculty meetings in Hagen, in a workshop with the European Forum fellows at the European University Institute, in panels at the European Union Studies Association Conferences in Nashville and Austin as well as at the European Consortium for Political Research General Conference in Budapest, in an Economic and Social Research Council workshop at the University of Newcastle, in various workshops of the EU network of excellence CONNEX (Connecting Excellence on European Governance), in a British Academy workshop in London, and in a seminar at ARENA, the Centre for European Studies in Oslo.

I am indebted to a number of colleagues who contributed important ideas, suggestions, and criticisms at various stages during the completion of this project. In particular, I would like to thank Katrin Auel, Stefano Bartolini, Nathalie Behnke, Gwendolyn Bunse, Lars-Eric Cederman, David Coen, Maria Green Cowles, Kenneth Dyson, Michelle Cini, Klaus H. Goetz, Sonja Lehringer, Andrea Lenschow, David Lowery, Johan P. Olsen, Simona Piatoni, Salvatore Pitruzello, Thomas Risse, Sabine Saurugger, Philippe C. Schmitter, Gerald Schneider, Bo Strath, Ulf Sverdrup, Sid Tarrow, Gunnar Trumbull and Tony Zito for their helpful comments and suggestions. Joachim Behnke, Bernhard Boll, Richard Breen and Ulrich Kohler gave helpful advice on different aspects of the data analysis. The commentaries of the three anonymous reviewers were very useful when revising the manuscript for publication. During the final revisions and the completion of the manuscript I benefited very much from the support of Angelika Hüpen, Svenja Neumann and Jonas Zimmermann.

While the book includes some chapters that are based on previously published articles, these have been modified in accordance with its core argument that institutional contexts, resource dependencies and organizational characteristics need to be taken into account when explaining interest representation in the EU multi-level setting.

Chapter 2 includes material previously published in 'Interest groups in EU policy-making', *Living Review in European Governance* 3(4) (2008), www.livingreviews.org/lreg-2008-4, reprinted with friendly permission from the Publisher of the Living Reviews in European Governance.

Chapter 5 is a revised version of 'Multi-level Governance and Business Interests in the European Union', *Governance: An International Journal of Policy, Administration and Institutions* 17(2): 211–45 (2004), reprinted with friendly permission from Blackwell Publishers.

Chapter 6 draws on some arguments made in 'Interest Groups and Social Movements', in Paolo Graziano and Maarten Vink (eds), *Europeanization. New Research Agendas*, Basingstoke: Palgrave Macmillan 2007, 167–81, reprinted with friendly permission from Macmillan Publishers Limited.

Chapter 7 modifies the discussion in 'The Access of Business Interests to EU Institutions: Towards Elite Pluralism?', *Journal of European Public Policy* 14(3): 384–403 (2007), reprinted with friendly permission from Taylor & Francis.

Chapter 8 is a revised version of 'Institutional Context, Organizational Resources and Strategic Choices: Explaining Interest Group Access in the European Union', *European Union Politics* 8(3): 329–62 (2007), reprinted with friendly permission from SAGE Publications.

Abbreviations

ANOVA	Analysis of variance
BDI	Federation of German Industry (Bundesverband der Deutschen Industrie)
BEUC	European Consumers' Organization (Bureau Européen des Unions de Consommateurs)
BIAs	business interest associations
CBI	Confederation of British Industry
CEEP	European Centre of Enterprises with Public Participation and of Enterprises of General Economic Interest
CEFIC	European chemical industry council
CEO	Chief Executive Officer
CFSP	common foreign and security policy
COFACE	committee of family organizations in the European Union
CONECCS	Consultation, the European Commission and Civil Society
CoR	Committee of the Regions
Coreper	Committee of Permanent Representatives
df	degrees of freedom
DG	Directorate-General
DTI	Department of Trade and Industry
EC	European Community
ECJ	European Court of Justice
ECSC	European Community for Steel and Coal
EEB	European Environmental Bureau
EEC	European Economic Community
EFPIA	European Federation of Pharmaceutical Industries and Associations
EICTA	European Information, Communications and Consumer Electronics Technology Industry Association
EIF	European Industry Federation
EMU	Economic and Monetary Union
EP	European Parliament
ESC	Economic and Social Committee
ESPRIT	European Strategic Programme for Research and Development in Information Technology

ETUC	European Trade Union Confederation
EU	European Union
EurActiv	European Public Affairs Directory
EURATOM	European Atomic Energy Community
EURELECTRIC	European Grouping of the Electricity Supply Industry
EURO COOP	European Community of Consumer Cooperatives
EUROLOB	Survey on lobbying in the European Union
GDP	Gross Domestic Product
GEODE	European group of energy distribution companies and organizations
IMP	Internal Market Programme
LME	liberal market economy
MEP	Member of the European Parliament
MLG	multilevel governance
NGO	non-governmental organization
OECD	Organization for Economic Cooperation and Development
OEEC	Organization for European Economic Cooperation
SEA	Single European Act
SMEs	Small and Medium Sized Enterprises
se	standard error
ss	sum of squares
TABD	Transatlantic Business Dialogue
TAF	Trade Association Forum
UK	United Kingdom
UNICE	Union of Industrial and Employers' Confederations of Europe
UNIPEDE	Union Internationale des Producteurs et Distributeurs d'Energie Electrique

Part I
The theoretical and empirical study of state–business relations in Europe

1   Introduction

European integration has prompted a large number of societal and economic interest organizations to promote their cases before the European Union (EU) institutions. These organizations transport socio-economic interests onto the EU level, are sources of information to the EU institutions, exert influence on the EU policy-process, cooperate in the implementation of EU policies and deliver their members' compliance with European decisions, to name only a few of their important functions. The EU institutions have long recognized the relevance of interest groups. They have accorded to the cross-sectoral European employer associations and trade unions the status of social partners in the social dialogue. In other policy areas, they have established expert committees in which interest organizations routinely represent their members and domains. The Lisbon treaty further strengthens the role of interest groups and civil society in EU decision-making by introducing provisions for a participatory democracy at EU level.

Interest organizations seem particularly important to EU politics because the European Union lacks some channels of representative democracy that are crucial in its member states when tying state institutions to citizen preferences. The use of concepts such as associative democracy or participatory democracy in the analysis of EU politics signals that interest groups might help to fill a void that political parties leave in the EU, linking the EU institutions closer to the citizens of the union. Partly due to the transformation of the European nation state, the importance of electoral and party politics appears to be in decline (Bartolini 2005; Balme and Chabanet 2008) and the 'authoritative allocation of values' seems to migrate into policy networks (van Waarden 1992; Falkner 2000) and negotiation systems (Mayntz and Scharpf 1995) in which interest groups assume prominent positions. However, despite the important political role that is ascribed to them and despite numerous empirical studies, our knowledge of interest organizations in the EU is limited (see also Beyers, Eising and Maloney 2008). There are notable gaps in the study of EU interest representation and several scholars have arrived at different conclusions regarding the role of interest groups in EU politics (see Chapter 2).

Empirical and theoretical scope of the book

Against this background, this study seeks to enhance our knowledge by describing and explaining the adaptation of domestic interest organizations to the EU multilevel system. European integration and globalization, especially during the two decades which followed the end of the Cold War, correspond with an increase in the transnational flows of capital, goods and information, and confront the nation state with new trans-border challenges. Contemporary governance features a growing importance of non-governmental actors and a rise of transnational networks straddling frontiers and levels of governance. This has tremendous consequences for how interests organize and how views of citizens are represented by, through, and within interest organizations. While the coincidence of boundaries in the past led to nation state institutionalization of interest representation, contemporary de-bordering leads to its reconfiguration in the EU multilevel setting.

As a result of these changes, it is now common to claim that interest groups need to follow a 'dual strategy' (Mazey and Richardson 2002; Kohler-Koch 1997) and must represent their interests both in the member states and at the EU level in order to exert influence on EU policies. Some studies have identified groups that pursue such multilevel strategies and others suggest that the EU provides exit options to domestic actors that can lead to major realignments in national systems of interest representation (see Bartolini 2005: 304–8). But, so far, we know surprisingly little about several important issues linked to this institutional transformation: To what extent is this course of action pursued? Which groups pursue it? Under what conditions do they employ it? And what are the effects on domestic interest group systems? Attempting to answer these questions, I seek to advance our knowledge about the adaptation of national interest groups to the European Union and our insights into how multilevel governance operates in the EU. While there is a burgeoning Europeanization literature that investigates the impact of the EU on domestic political systems and in the international arena since the 1990s (Kohler-Koch and Eising 1999; Goetz and Hix 2000; Cowles, Caporaso and Risse 2001; Héritier *et al.* 2001; Schmidt 2002, 2006; Dyson and Goetz 2003; Graziano and Vink 2007), there have only been few studies on how interest groups responded to the integration process.

Before outlining in more detail the basic ideas and arguments to come, it is necessary to clarify what I mean by the term interest organization. In this study, I use the terms interest organization and interest group interchangeably. In essence, three factors define the terms (see Beyers *et al.* 2008): *organization, political interests* and *informality*. *Organization* relates to the nature of the group and excludes broad movements and waves of public opinion that may influence policy outcomes as interest groups. Interest group politics concerns aggregated individuals and organized forms of political behaviour. *Political interests* refers to the attempts these organizations make to influence policy outcomes. This aspect is often called *political advocacy*, which refers to all efforts to push public policy in a specific direction on the behalf of constituencies or a general political idea. *Informality* relates to the fact that interest groups do not normally seek public office or compete in elections, but pursue their goals through frequent informal interactions with politicians and bureaucrats. This, however, does not rule out that important facets of state–group relations in capitalist democracies can be heavily institutionalized. Not all interest organizations are permanently involved in politics, for some political activities are more sporadic and ephemeral. Note also that not all interest organizations are groups *strictu senso*. Some interest group scholars consider institutions such as hospitals, universities, firms or local governments to be interest groups or interest organizations (see Gray and Lowery 2000). These institutions show some level of organization, they exhibit policy preferences and their capacity to mobilize resources makes them potentially powerful. Accordingly, it makes sense to conceive of them as interest organizations that are equivalent to interest groups, although they are not aggregating (or grouping) the preferences of some constituency.

This book is based on the idea that *institutional contexts, resource dependencies* and *organizational characteristics* explain, to a considerable degree, how interest groups adapt to EU policy-making. Institutional theory stresses that *institutions* structure political, social and economic processes. They do not fully determine the outcomes but they set the rules of the game, endow the actors with resources, define their roles and channel their perceptions, interests and behaviour, both by providing opportunities and setting constraints (Hall and Taylor 1996; March and Olsen 1989; Steinmo, Thelen and Longstreth 1992). As a result, the actors make choices depending on their expectations of how these rules and structures affect the outcomes they desire (see also Czada 1991: 259). An institutional perspective places the emphasis on the structured relations, the enduring division of labour, and the rules of the game that emerge within the EU institutional context because these affect the strategic choices and the political behaviour of the actors.

Resource dependence theory complements this perspective. According to this approach, the EU and the national institutional contexts are important for understanding what decisions interest organizations take. The EU institutions and these organizations are interdependent: neither of them controls 'all the conditions necessary for the achievement of an action or for obtaining the outcome desired from the action' (Pfeffer and Salancik 2003: 40). On the one hand, EU institutions depend on business interests to ensure the flow of policy information, the cooperation and the political support that are necessary to formulate policies that solve problems and find acceptance. On the other hand, business interests depend on their access to EU policy-makers to receive information about and exert influence on EU policies because state actors have some degree of autonomy when designing these policies. Accordingly, I seek to identify the strategic actions in which these organizations engage to obtain support from their institutional environment.

Finally, I argue that *organizational characteristics* are important determinants of the responses of business interests to the European Union. In that respect I distinguish among large firms, national associations, and EU associations because these different forms of organization are in control of different exchange goods and are placed at different locations in the EU multilevel system. Regarding business interest associations, I also analyse the impact of organizational domains and resources on their choice of organizational strategies and their political behaviour in the EU multilevel setting.

Throughout, the analytical method consists in the development of explicit concepts and categories that shed light on the adaptation of domestic groups to the EU as well as in the empirical test of explanatory causal hypotheses. Each chapter tests competing theoretical propositions to support, modify or disconfirm long-standing conjectures about interest group activity in the European Union. The aim is to generate mid-level generalizations about the role business interests play in EU policy-making, the patterns of interest intermediation in the European Union, and the EU impact on domestic interest representation.

The following chapters develop these ideas more fully and outline in detail the domestic institutional contexts in France, Germany and the United Kingdom. Focusing on interest organizations from these countries holds important background factors constant while important elements of the institutional contexts vary. These nations have different varieties of capitalism and modes of interest intermediation. France is grouped among the Mediterranean market economies and has a statist regime of interest intermediation, the United Kingdom (UK) is held to be a liberal market economy with pluralistic traits, and Germany falls into the camp of coordinated market economies and is characterized by corporatism. The empirical analysis demonstrates that the associational settings display distinct national traits but that these cross-national differences are far less noticeable than is often asserted.

Having placed the interest organizations in their domestic contexts, I describe and explain how they have adapted to the European multilevel system. I start by characterizing the EU interest group system and by examining why national interest organizations join EU associations given that they specialize in representing their members' interests. In this respect, I test two competing explanations that centre on contextual factors and organizational features. I compare the importance of domestic political contexts and socio-economic dynamics, on the one hand, to the relevance of the organizational incentives that EU business associations offer their potential members on the other hand. Politico-economic structures and modes of interest intermediation seem to explain the overall membership pattern rather well, whereas the selective material incentives of EU associations say little about how many of their potential members join them. This finding alludes to the importance of domestic institutional contexts for political behaviour and calls into question the Olsonian logic of collective action.

Thereafter, I move beyond the analysis of the formal membership patterns of EU associations, discussing at what levels of government and at what stages of the EU policy cycle interest organizations represent their interests in the EU multilevel system. Drawing on European integration theories, I test three different hypotheses about the impact of the EU institutional context on interest representation. In brief, liberal intergovernmentalism suggests that interest groups remain embedded in domestic institutional contexts, neofunctionalism posits their move to the EU level and multilevel governance claims that domestic interest groups become vocal at both the EU level and in the member states. The findings indicate that the multilevel governance approach captures the responses of interest groups best. Nonetheless, it is important to note that only a minority of national organizations have evolved into multilevel players who represent their interests routinely at both the EU level and in the member states. The majority of national interest groups remains rooted in domestic contexts and depends on other actors – European associations, national interest groups that act as multilevel players or national governments – to support their cases vis-à-vis the EU institutions. Accordingly, their positions in the multilevel setting and the division of labour within domestic interest group systems condition the responses of interest groups to European integration.

Then, I analyse the impact of the EU on domestic interest organizations and modes of interest intermediation in more detail, scrutinizing three different explanations for the adaptation of domestic groups to the EU: the degree of fit between the EU and national systems, organizational negotiation capacities, and the material resources of interest organizations. These results call into question the core hypothesis that has emerged in the Europeanization literature, namely, that the degree of fit between the EU and domestic settings matters most for the adaptation of domestic actors to the European Union. Rather, organizational resources and negotiation capacities impact more profoundly on the response pattern to European integration. All in all, I find that adaptation to the EU context leads to extensions and some modifications of established practices rather than a fully fledged transformation of domestic interest group systems.

Having so far focused on the vertical set-up of the EU multilevel system, I then seek to develop a comprehensive explanation of interest group access to the European Union institutions – the Council of the EU, the European Parliament and the European Commission. This explanation of the political exchanges between state and business takes into account the domestic contexts of the interest groups, their organizational structures, exchange goods and strategies. The analysis moves beyond the argument that the exchange of information is most critical for interactions among EU institutions and interest groups (Bouwen 2002a, 2002b; Crombez 2002). In a first step, I seek to explore the access of different forms of interest organization to EU institutions, identifying significant differences in the access of firms and associations. Nonetheless, the evidence qualifies the often-made assertion that large firms have invariably better access than EU business associations to EU institutions. In a second step, I deepen the access analysis, focusing on business associations. The outcome supports the idea that institutional contexts, organizational structures, resources and strategies must be taken into account when explaining the access of interest groups to EU institutions. The results highlight important general features that mark EU interest representation. These are the division of labour among EU and national associations; organizational resources such as money, information and economic clout; and the extent of EU political regulation that affects the interest groups and their members. The findings also point out the contingencies emanating from the EU institutional context such as varying consultation criteria of the EU institutions.

The remainder of the introduction presents the data and the methods of the study in more detail. Thereafter, the plan of the book is outlined.

Data, cases and methods

The empirical analysis is based on an original data set (EUROLOB – Lobbying in the European Union) covering 800 business associations in Germany, France, the United Kingdom and at the EU level, as well as on 34 large firms from these three large member states. In some chapters, complementary evidence is drawn from the CONECCS database (Consultation, the European Commission and Civil Society) of the European Commission. CONECCS covers EU-level interest groups and allows extension of the comparison to the EU-15.[1] In the EUROLOB survey, the interest organizations provided information on:

- their contacts and relations with national and EU political institutions;
- their activities during different phases of the policy-making process;
- their links and relations with other interest groups;
- their organizational characteristics; and
- the features of the economic sector in which they operate.

The questionnaire used in gathering the EUROLOB data is printed in the appendix to this book. The empirical scope of the project is larger than that of many other studies about interest groups in the EU to achieve more robust analytical results than case studies can deliver. This study combines Lijphart's comparable cases research strategy (1975) with statistical methods. Important context variables are controlled by focusing on *specific types of interest organization*. The emphasis is placed on business interest associations and large firms. Furthermore, these actors are located in *member states with several common features*. The study is targeted at testing theoretically derived explanations rather than at manufacturing fancy hypotheses even though, in that respect, the differences between quantitative and qualitative studies should not be overdrawn. The cross-sectional analysis is based on a survey that was conducted between June 1998 and March 1999 and gives an account of the adaptation of interest groups to the European Union at the turn of the millennium.[2] Major institutional reforms of the EU – the Single European Act, the Maastricht Treaty and the Amsterdam Treaty – had been decided and implemented before this survey was completed so that many interest organizations in the three long-standing EU member states had at that moment already responded to European integration in one way or another. Accordingly, the survey covers the responses of these national interest organizations after long years of experience with European politics.

The EUROLOB survey focuses on two classes of actor. It was addressed to 1,998 German, French, British and EU *business associations* asking them to specify their patterns of interest intermediation. In addition, 68 *large firms* in these countries have been questioned. The study is not limited to a specific economic sector like so many other studies of interest groups in the EU but is cross-sectoral: Economic sectors from agriculture, industry and services are included. None of the sectors dominates the sample. The largest branch is trade with a share of 13.8 per cent of all associations. Owing to its large size and broad sectoral coverage, the analysis should give a good indication of the cumulative responses of business interests to European integration after almost 50 years of the integration process. But note that no time-series data are available (yet) on this topic and that only few questions in the questionnaire cover the time dimension. Overall, 834 responses

Table 1.1 Rate of return of the survey

	EU associations	German associations	British associations	French associations	Multinational firms	Total
Trade associations addressed	420	727	501	350	68	2,066
Questionnaires returned	185	322	206	113	34	860
Questionnaires excluding international associations	162	321	204	113	34	834
Rate of return excluding international associations	40.8	44.2	40.9	32.3	50.0	40.9

were received (see Table 1.1). Twenty-six of the respondents were identified as international associations and omitted from the analysis so that the effective rate of return amounts to 40.9 per cent. The return rates for the different sub-groups range from 32.3 per cent in the case of the French associations to 50.0 per cent in the case of the large firms.[3] Although providing a reasonable rate of return on which inferences can be based, the sample might disproportionately cover those organizations that are affected by EU regulation and have the capacity to deal with EU institutions. The analysis of the non-responses indicates that more than 60 per cent of the non-respondents did not answer because of a lack of staff.[4] Another 15 per cent are not politically active at EU level; that is, they don't have contacts with EU institutions. Finally, some 22 per cent of the associations do not generally respond to surveys. I did not correct this by statistical weights because the structure of the European business interest group population is not well known.

The study concentrates on business interest organizations as units of observation to control for some organizational features. I have excluded the political activities of individuals, social movements and public interest groups because their logic of action differs from that of business interest groups (for general discussions, see Olson 1965; Offe and Wiesenthal 1985). Social movements and public interest groups thrive to a greater extent on normative values than business interest organizations which seek to realize material gains for their member firms (Offe 1995). When targeting EU policy, social movements tend to address national and regional political authorities rather than EU institutions because it is notoriously difficult for them to engage in cross-border protests and media events (Balme, Chabanet and Wright 2002; Balme and Chabanet 2008; Imig and Tarrow 2001b, 2001c; Rucht 2002). To represent their causes at the sites of the

EU institutions, they tend to rely on their European interest organizations. In contrast to these informal alliances, firms and business associations have clearly delineated domains, memberships, operational rules and role definitions. The representation of interests by these organizations can be expected to be more durable than that by individuals or informal movements. In sum, this study focuses on formal organizations that are more likely to act on the basis of material interests and economic rationality than the other interest groups. Moreover, their organizational properties do not hinder them as much as social movement organizations to take political action in Brussels.

Focusing on business associations means also that the analysis covers the largest family of interest organizations at the EU level: 79.9 per cent compared to only little more than 20 per cent that are non-economic interest organizations (Commission General Secretariat 2002). In addition, the 34 large British, German or French firms included in the analysis represent the approximately 250 firms that have opened offices in Brussels to represent their interests vis-à-vis the EU institutions. They serve as a contrast group to investigate whether the political activities of these resourceful corporate actors deviate significantly from those of business associations.

The focus on three large member states of the EU – France, Germany and the United Kingdom – controls some country-specific factors such as population size, level of economic and technical development, the economic weight of these countries in the EU, their formal decision-making rights in EU politics and their long duration of EU membership. The three countries differ from other EU member states in several respects: They are the largest; they are founding (France, Germany) or long standing (United Kingdom) members of the European institutions; and they belong to the group of established liberal democracies and economically advanced member states. As the largest member states, they have a great number of interest organizations that cover a broad spectrum of interests, whereas smaller member states have fewer interest organizations that may cover a narrower range of interests. These countries have greater formal decision-making rights (in qualified majority decisions) and tend to have greater political clout in EU decision-making than the smaller member states. As a result, interest organizations from these countries may be more inclined to rely on their governments as representatives for their interests than organizations from other member states. However, the reliance of domestic interest organizations can also hinge upon other factors such as the national coordination of EU policy (Kassim, Peters and Wright 2000), the socialization of the associations in the EU and their standing in domestic politics (see also Chapters 6 and 8).

German, French and British interest groups have been socialized into European politics for a long time so that they should be used to integrating EU institutions into their strategies of interest representation. As a result, they may find it easier to act within the EU multilevel system than interest groups from the new Eastern and Southern European member states or from the Northern member states that joined the EU only in the mid-1990s. Being situated in economically advanced member states, the composition of and the resources available within the German, British and French interest group populations may differ also to some extent from that of the worse-off Southern or Eastern European member states. Note also that the latter have interest group systems that have only relatively recently come into being, making for a relatively weak civil society and business interest group infrastructure in these countries (Wiesenthal 1996; Borragán 2003). Hence, the ability of the Eastern European groups to act in EU politics seems more constrained than that of the Western European groups whereas their susceptibility to EU influences may be greater. The implications of this will be analysed in more detail in Chapters 4, 5 and 6.

Evidently, it would be desirable to include associations from all EU member states and some non-member states as control variables in the analysis. But this would require a research team in all of these states, for which resources did not allow. Due to pragmatic limitation, the findings presented here cannot be easily translated into the contexts of the Southern member states (Portugal, Spain and Greece) whose economic structures diverge somewhat, or into the contexts of those member states that entered the European Union only in 1995 (Sweden, Finland, Austria) because these were only later exposed to the full influence of the European Union. This holds all the more for the recent accession countries of the Eastern enlargement whose economic structures still diverge profoundly from those of the large EU member states and whose interest organizations have only evolved during the political transformation of these states into liberal democratic systems.

Notwithstanding these similarities, important variations remain among the three countries, which allows for assessing the importance of domestic political structures, modes of interest intermediation, and varieties of capitalism for the representation of interests in the European Union. The political structures of the three countries diverge in several respects (see Chapter 3). It is common to include France and the UK among the 'strong states' (Atkinson and Coleman 1989) because their centralized political structures grant state institutions great capacities to define and implement policies relatively autonomously. In contrast, Peter Katzenstein (1987) has drawn attention to the 'semi-sovereignty' of the German state. Hence, if centralized and decentralized political structures have an impact on EU interest representation, there should be significant differences between the German associations and firms, on the one hand, and the British and French interest organizations, on the other. Moreover, the national modes of interest intermediation in these countries are said to vary significantly. Germany is usually considered among the countries with a corporatist tradition of intermediation (Streeck 1999, Voelzkow 2000), France is held to be statist (Schmidt 1996) and the UK is often included among the pluralistic EU member states (G. K. Wilson 1990). Finally, these countries display different varieties of capitalism (Hall and Soskice 2001a, 2001b) that affect the role of business interest organizations as coordination devices in the economy: France is said to fall in the camp of 'Mediterranean' capitalism; Germany is held to be a 'coordinated market economy'; and the UK falls among the 'liberal market economies'. Accordingly, we should witness significant differences among the French, German and British associations when it comes to representing interests in the European arena and coordinating activities in domestic markets.

Plan of the book

The book is organized in three main parts. First, this introduction and the following two chapters give an overview of the research questions, the basic concepts, the theoretical approach and the national systems of interest intermediation. In Chapter 2, I review the literature on interest groups in the EU and outline the resource dependency perspective in more detail. I also discuss the options that firms have to represent their political interests, ranging from individual lobbying to various forms of collective action and hiring political consultants. Drawing on institutional theory, in Chapter 3 I analyse the domestic contexts in which French, German and British business interest organizations are placed. Based on the EUROLOB data, the argument is that studies on the national varieties of capitalism and modes of interest intermediation are in need of being fine-tuned even if some national differences remain.

Part II of the book concentrates on the adaptation of national interest organizations to the evolving structure of multilevel governance in the European Union. In Chapter 4, I describe the evolution and the structure of the EU interest group system and discuss the reasons why national interest organizations join EU-level groups. I consider both contextual factors and organizational incentives to explain the decision to join. Chapter 5 discusses the shape of interest representation in the EU multilevel system. Testing competing propositions about the allocation of political competencies in the multilevel system – centralized, decentralized and federalized – I develop an empirical typology of interest organizations according to their activities in the multilevel system: niche organizations, occasional players, national players, EU players and multilevel players. According to the composition of these types, interest representation in the EU approximates a federalized structure of multilevel governance. In Chapter 6, I look in more detail into the EU impact on domestic interest organizations and interest intermediation. I put three hypotheses to the test that seek to explain how interest groups adapt to the EU: the degree of fit, the negotiation capacities of interest organizations and their material resources. The findings suggest that the negotiation capacities and material resources of the groups may be more important for their adaptation to EU politics than the degree of fit between domestic and EU modes of interest intermediation.

Part III of the book focuses on those factors that explain the access of interest organizations to EU political institutions. It integrates institutional contexts, organizational structures and strategies as well as resource dependencies among public institutions and private actors in a theoretical explanation of interest group access to the EU institutions. In Chapter 7, I test the proposition that the access of different forms of organizations – EU associations, national associations and large firms – varies systematically, giving rise to biased interest representation and a form of elite pluralism in the EU. Even though this analysis yields significantly different access patterns for the different forms of organization it does not necessarily support the conjecture that elite pluralism marks the EU. In Chapter 8, I deepen this analysis focusing on national and EU business associations. This analysis brings together several elements of this book and controls for the impact of various contextual factors, exchange goods and organizational features. The outcomes support the argument that institutional contexts as well as organizational structures, resources and strategies must be taken into account when explaining the access of interest groups to EU institutions. They highlight both important general features that mark EU interest representation and variations that are due to the segmented institutional context. The conclusion summarizes and evaluates the findings.

2 Studying interest groups in the European Union
The theoretical terrain

There is a plethora of studies on interest groups in the European Union that have generated a wealth of insights. These analyses demonstrate quite well why national groups join in the circuit of EU collective action and what strategic options are generally open to them, but they also have notable gaps, have brought about some areas of controversy and display some contradictions in their findings.[1] Even though political scientists have long discussed the roles and functions of interest groups in the EU polity, their attention has been discontinuous and focused on different aspects of EU interest intermediation. I argue that five factors account for this state of the art in EU interest group research: the complexity of the subject matter itself; different conceptual and theoretical perspectives, the changing nature of the European polity, the focus on specific units of observation and a methodological preference for case studies. After this review of the literature on interest groups in the EU, I lay down the essential resource dependency perspective on state–business relations that informs this study.

The large size of the interest group population and the manifold differences between the groups (see Chapter 3 for details) pose significant problems when we move to empirical analyses. In this respect, we encounter a substantial difference between the study of political parties and interest groups. The former can be modelled as being principally concerned with electoral politics, public office or public policy. The activities and strategies of interest groups are much more diverse and diffuse. While political parties have a rather general policy agenda that covers many issues, many interest groups specialize in a small number of policy areas. Accordingly, it is difficult to draw general conclusions concerning their organizational structures, functions, strategies or influence. Most of the time, findings are restricted to particular types of group and to specific policy areas or issues.

This goes hand in hand with a broad range of conceptual and theoretical traditions from which interest groups are studied and that have led to rather different and demarcated perspectives on them. EU interest group research has moved from theoretical perspectives that were derived from international relations and comparative politics approaches, towards modes of analysis that are rooted in policy studies, normative approaches of associative and deliberative democracy and approaches focusing on multilevel governance and the Europeanization of interest groups. While highlighting the many facets of interest groups, the sheer variety of perspectives can impede the accumulation of knowledge about interest groups. A brief review of the major theoretical perspectives illustrates that proposition.

Until the 1980s, two international relations approaches – neofunctionalism and intergovernmentalism – dominated the study of European integration. Both consider the impact of interest organizations on the integration process but offer different theoretical lenses on their political role. Neofunctionalists (Haas 1958) were the first to study the role of interest organizations in the European Community (EC). Their main research interest was in the changing nature of international relations after the Second World War and the build-up of a supranational political organization (Kohler-Koch 1992). To them, business associations and trade unions were among the driving forces of European integration.[2] They appreciated the engagement of economic interest organizations in European institutions because they expected them to contribute not only to the deepening of European integration and the peaceful resolution of conflicts but also to an increase in economic welfare throughout the EC. During the set-back of the integration process in the 1960s and 1970s these questions lost in relevance while others gained in prominence. Continued member state resistance to important integration measures led Stanley Hoffman (1966) to an intergovernmental account of European integration and Ernst Haas (1975) to question the usefulness of regional integration theory altogether.

Only the revival of European integration in the mid-1980s started a new search for the leading actors of this transformation. Whereas authors in the neofunctional tradition (Sandholtz and Zysman 1989) emphasized once more the contribution of business interests to this transformation, scholars rooted in the intergovernmental tradition of international politics viewed the integration process as the outcome of bargaining processes among the large member states. They maintained that interest groups did not have a great say in major policy decisions and, in any case, represent their interests only to their national governments, who act as gatekeepers to the EU (Moravcsik 1998). Hence, the influence that interest groups wield on EU policy-making is sometimes contested on grounds of theoretical assumptions rather than empirical evidence.

Scholars rooted in the comparative politics tradition discovered the emerging political system of the European Community only in the 1970s. They were mostly interested in how interest intermediation in the EC operated and what role associations played in EC decision-making (Meynaud and Sidjanski 1971; Schwaiger and Kirchner 1981). This change in the analytical perspective also introduced new normative standards for judging the role of interest groups in the EC. Whereas neofunctionalists had viewed group activities favourably, some comparative politics scholars branded the pursuit of narrow-minded group interests and highlighted the dangers of a biased representation of interests. Based on the critical debate of the American group approach from the late 1960s onwards, James Caporaso criticized the pursuit of narrow-minded self-interests, claiming that interest groups would endanger the legitimacy of the European institutions and the integration process (Caporaso 1974: 180).

Later, the emphasis shifted to the patterns of interest intermediation and the conditions of collective action in the EC (Averyt 1975, 1977). The dependence of EC level interest intermediation on national interest group systems came as much into focus as the new options the EU institutions entailed for national interest groups (Burkhardt-Reich and Schumann 1983; Kohler-Koch *et al.* 1988). In that respect, several authors arrived at the conclusion that the European institutional setting promoted informal, sectoral and pluralistic patterns of interest intermediation rather than formal, cross-sectoral and corporatist patterns (Averyt 1975; Schmitter and Streeck 1991). Following this line of reasoning, some form of pluralism is held to be characteristic of EU interest intermediation (Coen 1998; Schmidt 1999; Cowles 2001). However, even this assessment is not without its critics. Other studies found more institutionalized and quasi-corporatist patterns of interest intermediation (Andersen and Eliassen 1991: 175; Falkner 1998; Mazey and Richardson 2002: 124).

Such variations can be traced to the pronounced institutional segmentation of the EU and the autonomy of its functional domains that will be explored in Chapters 7 and 8. Authors highlighting the segmentation of EU institutions find it impossible to identify cross-sectoral patterns of interest intermediation. Instead, they suggest that the EU patterns are specific to sectors, policies or even issues (Greenwood and Ronit 1994; Falkner 2000; Baltz, König and Schneider 2005). Following this logic, since the 1980s, policy studies have enriched empirical research on interest groups in the European Community. While mostly seeking to describe or explain the evolution of EU policies, several studies also analyse in great detail how organized interests adapted to European policy-making and what influence they had on EU policies. Featuring the importance of sectoral or policy characteristics, they place sectoral negotiation systems or policy networks at the heart of their analysis (Grande 1994; Börzel 1997; Peterson 2003) sometimes downplaying the importance of cross-sectoral influences.[3]

Studies that discuss the contribution of interest organizations to European democracy and governance also arrive at fundamentally different conclusions: According to Hubert Heinelt, whose analysis is anchored in de Tocqueville's tradition of civil society studies, the participation of interest groups in EU policy-making can be a cure to the democratic deficit of the EU (Heinelt 1998). But following James Caporaso (1974), whose empirical analysis is rooted in a critical appraisal of the pluralist perspective on interest groups, their 'hedonistic' activities may put in danger the legitimacy of the whole integration process. In recent years, the study of social movements and political protest in the European Union gave this debate new impetus (Imig and Tarrow 2001a; Balme, Chabanet and Wright 2002, Balme and Chabanet 2008). While associations and social movements used to be studied separately, both literatures are now coming together. This is partly the result of political discussions to confront the democratic deficit of the European Union. In particular, the European Commission and the Economic and Social Committee emphasize ways to make the political participation of civil society organizations more effective and democratic (see Commission 1999, 2001, 2002). The theoretical debate on this topic focuses on the possibility of deliberative and associative democracy in Europe and its prerequisites (Pollack 1997; Heinelt 1998; Eriksen, Jörges and Neyer 2003). The renewed interest in normative questions has also come to spur empirical analyses of EU interest intermediation (Abromeit and Schmidt 1998; Eder, Hellmann and Trenz 1998; Warleigh 2001; Klein et al 2003), effectively linking the study of interest groups in the EU with democratic theory.[4]

The contribution of interest groups to European governance is also ambiguous. In part, this is due to a focus on different research topics and policy areas. Based on their analysis of the EU harmonization and standardization processes, Volker Eichener and Helmut Voelzkow (1994c) conclude that interest groups enhance the governability of the European Union. Analysing the role of interest groups for migrant inclusion, Andrew Geddes (2000) contends that these groups contributed to political change in the EU by placing new issues on the political agenda and framing parts of the EU policy discourse. But looking at the organizational characteristics of some 50 EU-level interest groups, Justin Greenwood and Ruth Webster (2000) find that these organizations are unable to act as routine governance partners of the EU institutions. And in his study of EU transport liberalization, Mark Aspinwall (1999) maintains that vested domestic interests often stand in the way of political change.

Other analyses draw attention to the issue of collective action. Analysing the impact of the organizational features of EU associations on associative activities (Schwaiger and Kirchner 1981; Greenwood 2002a) they are usually rooted in Mancur Olson's logic of collective action and in the study of organizational incentives (Greenwood and Aspinwall 1998). In this area, a broad consensus has emerged that it is common for domestic organizations to join EU-level groups because the costs of non-membership can be considerable (see Chapter 4). The specific material incentives that EU associations have to offer are less important. However, we know less about the conditions under which EU-level interest organizations are actors in their own right, serve as political forae in which the members discuss their political options or are instruments of their dominant members.

Given the growing range of EU activities and their impact on the member states, several studies emphasize that the EU must now be analysed as a system of multilevel governance (see Jachtenfuchs and Kohler-Koch 1996, 2003; Benz 1998; Kohler-Koch and Eising 1999; Ansell 2000; Marks and Hooghe 2001; Hooghe and Marks 2003) in which European, national and regional political processes are closely linked and in which interest groups and social movements have come to participate regularly in EU policy-making and policy-implementation (see Chapter 6). Whereas the multilevel governance approach seeks to capture European governance in a perspective that encompasses the different territorial levels, Europeanization studies maintain the analytical separation of different levels. Europeanization studies of interest representation concentrate on the impact the EU has on national interest groups and patterns of interest intermediation (Schmidt 1999; Falkner 2000; Cowles 2001). Usually, they have a comparative design to identify cross-national similarities and differences, denote areas of convergence and trace the causal mechanisms of these processes (see Chapter 6).

In sum, the theoretical and empirical scope of EU interest group studies has widened tremendously in recent years. At the same time scientific controversy about the adequate theoretical and methodical approaches to EU interest intermediation has intensified. The field has moved beyond the stage of adapting the approaches developed in other fields of study to the EU context.[5] Most notably, the concepts of multilevel governance and Europeanization feed back into comparative politics and international relations. For example, the former gives new impetus to research on comparative federalism (Marks and Hooghe 2001, Nicolaïdis and Howse 2001; Benz and Lehmbruch 2002; Hooghe and Marks 2003) and to studies of international organizations and their linkages to national politics.

In regard of the complexity of the field and the variety of theoretical lenses, it is not likely that a single theoretical perspective to the study of interest groups in the EU will evolve. In some measure, contradictory normative and theoretical statements are indicators of a vibrant scientific debate that has not yet reached its dead end. However, given that many theoretical assumptions in these studies are implicit rather than explicit and that several analyses do not put competing theoretical propositions to the test, progress in the sense of an accumulation of findings is less than is desirable. As Baumgartner and Leech (1998: 21) have put it for the US literature, such progress will come only 'from an increased willingness to be explicit in our theoretical perspectives, from clear statements of the limits of our chosen theoretical perspectives, [and] from concerted efforts to build on the findings of others'.

A further reason for the lack of coherence in the study of interest organizations is the change of the European political system over time. What was once a sector-specific European Community for Steel and Coal (ECSC) has little in common with today's political union which regulates not only many economic and social activities but has also acquired substantial powers in justice and home affairs as well as in foreign and security policy. The EU institutional system has become far more complex than it was in its beginnings (Tömmel 2005) even though its core institutions – the Commission, the Parliament and the Council – were then already in place. It is now also closely 'fused' with the political systems of its member states (W. Wessels 1992). All in all, the trend is towards multilevel policy-making and regulation even if its progress is uneven across different issue areas. Moreover, the subsequent enlargements have raised the membership to 27 member states and added to the complexity of interest intermediation in the EU. As a consequence of these developments, the composition of the interest group system has changed over time, co-evolving with the EU institutions (Eichener and Voelzkow 1994a, 1994b). Today there are more types of actor and a greater variety of interests present at EU level than in the 1950s and 1960s. Chapter 3 discusses these changes in more detail.

The fourth impediment to accumulating knowledge about interest groups in the EU is that most studies concentrate on a sub-species of the interest group population in the EU, that is, the EU-level interest group. This leads to notable gaps in the study of interest organizations in the European Union. Only with the onset of the Europeanization debate has the role of domestic interest groups in EU politics come to attract greater attention (Sidenius 1999; Lehmkuhl 2000; Cowles 2001; Eising and Jabko 2001). The same holds for the study of firms (MacLaughlin, Jordan and Maloney 1993; Coen 1997; Cowles 1997; Bouwen 2002a, 2002b), social movements (Imig and Tarrow 2001a; Balme *et al.* 2002; Balme and Chabanet 2008) and professional consultants (Lahusen 2002, 2003; Michalowitz 2004).

Finally, the preference of most scholars for case studies or comparative studies with a small 'N' must not be neglected. As a consequence, crucial concepts and research designs vary significantly in different studies. Concepts such as access, influence, power or networks are defined and measured in different ways, reducing the comparability of findings. While this problem can also arise in quantitative studies that cover many interest organizations, due to the sheer number of small 'N' analyses it is more pertinent in the case study tradition. Chapter 6 highlights how different definitions of pluralism and different characterizations of the same country – the United Kingdom – lead to very different results in Vivien Schmidt's (1999) and Maria Green Cowles' (2001) studies on the Europeanization of interest intermediation in France, Germany and the United Kingdom. Even well-designed case studies tend to use slightly different definitions of key concepts or apply causal explanations which render them incomparable with other studies – unless one climbs the 'ladder of abstraction' to its very top (Sartori 1984). Given the different definitions of core concepts in interest group studies, their meaning is in danger of becoming vague and ambiguous (see Sartori 1984).

Methods such as process tracing or counterfactual analysis certainly increase our understanding of a specific case. In particular, case studies that involve the 'generation, testing, revising, and retesting of explanatory propositions within the same complex material' (Rueschemeyer 2003: 315) increase our insights. However, even observers who are sympathetic to the in-depth study of single cases concede that it 'cannot deal effectively with factors that are largely or completely held constant within the boundaries of the case' (Rueschemeyer 2003: 332; see also Mayntz 2002: 16). The logical consequence is that the focus on a few large cases does 'not allow us to come to reasonable conclusions about our assumptions regarding underlying causal patterns' (Rueschemeyer 2003: 333). These problems are by no means unique to EU interest group studies. In their review of the US literature, Baumgartner and Leech (1998: 6) arrive at the conclusion that the 'addition of vast amounts of new observational data' on interest groups 'has not led to a comparable increase in our understandings of the roles and impacts of groups in politics' because of a similar emphasis on case study methods.

Despite the immense number of case studies, the preference for small 'N' analysis is an important reason for the lack of agreement on the role that interest groups play in the European Union. It has three main consequences. First, the proclivity for small research projects is often matched by narrow theoretical concerns so that the theoretical ground covered is smaller than it could be. Second, due to the preference for case studies, findings in one issue area are often transferred to other areas of EU politics even though they may not fit these issue areas because they have different characteristics, leading to the 'overstretching' of findings (see Sartori 1984). Finally, several case studies are set up as descriptive accounts rather than as contributions to a systematic theory of interest groups in the EU, which aggravates these problems. The complexity of the field is an important explanatory factor accounting for the prevalence of case studies in this area. While the case study method can shed much light, it does not always enhance the development and accumulation of literature. Only in recent years have quantitative studies (see the contributions in Coen 2007) and combined quantitative and qualitative approaches (see Dür and De Bièvre 2007) gained more ground in the study of interest groups in the EU.

This study seeks to address some of the problems that have been discussed. First, it draws on generic social science concepts and theories to broaden the theoretical base of interest group studies and enhance their compatibility with other research in other areas of comparative politics and EU studies. It builds on institutional theory, organization theory and theories of resource dependency to analyse to role of interest organizations in EU politics. Second, it incorporates both EU-level groups and national groups to analyse the impact of location in the EU multilevel system and of national characteristics on interest intermediation. However, the study is focused on business interest organizations to control for various organizational factors. Finally, the study looks at a large number of cases to allow for theory testing and enhance the generalizability of findings. The following section of this chapter develops the resource dependency perspective on which the exchange between state and business is based.

Business, the state and political exchange

Resource dependency and political exchange in state–business relations

Why do firms engage in collective political action? In his critique of classic pluralism, Charles Lindblom (1977: 170–88) argues that business assumes a privileged position in capitalist democracies. Since the performance of the economy critically influences the prospects of government and opposition parties to win the next election, businessmen would appear to government officials as functionaries that perform indispensable public functions (Lindblom 1977: 175). Accordingly, their exercise of political authority over commercial activities is curbed by concern about 'its possible adverse effects on business, since these may cause unemployment and other consequences that government officials are unwilling to accept' (Marsh 1983: 5). Lindblom (1977: 180) suggests that political authority will therefore be confined to issues of secondary interest to business and not extend to those that are fundamental to its interests. Among the latter are 'private enterprise itself, private property in productive assets, and a large measure of enterprise autonomy, for example'.

Obviously, this raises the question why firms engage in overtly political behaviour and collective interest organization (Schmitter and Streeck 1981: 10–11). Resource interdependencies of state and business are key to answering this question. On the one hand, firms cannot be sure to be so privileged that their interests are safe and sound with the state institutions (Marsh 1983; Vogel 1987). Their investment power does not always allow them to exercise a veto on public policies that are detrimental to their interests. 'Investment strikes' in response to government policies may lead to a decline in their profitability or a devaluation of their assets (Marsh 1983: 7). Even the so-called 'global players' among the firms are said to continue to depend in great measure on their national home markets for qualified personnel, research and development activities and so forth. Hence, business cannot always use its investment power in disruptive activities. Furthermore, what in Lindblom's perspective are but secondary issues – political de- and reregulation, government taxation or distributive policies – all extract resources from firms or circumscribe the scope of their property rights. Accordingly, they may well turn out to be primary issues to individual enterprises because they effect their commercial prospects.

Moreover, state actors do not always take business interests as much into account as firms may desire. Government receptivity to business concerns varies over time, across issues and in different political settings as well as economic circumstances (Vogel 1987). The build-up of elaborate welfare state regimes and the increasing use of social regulation across Western Europe (Majone 1996) have redistributed income to wage owners, protected consumer interests and supported environmental and social groups within society. These developments indicate that government officials can at least occasionally enjoy some autonomy from business interests.[6] What is more, the interests of different factions of business can vary considerably (J. Wilson 1973), and business can be challenged by countervailing forces such as trade unions or environmental groups. To some extent, firms may be able to make the necessary adjustments in the economic market place or seek to get around compliance with political regulation (Camerra-Rowe 1994: 30). But many firms are aware of the need for individual or collective activities in the political market place. In sum, when its perceived benefits increase, firms are more likely to resort to political interest representation, seeking to exert influence on political decisions, control the vagaries of the market place or contain countervailing forces.

On the other hand, in order to intervene effectively in society and markets, the state apparatus and its bureaucratic machinery 'must link up with the workings of the market' (Rueschemeyer and Evans 1985: 51) because they depend on 'the maintenance of some reasonable level of economic activity' (Block 1977: 15) both for the financing of state operations and for maintaining political support' (Rueschemeyer and Evans 1985: 62). State actors in advanced capitalist democracies consult and involve business to ensure the flow of information, cooperation and political support that are necessary to formulate policies that solve problems and find acceptance (see Rueschemeyer and Evans 1985: 62).

Firms and business associations have different resources at their disposal that can be exchanged with the political actors. For instance, they can supply government officials with information about the likely consequences of public policies in the market place. Firms command knowledge that is crucial when setting technical standards or regulating markets and business associations can provide information about how their members assess governmental policies and whether they are likely to comply with them. Business support may allow some government officials to implement their political preferences against those of others. In addition, business interest groups may give legitimacy to the government policies of which they approve and win larger acceptance for them. Finally, it is not uncommon that interest organizations help to implement public policies and enhance the governance capacities of the state or simply reduce its workload. Therefore, policy-makers in many nations have 'recognized the virtues of functional representation' through business interest associations (BIAs) (G. Wilson 1990: 83) and promote the representation of business interests.

Already back in 1936, Pendleton Herring argued that liberal democratic states need to establish 'a working relationship between the bureaucrats and the special interests – a relationship that will enable the former to carry out the purpose of the state and the latter to realize their own ends' (quoted in Aberbach, Putnam and Rockman 1981: 9). In his analysis of economic planning in the 1960s, Andrew Shonfield (1965: 389) renewed 'Herring's law':

> the increased range and subtlety of the relationship between the public and the private sectors have made it less feasible to govern effectively by decree. The system will not function unless private organizations give their willing collaboration to the pursuit of public purposes. What is therefore required is the opposite of a bully state – rather a wheeling and dealing type of public authority constantly seeking out allies, probing and manoeuvring for the active consensus.

Since then, governance capacities have spread across a multitude of societal and economic organizations and the emergence of inter-organizational networks has become a characteristic feature of advanced capitalist democracies (Mayntz 1992; Rhodes 1997).[7] It is now

> fairly common that in earlier stages of the legislative process bureaucrats discuss bills and regulations with group representatives. Everywhere we encounter a multitude of advisory committees with the participation of group representatives, and it is not uncommon that similar bodies participate in policy implementation.
> (Lehmbruch 1991: 123)

The actors: firms, alliances, associations and consultants

Firms have different options how to represent their political interests to government officials. They can act alone, form alliances, join business associations or hire consultants. I will now discuss the underpinnings of the political behaviour of business and analyse the characteristics of these different formats.

I make three *behavioural* assumptions about business interest organizations. First, it seems reasonable to assume that they are self-interested actors. Firms and business associations are economic interest organizations so that their actions are usually meant to serve the promotion of their material benefit or that of their members (Olson 1965; Moe 1980). Second, I assume that the rationality of these organizations is bounded. They choose their actions from a set of alternatives that are ranked according to a transitive preference ordering and they evaluate their options according to a general rule. However, they do not necessarily possess full information about the decisional situation, face computational limits in processing the information that is available to them, and may therefore not always be able to make the best possible choice. They make their decisions 'on the basis of their imperfect perception of the objective situation, and subject to a number of limitations on their information and skills' (Moe 1980: 18). Because of their bounded rationality, they engage in patterned, routine behaviour that is conditioned by their organizational characteristics as well as by their economic and political environments. In the following chapters I suggest that it is the modes of interest intermediation and the varieties of capitalism in which they are nested that shapes their behaviour. Finally, I assume that these organizations seek to survive. As a consequence, their behaviour is to a large extent 'determined by the requirements of organizational maintenance and enhancement' (J. Wilson 1973: 13). In the long run, firms survive if they make profits, and associations survive if they are able to secure a sufficient stream of resources from their environment and from their members (J. Wilson 1973). Accordingly, business associations must satisfy two varieties of self-interest that may not always be mutually compatible: organizational survival and their members' interests.

As organizations, firms and business associations have clearly delineated domains, memberships and operational rules. They define quite precisely the roles of the persons who join them, and who act and speak for them even though they do not necessarily speak with one voice. Due to their internal differentiation, the policy positions and political actions of firms and business associations can well be the outcome of internal conflicts (Mayntz 1986: 180). Firms and associations stand for two distinct classes of organization: they are corporate actors and collective actors, respectively. This makes it necessary to analyse the most important features of these organizations and their consequences for political action. *Firms* are corporate actors in the economic market place and are in full command of their organizational resources. They are directed by a 'hierarchical leadership representing the owners or beneficiaries' (Scharpf 1997: 56; see also Salisbury 1984: 68). They can speak more easily with one voice than business associations even though sub-holdings may enjoy substantial autonomy in their courses of action.

It is useful to distinguish here between small and large firms. Whereas small firms are usually directed by their owners, large firms have a professional management that enjoys a high degree of autonomy from the owners of the firm or the beneficiaries of their activities. These are usually not involved in defining the firm's course of action. At most, they have the 'collective power to select and replace' the firm's leadership. Firms have a professional staff that is expected 'to follow the rules adopted in central decision processes and the ... directives of the leadership' (Scharpf 1997: 56). The representation of political interests is not their primary purpose; their political interests are derived from their economic goals.

Depending on their economic activities, firms have a more or less wide range of policy concerns. They allocate a fraction of their resources 'to policy-relevant tasks if and when these are perceived as useful to the maintenance and enhancement of the enterprise' (Salisbury 1984: 68). Their preferred mode of representation depends on their organizational resources and on its costs relative to other courses of action: in general, firms will choose that mode of representation that they perceive to be most effective or efficient (Camerra-Rowe 1994: 30–1). Accordingly, they do not necessarily join business associations and channel their political activities through them. Instead, they can take unilateral action, hire lawyers or political consultants or build informal alliances with actors that have convergent interests (see Offe and Wiesenthal 1985: 179). These options are now discussed in more detail.

Firms can act *unilaterally* only when they have sufficient political clout and adequate resources. The large firms on which this study concentrates find it easier to represent their interests individually than small and medium sized enterprises (SMEs) that gain power only through collective organization and representation. Lobbying alone requires the build-up of substantial public affairs capacities that are usually beyond the financial means of SMEs. The SMEs are also more dependent on the services that business associations provide than large firms because of the high expense of producing them individually (Offe and Wiesenthal 1985: 175, 189). The advantage of lobbying alone rather than in a collective effort is that firms do not need to grant concessions to coalition partners or members of associations when pursuing their interests. Evidently, the drawback is that a firm speaks then only for itself and not for a broader constituency, which may reduce its chances to prevail in EU politics.

Hiring a *consultant* or a lawyer who looks after the firm's interests establishes a client relationship in which the firm pays the consultant for political services or the attainment of political goals. This client relationship usually entails a narrower set of policy concerns and smaller range of political activities than 'the idea of constituency representation' by business associations (Salisbury 1984: 71). Generally, it 'is more specialized in subject matter' and 'more limited in scope and time, than constituency representation' (Salisbury 1984: 71). Firms employ commercial lobbyists for specific purposes or on a continuous basis in order to save the cost of developing equivalent in-house public affairs capacities and to help them achieve their political aims more effectively. They choose the lobbyist who 'appears to offer the best promise of success' (Moe 1980: 52) which, in turn, depends on the issue, the institutional context, and the competition among interest groups.

Political coalitions or alliances are here defined as mostly informal and semi-permanent arrangements among 'actors pursuing separate but, by and large, convergent or compatible' political purposes (Scharpf 1997: 55). The partners in the alliance keep their separate action resources under their control but use them in coordinated strategies. Such coalitions can only act by agreement, and their course of action is dependent on its perceived utility for each of the involved actors. Hence, the members' and the coalition's interests are tightly coupled even though a longer-term membership 'may facilitate agreement to individual decisions, that, when viewed in isolation, are unattractive to some members' (Scharpf 1997: 55). Such semi-permanent coalitions are sustained in continuous interactions[8] whereas issue-specific coalitions in which each of the component organizations seeks to realize its issue-specific policy goals tend to be more short-lived (see Pollack 1997).

Finally, *business associations* are collective actors. They are more or less permanent organizations that represent members who pursue compatible purposes. Membership is usually voluntary. The members hold crucial action resources collectively in the associations which act as representatives of their members or the constituency they stand for.[9] They seek to advance the interests of these constituencies in policy-related activities (Salisbury 1984: 70–1). Business associations typically 'depend on and are guided by the preferences of their members' (Scharpf 1997: 54) who are entrepreneurs, managers or, which is more usual, firms. The associations have to supply incentives to these actors so that these 'will become, or remain, members and will perform certain tasks' (J. Wilson 1973: 13). As a rule, associations have a dual organizational structure consisting of their professional staff and the voluntary work of their members. Despite the dependence on their members' contributions in some business interest associations the professional leadership has substantial leeway in defining and representing members' interests. Even though it is generally held that they 'specialize in the aggregation, definition, advancement and defense of the collective goals in the political realm (interests) of a distinct group of producers' (Schmitter and Streeck 1981: 33) and employers, political interest representation need not be the main aim of business associations (J. Wilson 1973: 10). Several business interest associations specialize in providing legal or economic services to their members or in regulating market entry, market standards and market behaviour.

There is a good reason for firms to prefer other alternatives over joining an association when it comes to representing their interests. Membership in a business association has some costs. First, it may be costly in financial terms. However, usually, for large firms the cost of membership is relatively low in relation to their income (J. Wilson 1973: 144) so that this does not often get in the way of joining an association. For smaller firms, these costs can be non-trivial so that they are more sensitive to the association's value for their money. Second, joining an association implies a mid- to long-term commitment whereas the pursuit of some political aims may have a much shorter time horizon. If further collective action is obsolete after the realization of these goals or after the policy has been formulated, firms may prefer unilateral action or hire political consultants for the job. Only the need for relatively continuous political activities – or other material incentives – will spur them to join business associations. Third, within the association, the firms' interests may be subdued to other considerations. Relying on collective action in business associations usually involves some sacrifice of the firms' self-interests: firms are not in full command of the policy positions taken by the associational staff. To some extent, information asymmetries in favour of the associational staff may even give rise to opportunism, moral hazard and shirking.[10] Moreover, their membership subjects firms, which are competitors in the economic market place, to the same rules and strategies in political processes and to the acceptance of joint positions (Schmitter and Streeck 1981). Such problems may prevent them from joining a business association.

However, firms weigh the cost of membership against the cost of non-membership which can be substantial and may endanger their survival. Being an outsider, it is difficult for a firm to influence the political activities of a business association (unless it has a crucial position in the market that needs to be taken into account): it can neither contribute to the adoption of policy positions that are in its favour nor prevent the association from taking a policy stance that is detrimental to its own interests. In addition, non-membership cuts the firm off from important information about state activities and its competitors' points of view as well as from the services the association provides. The consequence is that a firm needs to step up its in-house public affairs activities and supply of services or that it must buy them from commercial suppliers. Hence, the opportunity costs of non-membership amount easily to a multiple of membership costs. It is therefore likely that firms seeking organizational survival will minimize these risks and join the relevant associations in their economic domain. The history of national business associations supports that proposition. Many national business associations emerged in response to market failures and crises, the collective political mobilization of labour and counter-pressure by trade unions and increased state activity that raised the perceived value of collective action to firms (Liefmann 1897; Truman 1951; Schmitter and Streeck 1981; Offe and Wiesenthal 1985).

Economic globalization and neoliberalism as sources of change

Concentrating on the effects of the transformation of the institutional setting in Europe by no means implies that this is the only or the most important factor of change that bears on large firms and business interest associations (see also Grote and Lang 2003). Currently, these organizations are subject to a variety of pressures. Among the most important drivers of change are the market and functional pressures which result from the so-called *globalization of the economy* and *ideational effects*, notably the consequences of the neoliberal surge. I discuss these two factors to illustrate their consequences and put the importance of the European Union for domestic interest organizations into perspective.[11] I argue that the European Union has become the most important regional regime in Europe to buffer the pressures arising from economic globalization and promote neoliberal policies that are supposed to strengthen economic competitiveness.

The globalization of markets and technologies

Theories of globalization point to the numerous forces, both technological and competitive, affecting markets within the international political economy. It is said that these forces engender a reconfiguration of societal actors, as they alter opportunity structures, causing actors to adjust their organization, strategies and preferences accordingly (Armstrong and Bulmer 1998). Supposedly, these actors have to adapt to a new global economic, technological and political environment to ensure their continued survival. For example, impinging upon labour and product markets, economic globalization affects the interest definitions of firms, potentially reducing the relevance of associations as interest *intermediaries* for them. With the uncertainty that globalization engenders, both firms and individuals, as well as the organizations representing them, seek new ways to minimize the risks involved and profit from the opportunities that the new environment brings.

Large firms have been particularly adept at capitalizing on the opportunities that market changes have offered; but they have done so in diverse ways. While these companies have certainly not become stateless, they have extended their international economic activities considerably (for many, see Pestoff 2000; Hassel *et al.* 2000). Indeed, due to the internationalization of their economic activities, it would appear that the national level is losing some of its relevance for these actors; even if the domestic market is still an important base for production and research facilities.

As a consequence of these developments large firms are more likely to question the role traditionally played by their interest intermediaries in this new environment. They may begin to see them as unnecessary constraints upon their autonomy, and as a result suggest that existing associational structures be reformed. For large firms the downsizing and organizational rationalization of associations is often seen as a remedy to the problems caused by market change. Merging business interest associations to save costs or admitting 'foreign' firms such as IBM or Toyota as members in them entails substantial change in the logic of membership (see Schmitter and Streeck 1981).

By contrast, small firms, or rather those not inextricably linked to large firms in a supplier relationship, are likely to react to more intense competition by making additional demands on political actors via their associations. They will do this to enhance their own security (on the Swiss case, see Kriesi 2000). Competitive pressures are not felt equally by all sectors of the economy. In a field such as health care, where the boundaries between national systems are deeply entrenched, professional bodies are relatively insulated from direct global competitive pressures to the extent that national cleavages outweigh sectoral similarities when it comes to representing interests in international contexts (see Lovecy 1999).

Highly internationalized sectors such as chemicals and sectors with a high rate of technological change such as telecommunications and information technology have been subjected to tremendous functional pressures that have had important effects on interest organization, paving the way for the reconfiguration of the sector and the associational landscape (Schneider 2001; Blank 2002; Grote and Lang 2003). One of the consequences of these changes has been an increase both at the EU level and at the global level in issue-specific interest alliances and in interest organizations constructed on the basis of direct firm membership. Yet even in these dynamic sectors the relationships between global and EU-level interest organizations and activities have not followed a single overarching logic, demonstrating the considerable discretion that actors have with regard to the market effects and the different responses that have resulted.

Hence, the impact of international competition on trade associations is by no means straightforward. On the one hand, it can enhance the pressures of members on associations to cut costs, streamline activities and develop a reasonable division of labour with other associations (see Boleat 2000; Wartenberg 2000). Intensifying the competition among the associational members, they may even decrease their willingness to cooperate. On the other hand, it can lead to the emergence of new associations and to the strengthening of associational systems of quality control and standardization (van Waarden 1994: 238; Coleman 1997). It is often argued that the impact of these forces is channelled through established institutional settings such as the varieties of capitalism or domestic modes of interest intermediation (see Chapter 3).

Ideational effects: the neoliberal surge

The demise in the 1970s of Keynesianism as the dominant economic paradigm, and the rise of neoliberalism since the 1980s in economic policy-making, were at the root of the introduction of deregulatory, monetarist and privatization policies by governments of both right and left. Underpinned by the belief that 'the competitive market system, left to its own devices, free of government interference, will produce superior results, in terms of efficiency and social justice' (Helm 1989: 12) these policies formed the core of the neoliberal policies in Western Europe. However, the ascendance of neoliberalism did not lead to the wholescale convergence of policies in Western Europe. While it led to the introduction of neoliberal policies in some countries and in certain sectors, it also opened the door to what became a far-reaching debate about the extent to which market solutions to economic (and political) problems were appropriate in all cases, given the diversity of sectoral contexts and political systems within the region.

By way of an example, this debate, which focused attention on the limits of regulation and the role of governance mechanisms beyond the state, contributed to a 'renaissance of concertation through social pacts' in the 1990s (Ebbinghaus and Hassel 1999: 6). Relatively stable tripartite agreements were concluded among the state, trade unions and employers' associations in Ireland, Finland, Italy, the Netherlands and Denmark. However, in those countries where stable agreements *were* negotiated, their nature differed substantially from the neocorporatist concertation and the Keynesian wage policies of the 1950s to 1970s, that is, from a system of 'wage contention in exchange for near-full employment and side-payments in increased, state-provided, welfare' (Schmitter and Grote 1997: 14). The new social pacts of the 1990s have both a wider and a narrower scope: wider in the sense that they imply, whether simultaneously or sequentially, a reform of the welfare state, labour relations and employment policies; but narrower in the sense that they are closely tied to the strengthening of national competitiveness and the reform of public finance as embodied in the convergence criteria for Economic and Monetary Union. Thus, social pacts combine liberalization and flexibility on the one hand, but on the other they also provide some compensation for labour (Ebbinghaus and Hassel 1999).

However, in Greece, Spain, Portugal, Belgium, Germany and Sweden such pacts either excluded one of the social partners or were not as successful as in the other cases; and in some countries such concertation has, at least for some time, *not* been a major element in the reform of the welfare state and of labour relations. In statist France, for example, there is only little evidence of increased cooperation between the French state and the 'social partners'. Rather, the abandonment of national wage bargaining and the decentralization of labour relations in the 1980s led to the introduction of plant-level wage bargaining, and even, according to Ebbinghaus and Hassel (1999), to employer-imposed wage settlements.

In the United Kingdom the retrenchment of the welfare state and the reform of labour relations were the result of unilateral state action. Despite the election of a Labour Government in 1997 there were subsequently no significant moves towards strengthening trade unions and reintroducing tripartite negotiations. However, these two cases should not lead us to conclude that the effects of neoliberalism imply any convergence upon a single model. While the statist France and the neoliberal British Conservative government adopted a more market-orientated and pluralistic organization of labour relations, the same cannot be said of all West European states.

On the face of it, we might have presupposed that the introduction of a neoliberal agenda would weaken organized interests across the board in Western Europe. After all, from a neoliberal standpoint, associations are often deemed little more than cartels of actors, intent on protecting the interests of their members in a conspiracy against the public interest and free trade (Coleman 1997). However, from the above examples, we might surmise that the surge of neoliberal ideas that has swept Western Europe has been received very differently in different states. National institutional configurations shaped the responsiveness of countries to the neoliberal agenda and responses to globalization pressures.

Hence, European integration is by no means the only driver of change in firms and business interest organizations. Nonetheless, in Europe, the European Union is the most important regional regime that is supposed to cope with and buffer the pressures arising from the globalization of the economy. Furthermore, as European integration has for a long time meant the integration of member state markets and later also the build-up of the European Monetary Union, European institutions have clearly supported the rise of neoliberalism within Europe. Today, the authority of the European Union covers a greater number of policy areas and reaches deeper into the member states than does any other international regime. Moreover, the sharing of national regulatory powers with EU institutions has transformed the domestic environments of the member states and has embedded domestic actors in a multilevel political system. Thereby, it has transformed the arenas in which interests are defined and pursued, both offering new opportunities and imposing constraints, while also challenging intra- and inter-organizational routines and modes of interest intermediation. These are the reasons why this book is concerned with the effects of the Europe-wide institutional transformation of the state on interest organizations. Its concern is not so much with the responses of these organizations to specific pieces of EU legislation but with their adaptation to the enduring constraints and opportunities that the transformation of the institutional setting entails. Accordingly, emphasis is put on the structured relations, the enduring division of labour and the rules of the game that emerge within this institutional structure because these affect the strategies, the choices and the behaviour of the actors.

3 State–business relations in the EU member states

In all advanced capitalist democracies, state institutions and business interest associations (BIAs) maintain frequent and close relations. In several countries, trade associations have been granted formal powers in the making and implementation of public policies. Nonetheless, according to many observers, the nature of these political exchanges varies significantly across nations. Social, economic and political institutions as well as established ideas about state–society relations are at the root of these differences (Katzenstein 1978a; Hall 1986; Lehmbruch 1991; Hall and Soskice 2001a, 2001b). National modes of interest intermediation and varieties of capitalism are said to channel how functional exigencies are dealt with in political-economic systems. They should also lead firms and business associations to respond in different ways to European integration, causing them to chart different courses of coordinating the economy and representing business interests.

In this chapter, I therefore outline the prevalent images of state–business relations in France, Germany and the United Kingdom, emphasizing that they are shaped both by national political institutions and the characteristics of national capitalism. Then, I analyse these perspectives on the basis of the EUROLOB data. The main finding of this chapter is that there remain indeed national differences but that these are confined to rather specific aspects of national state–business relations. The prevailing distinctions of national state–business relations seem overdrawn and need to be fine-tuned.

National institutional orders: varieties of capitalism and modes of interest intermediation

Despite potent functional exigencies and manifold political exchanges between state and business everywhere, state–business relations are still said to vary across nations, sectors, issues and time. I trace these differences to the evolution and workings of economic and political institutions (Katzenstein 1978a, 1978b, 1978c; Hall 1986; Hall and Soskice 2001a) and to the perpetuation of the leading ideas about state–society relations (Lehmbruch 1991; Kohler-Koch 1999; Schmidt 2002) that mediate the functional pressures arising from European integration and economic globalization. The firms and business associations in any

Table 3.1 Modes of interest intermediation and varieties of capitalism in France, Germany and the United Kingdom

		National capitalism		
		Liberal market economy	Coordinated market economy	Mediterranean market economy
Mode of interest intermediation	Pluralism Corporatism Statism	United Kingdom	Germany	France

Sources: Siaroff 1999; Hall and Soskice 2001b; Schmidt 2002.

political economy face a set of institutions that are not fully under their control (Hall and Soskice 2001b: 15).

These institutions structure political and economic processes and are not simply arenas in which actors can pursue their interests. They do not fully determine the outcomes but they endow the actors with resources and define their roles so that they channel their perceptions, interests and behaviour, by both providing opportunities and setting constraints (March and Olsen 1989; Steinmo, Thelen and Longstreth 1992; Hall and Taylor 1996). As 'guidance devices', institutions reduce the complexity of decision situations and form an important set of reference points (Kratochwil 1989). Integrating some conflicts into politics and excluding others (Schattschneider 1960), they bear on the chances of BIAs prevailing in the political process. As a result, the actors make choices depending on their expectations of how these rules and structures affect their pay-offs (Czada 1991: 259).

Selecting France, Germany and the United Kingdom for closer inspection controls important background variables. These countries are the three largest member states of the European Union. They have not only the largest populations but also the largest economies in the Union. Their citizens elect relatively more members of the European Parliament than those of other member states; and the three countries wield greater decision-making powers in qualified majority voting in the Council of the EU than smaller member states. All three countries joined the European institutions a long time ago. While France and Germany were founding members, the United Kingdom (UK) joined the European Community (EC) in its first enlargement in 1973. Like the other EU member states, these countries are representative democracies so that they display notable political-economic similarities.

However, this choice of countries also involves substantial variation in state–business relations which condition the adaptation of firms and business associations to European politics. Notably, the three countries display different modes of interest intermediation and varieties of capitalism (see Table 3.1). The mode of interest intermediation impacts on the political role of BIAs and firms and the variety of capitalism shapes the role these organizations play in coordinating the national economies. Gerhard Lehmbruch (1991: 148) has argued that such inter-organizational constellations are often the outcome of 'collective historical experiences'. These patterns are relatively stable over time and change only due to crucial events and important new demands. They should also be reflected in the access of interest organizations to political institutions and can facilitate or get in the way of contacts with EU institutions.[1] The literature on state–society relations distinguishes among three major *modes of interest intermediation*: pluralism, corporatism and statism. The three countries display different modes of interest intermediation. Usually, Germany is said to fall in the corporatist camp (Streeck 1999), France is held to be the prototype of statist interest intermediation (Schmidt 1996) and the United Kingdom is frequently ranked among those countries characterized by pluralism (Siaroff 1999).

These modes vary in several respects: in the role of state actors; the patterns of interaction; the dominant actors; and the role of private actors in policy formulation and implementation (see Schmidt 1996, 2002; Siaroff 1999; Eising and Kohler-Koch 1999a). In the *statist* mode, the state is an authority above society, legitimated by democratic vote and pursuing a common 'national' interest. State actors are the dominant actors in policy formulation, with interest groups playing only a minimal role. Participation in policy formulation is limited to a small number of organized interests. Indeed, many interest organizations are included in political processes only after the basic contours of the policy have been outlined, often politicizing the later stages of the policy-making process, so that policy implementation becomes characterized by 'the politics of accommodation' (Schmidt 1999: 167). In the EU, France and Greece are often regarded as statist countries.[2]

In *corporatism*, the boundaries between state and society are blurred (see Lehmbruch 1977; Schmitter 1979). The state institutions act as mediators who try to integrate the conflicting interests of peak associations that are fully representative of their functional domains. The associational setting is highly centralized and well integrated. In their negotiations, the state and the peak associations seek to build consensus over the problems plaguing particular sectors. The actor constellations are relatively closed and stable over time, and interest groups are on an equal footing with state actors even though these occasionally invoke the threat of political regulation to increase the incentives for the interest organizations to come to an agreement. State institutions provide the peak associations with rights to formulate binding rules in specific issue areas and/or implement these rules. Hence, interest organizations assume quasi-public functions. In return, it is expected that they mediate between state and member demands, thus effectively reconciling public and private interests. Among the EU member states, Denmark, Sweden, Finland, Austria, the Netherlands and Germany are commonly regarded as corporatist countries.

In *pluralism*, state and society are separated. The state's role is that of a referee mediating the pursuit of individual interests. Fragmented organized interests that represent narrow membership concerns lobby government to accommodate their goals. The organizations compete and bargain in order to build minimum winning coalitions. These are generally fluid and depend on converging interests. The interest organizations represent members' interests and do not mediate between state and member demands. Nor do they assume important regulatory functions. Among EU member states, the UK, Belgium, Ireland and Italy are often held to be pluralist.

Next, the countries chosen for this study can be said to represent different *varieties of capitalism*. The literature on this analyses the economic behaviour and performance of firms to assess whether the different varieties of capitalism lead to different economic outcomes. I am less concerned with the functional assumptions this approach entails about the economic performance and pathways of divergent institutional configurations. Rather, I concentrate on the consequences of these arrangements for the political representation of business interests and for the role that business associations play as coordinating devices in the economies of the EU member states.[3] The literature on the varieties of capitalism distinguishes between two major types of capitalism – liberal market economies and coordinated market economies.[4] Several countries that display more ambiguous modes of economic coordination are sorted in a third variety that has been called 'Mediterranean' capitalism. Analyses in this tradition place the UK and the other Anglo-Saxon OECD-countries among the liberal market economies. Like other Southern European countries, France is held to be a Mediterranean market economy. And together with several small and economically advanced EU member states such as Denmark and the Netherlands, Germany is regarded as a coordinated market economy (Hall and Soskice 2001b: 21).[5]

In *liberal market economies*, 'firms coordinate their activities primarily via hierarchies and competitive market arrangements' (Hall and Soskice 2001b: 8). Market arrangements are supposed to be 'highly efficient means for coordinating the endeavors of economic actors' (ibid.) and characterized by arm's-length exchanges in the context of competition and formal contracts. The economic actors on these markets respond to price signals when supplying or demanding goods and services. Non-market and non-hierarchical modes such as inter-firm networks and business associations play a far lesser role in coordinating economic activities. The market arrangements are deemed to provide 'highly effective means for coordinating the endeavors of economic actors' (ibid.). By contrast, in *coordinated market economies* firms rely to a greater extent on strategic interactions that are based on non-market relationships to coordinate their endeavors with other actors (ibid.). Such mechanisms usually entail more cooperative, as opposed to competitive, relationships to develop the firms' core areas of competency. Among them are far-ranging ownership linkages and cooperation within encompassing business associations. *Mediterranean* capitalism deviates from these two polar types in that the economic collaboration is based more on common career patterns of the companies' managers and on their close ties with the state bureaucracy. Personal networks and extensive ties among managers and politicians are even more important coordination devices than business associations and also prevent a major political role for BIAs. This pattern is said to equip these economies with specific capacities of non-market coordination in some sectors of the economy such as finance and more liberal arrangements in others such as labour relations (Hall and Soskice 2001b: 21).

It is no coincidence that France, the UK and Germany combine distinct modes of interest intermediation with specific varieties of capitalism. Both typologies and institutional configurations hinge as much upon the extent to which the economic and political actors cooperate rather than compete as upon a liberal or interventionist role of the state in economy and society. Hence, in the UK, competitive market relations conform to bargaining in the political market place. In Germany, collaboration in the coordination of economic markets is associated with cooperative ways of resolving conflicts of interests. In France, a strong role of the state in the governance of the economy corresponds with its dominant position in state–society relations. Hence, the three countries represent typical configurations of national state–society and state–economy relations that are likely to cause substantial variations in the responses of firms and business associations to the EU.[6] Therefore, I will now take a closer look at the three countries and discuss how the historical interaction between political institutions and national capitalism has come to shape business interest representation.

State institutions, national capitalism and state–business relations

The United Kingdom

In Britain's liberal market economy (LME) (see Hall and Soskice 2001a, 2001b), firms coordinate activities mainly through markets and hierarchies. Partly, this mix stems from the historical evolution of state, market and society in Britain (St. Blank 1978; Katzenstein 1978c). As in France, the British institutions of government had been in place before the nation was formed. Early parliamentary sovereignty and democratic control through the extension of suffrage limited the interventions of government in economy and society. In combination with an atomistic form of competition due to early industrialization, this led political and economic actors to favour liberal economic policies at home and abroad. The emergence of a modern and centralized civil service in the late nineteenth century with its 'prescribed role as neutral arbiter, rather than creative shaper' of state–society and state–economy relations (Katzenstein 1978c: 326) also inhibited the emergence of close ties with economic and societal interests. The passivity of the state in directing strategies of industrial growth did not make it necessary for the economic actors to organize their interests centrally. At the same time, the growth of the advanced financial community shifted power from industry to finance, which was geared to facilitate capital exports (Windolf 2002: 52) so that finance and industrial capital were effectively separated (Lütz 2002: 75).

As a consequence of these developments, it is still less common to use business associations as coordinating devices in governing inter-company relations than it is in coordinated market economies. Relying greatly on market relations and formal contracts to coordinate their activities, inter-firm networks also play a lesser role than in France or Germany. Ownership linkages and interlocking directorates have comparatively low densities, there is a large number of quite isolated firms in these networks, and only a few firms hold multiple ownerships. Overall, this indicates a low degree of central coordination and control in the British economy (Windolf 2002: 49).

Observers stress that the British government maintains an 'arm's-length' relationship with business. State reluctance to intervene in private business decisions has been 'mirrored by industry's insistence on a hands-off policy' (Lane 1992: 68). Despite the brief period of economic nationalization and the formation of the welfare state during and after the Second World War, the philosophy of economic liberalism has been dominant throughout most of the period since. After the wartime economy the state, producers and labour quickly 'sought to restore the traditional distance between government and the economy' (St. Blank 1978: 101).

Nonetheless, there is a 'long tradition in Britain ... of consulting with affected interests' (Grant 1993a: 11). Several accounts of state–business relations suggest that business has acquired an insider status in British policy-making (Vogel 1986; Grant 1993a: 12). Direct contacts among firms and government are common in British state–business relations (see Grove 1962: 157). Several observers characterize the UK as a company state in which business associations play a lesser role as intermediary institutions than in more corporatist countries, such as Germany (Bennett 1997c: 19). British trade associations would not have as strong 'a tradition of self-organisation' as German associations (Lane 1997: 24). For a long time, the relation of business associations with government has not been 'legally anchored and formalised' as it has been in Germany (Lane 1997: 24; see also G. Wilson 1990: 82).[7] Only in the context of its initiative for better regulation has the Cabinet Office decided upon a code of practice on written consultation in November 2000 that is binding to all government departments and agencies. This code has introduced some transparency standards and a minimum consultation period of twelve weeks for all stakeholders.[8] It is to be used in conjunction with the code of good practice in policy consultations and policy appraisal that was also passed in 2000.

Before, the wide-ranging reforms of the Thatcher governments that limited interest group participation in British policy-making (for details, see Grant 1993a: 15) seeking 'to redistribute power between government and interests' (Hayward 1996: 241) brought to light that the centralization of power equips the British state with substantial capacities to structure state–business relations. However, it is generally acknowledged that many British policy networks and communities have survived the reversal of consultation patterns quite well intact. Under the subsequent Conservative and New Labour governments, the pendulum swung back in favour of greater consultation. The Department of Trade and Industry (DTI) emphasized the role trade associations could play in strengthening the international competitiveness of their member firms and developed 'a best practice guide' for the 'model trade association' (DTI 1996). Broadly speaking, the associations should be representative, resourceful, professional and used in cooperation with other actors. The DTI also provided financial support for benchmarking exercises and for establishing the Trade Association Forum (TAF) to promote the diffusion of best practices.[9] The New Labour governments broadened this agenda by engaging in a compact with the voluntary sector to promote and improve its participation in policy-making and implementation (Secretary of State for the Home Department 1998). Whereas these efforts worked somewhat as a 'change agent for UK trade associations', so far they have not restructured 'the essentially pluralist system of UK trade associations' (Greenwood 2004: 15). Nonetheless, they helped to reinstate the legitimacy of trade associations as interest intermediaries.

Due to such variations, it is controversial whether British state–business relations fall among the pluralistic practices (Siaroff 1999; Cowles 2001; Lütz 2002) or whether they must be regarded as statist (see Schmidt 1996, 2002, 2006) (see also Chapter 6). The configuration of a unitary state with a parliamentary democracy that is usually governed by a single majority party allows, in principle, for the possibility of unified and concerted government action that bypasses or even antagonizes important interest organizations (see Grande 1989: 355). However, characterizing Britain as statist underestimates the role of the leading ideas that have governed British state–society relations (see Richardson 1993: 88). British governments have usually not used their powers to the same extent as the centralized French state because the prevailing conceptions of state and society vary tremendously in these two countries (see also France, below). This feature led Kenneth Dyson (1980: 71) to label the UK a 'stateless society'.[10] In the British understanding, state and society are inextricably linked. Government and parliament are conceived of as bodies that are representative of society and not separate from it (Lütz 2002: 41) so that I side with those authors that characterize British state–society relations as pluralist.

Germany

In Germany's coordinated market economy, firms rely to a greater extent on non-market relationships to coordinate their economic transactions than British enterprises. Relational and incomplete contracting is more usual than in the UK. So are collaborative relationships in inter-firm networks that orchestrate economic activities. These networks are quite centralized, with some dense interlocks that incorporate nearly all the large companies. Several firms have multiple representations of firms in supervisory boards or ownership arrangements indicating a higher degree of centralized control than in the UK (Windolf 2002: 49). Hence, economic action is not only driven by supply and demand in competitive markets but also based on long-term and institutionalized patterns of strategic interaction. Business associations play a far greater role in Germany than in liberal market economies even if they have been stripped of a large number of regulatory powers by competition law. They support the diffusion of new technologies, are engaged in education and training programmes and have an impact on the strategic interaction of their members, by promoting the exchange of information among them and thickening their common knowledge.

Some of these characteristics can be traced to Germany's history as an industrial and national 'latecomer'. As a nation-state, Germany experienced economic, social and cultural integration before the full set of state institutions had been set up (Dyson 1980; Katzenstein 1987: 11). Its feudal past had a profound impact on its industrial revolution by uniting industry and agriculture and propelling Germany towards economic protectionism and foreign expansion. The executive-based state authority favoured a strategy of state intervention to keep up the momentum of the industrialization process. The state set up technical schools and universities to provide the industrial sector with trained personnel. Business responded to the increase in state intervention, the emergence of the labour movement and to the major economic crisis in the late nineteenth century by organizing its interests centrally in both employer and producer associations. German firms have specialized in heavy industry and manufacturing. Large universal banks provided industry with long-term finance thus forming an integrated whole with the industrial sector (Kreile 1978). The major industrial strategies were mapped by these universal banks and by the large firms that were frequently organized like cartels (Liefmann 1897) and well represented in the business associations. The defeat in the Second World War, the allied occupation and the German partition 'were a decisive watershed in German history' (Katzenstein 1978c: 329). They diminished the social and economic cleavages by eliminating the Prussian *Junkers*, levelling out the centre–periphery cleavage by reorganizing the structure of the states, and they bridged the conflicts between Protestants and Catholics through the formation of the Christian Democratic Union that opened itself to the two major religions. Nonetheless, in the economic sector, tight interlocks between finance and industry and within industry prevailed. Economic policy-making since the Second World War followed an 'export mystique' that was derived from the logic of the industrial structure as much as it was the result of a deliberative policy based on the consensus about the Social Market Economy and the 'principle that German competitiveness in world markets had to be maintained and strengthened' (Kreile 1978: 193).

In Germany, the leading economic idea of the Social Market Economy that dominates since the Second World War 'emphasises competition in the free market'. It 'eschews detailed intervention in industry but compensates labour for the social costs which the working of the market ... imposes' (Lane 1992: 66). This conceptual framework 'respects and perpetuates' the long-standing tradition of industrial self-regulation that is based on a 'dense network of trade associations and Chambers of Industry and Commerce' (ibid.). Despite its non-interventionist stance, the state does not remain 'aloof from industry concerns' (Lane 1992: 67) involving it in corporatist practices of policy-making and delegating self-regulatory powers in the implementation of public policies to it. These structural arrangements have, by and large, been transferred to the new German Länder after reunification.

France

French capitalism is held to be a more ambiguous form than liberal and coordinated capitalism – France has been called a 'Mediterranean' market economy that is marked by its history of state interventionism and a rather large agricultural sector. While the decades of economic planning after the Second World War left the public sector with strong capacities to intervene in the economy, some areas of the French economy, such as labour relations, display more liberal arrangements. According to several observers, collaboration among French companies is less based on market relations and associational arrangements than on the common career patterns of their CEOs both in the public and private sectors (Hancké 2001: 313). This makes for a greater reliance of French companies on state institutions than is the case in liberal or coordinated market economies. In addition, interlocking directorates and ownership linkages have come to play a great role in coordinating French inter-firm relations. But when compared to the encompassing and dense networks in Germany, French inter-firm networks exclude large segments of the economy. Paul Windolf (2002: 86–9) distinguishes between two types of network in the French economy. On the one hand, multilevel control networks are indicative of the public steering of the economy. They connect large private and state-owned corporations with each other and with the French financial corporations over which the state has exerted control for a long period after the Second World War. In these networks, 'state control, financial control, and managerial control are fused' (Windolf 2002: 90). On the other hand, in holding company networks, family owners construct complex linkages among firms in which the parent company holds shares of its subsidiaries which, in turn, dominate even smaller firms. Hence, arguably, business associations play a lesser role in French capitalism than they do in coordinated economies. For instance, French associations are said to be much less involved in vocational training programmes than German groups (Culpepper 2001).

The history of the French state provides part of the reasons for the emergence of these patterns. As in the UK, state power is highly centralized in France: 'the powerful executive, insulated bureaucracy, and high centralization make for a strong state in France' (F. Wilson 1993: 114, 123). As John Zysman (1978: 265) has put it: 'In France, ... one does speak of the state (*l'état*) as a powerful, independent force in political life, and the almost metaphysical notion of *l'état* as the unified authority of society has a powerful symbolic value in French politics.' The state bureaucracy has been created by the kings

> in their efforts to control the provincial nobles and administer the society without aristocratic mediation through agents directly loyal to the throne. Thus, from the beginning, the state has been an instrument of centralizing power created apart from the society, almost in opposition to it. As such, it was at least partially autonomous.
>
> (Ibid.)

After the French Revolution, the Napoleonic reforms endowed the country with a 'modern, centralized state machinery which has operated since then in a milieu in which state activism has been expected and dreaded'. For a long time, the French 'have subscribed to the view that the engine of industrial progress is the state, not the market' (Katzenstein 1978c: 329).

Until the Second World War, the French business community operated in a climate of peasants, shopkeepers and family ownership of firms, thus 'failing to overcome its position of relative backwardness' compared to Britain and Germany 'in the industrial revolution'. Therefore, after the Second World War, key segments of the French state embarked 'on a strategy of state-led growth' (Hall 1986: 140). The centrepiece of the French economic strategy was the system of economic planning that had important repercussions on state–business and, more generally, state–society relations. It led to close ties between state officials and individual firms, bypassing their associations and also other segments of the French society. As Christine Quittkat (2002: 88) has put it, 'la représentation *politique*, soucieux d'influencer l'ordre du jour politique au plus tôt en cultivant des contacts avec les personnes responsible de son élaboration, est occupé traditionellement par les grandes entreprises publiques ou quasi-publiques' (emphasis in original).[11] In part, the focus on direct relations between companies and government conforms to the French tradition that holds 'the state to be the principal guarantor of the public interest and views with suspicion the transmission of any particular demands' (Baumgartner 1996: 2). Going a long way back in French history (see Mény 1999), this view of state–society relations was expressed in the *loi Le Chapelier* (1791) whose intent it was 'to remove the *corporations* (guilds) from the positions of power and privilege that they had occupied under the ancient regime' (Appleton 2001: 49, italics in original). This retarded the development of interest groups and professional associations after the French revolution until they were 'explicitly recognized under the law on associations' in 1901 (Baumgartner 1996: 2).

As the French government has often used its capacities to promote its political preferences without consulting business in the formulation of its policies, it seems appropriate to characterize French interest intermediation as statist. In France, 'government decision-makers and decision-making organizations take a leadership role in policymaking and have primary control over structuring the "state–society relationship"' (Schmidt 1996: 47). Vivien Schmidt stresses that 'statist governments may take unilateral action at the formulation stage, in particular if it involves "heroic" policies', that is, policies that are salient to their political agenda and have a great symbolic value. However, statist governments 'do generally consult with the most affected parties at the implementation stage' where 'the result may be the politics of accommodation, co-optation or confrontation. What is more, where the policies are more everyday ones, accommodation or co-optation may begin already at the formulation stage, and private interests may hold sway' (Schmidt 1996: 48).

In sum, major political economy theories maintain that, despite the functional pressures for political exchanges in all advanced capitalist democracies, different state–business relations have emerged in France, the United Kingdom and Germany. The national varieties of capitalism and modes of interest intermediation make for very different relations among firms, BIAs and the state. Generally, German BIAs are supposed to play a larger role in the coordination of the economy and in the representation of interests than British or French groups. The next section scrutinizes this proposition empirically.

The interest group systems

The literature on varieties of capitalism and modes of interest intermediation suggests that the business interest group systems in the three countries differ significantly. Pluralism and statism make for more fragmented, competitive and ungovernable interest group populations than corporatism. Liberal and Mediterranean market economies grant associations only a negligible role as coordinators in the economy whereas these groups play an important part in coordinated market economies. Therefore, British and French trade associations are supposed to be much weaker than their counterparts in corporatist countries (Wilson 1990: 77; Schmidt 1996, 2002; Bennett 1997c: 15; Lane 1997: 24; Siaroff 1999; Boleat 2000: 16) with coordinated market economies.[12] They are said to be comparatively small in terms of membership, finance and staff. Only a small share of them should be able to play an active role as interest intermediaries and coordination devices in the economy.

Based on the EUROLOB data, I investigate whether these characterizations of the domestic associational systems hold true before analysing in the subsequent chapters the responses of the associations and firms to European integration. The survey provides information about the degree of fragmentation, integration and competition in national associational settings as well as about the resource endowment and functions of the associations. First, I analyse the fragmentation and integration of the interest group systems. Second, I scrutinize the resource endowment of the associations and the functions they fulfill. This helps to finetune and validate the analysis of the fragmentation and integration of the systems.

Fragmentation, integration, cooperation and competition

Fragmentation and integration

Associational systems consist of associations and the relations among them. They are usually composed of several tiers. Unlike in the study of party systems, no agreement has yet been reached on how to analyse the fragmentation of associational systems because they comprise far more organizations than party systems and are not grouped around a single ideological dimension such as the left–right axis. Building on the literature about party systems (Sartori 1976) as well as that about pluralistic and corporatist interest intermediation (Schmitter 1979), I consider four dimensions of associational systems to be particularly important: the degrees of fragmentation, integration, cooperation and competition.[13] These dimensions characterize the organizational segmentation in the system as well as the structure of inter-organizational relations. In this chapter, I use a combination of indicators to assess the degrees of fragmentation, integration, competition and cooperation. I apply two variance-seeking methods in the statistical analyses that are suitable for the investigation of nominally scaled variables and interval-scaled variables, respectively: Chi^2-tests and analyses of variance.

The degree of *horizontal fragmentation* indicates the extent to which an associational system is split into different organizations. A highly fragmented system is composed of a multitude of associations that have small organizational domains and are not linked to one another. In accordance with the studies on domestic modes of interest intermediation and varieties of capitalism, I expect that the French and

British associational systems are more fragmented than the German system, which yields the following proposition:

H 1 British and French groups have smaller domains than German associations.

As a first step, I analyse the sectoral domain sizes of the associations in each system assuming that smaller domains go hand in hand with a higher degree of fragmentation. Contingency tables and the corresponding Chi^2-tests indicate whether the domain size is related to the associational setting. Insignificant Chi^2-tests suggest statistical independence of the two variables whereas results at the conventional probability levels ($p = .05$ or $p = .01$) specify that the domain size is associated with national characteristics. The domain size of each association has been measured in three categories: sub-sectoral (i.e. industrial chemicals), sectoral (i.e. chemicals) and cross-sectoral (i.e. chemicals and pharmaceuticals).

Table 3.2 indicates that the differentiation and heterogeneity of business gives rise to a variety of rather narrowly defined collective interest organizations. Sometimes, 'businessmen have explicitly chosen a small domain or limited tasks, in order to keep the association homogeneous, minimize free rider problems, or to be able to profit from the differentiation of the state'. Many BIAs had therefore 'low start-up and maintenance costs' (van Waarden 1991: 67–8) and could draw on the resources of their member firms. In sum, the heterogeneity of interests that are embodied in the landscape of business interest groups and advanced by BIAs is quite pronounced (Streeck 1989: 258). At least 84 per cent of the associations in each system are organized at the sub-sectoral or sectoral level. Only a relatively small share of associations is organized across sectors contributing to the cross-sectoral integration of interests.

Notwithstanding these commonalities, the analysis also yields important differences. Roughly half of the British associations are sub-sectoral organizations that are grouped around specific products, production processes or economic functions. This holds only for one third of the French and German associations. As an interim result, the British system is more fragmented than the French and German systems. The major organizing principle in France and Germany is the economic sector: more than half of the French and German groups represent industrial or service sectors. Note also that a greater part of French and British associations are cross-sectoral than is the case in Germany. In all three countries, these cross-sectoral associations help to overcome the horizontal fragmentation of the interest group system by coordinating political and economic activities across sectors.

As a second step, I consider the vertical integration of the interest group systems. So-called higher order associations (see Schmitter and Streeck 1981) are an important mechanism in that respect. As associations of associations or associations of associations and firms (mixed-membership groups) they institutionalize membership relations among different interest groups and provide channels for encompassing collective action. I assume that a greater number of higher order associations in relation to direct membership organizations that organize

Table 3.2 Sectoral domain of national business associations (per cent of national associations)

Associations	Sectoral domain		
	Sub-sectoral	Sectoral	Cross-sectoral
G (N = 312)	34.0	56.7	9.3
UK (N = 187)	49.2	34.8	16.0
F (N = 108)	34.3	50.9	14.8

Note: Chi^2 (4) = 24.267 p = .000

Table 3.3 Type of members in national associations (per cent of national associations)

	Type of members		
	Individuals, firms and various organizations	Associations	Associations and firms
G (N = 308)	67.2	13.0	19.8
UK (N = 194)	73.2	4.6	22.2
F (N = 112)	62.5	7.1	30.4

Note: Chi^2 (4) 14.979, p = .005.

firms, individual entrepreneurs and other business related organizations increases the extent of *vertical integration* within the associational setting. Given the discussion of the domestic modes of interest intermediation and varieties of capitalism, the German interest group system should be more integrated than the British and French systems.

H2 *The German system of business interest groups is vertically more integrated than the British and French systems.*

Table 3.3 presents the membership of the national associations. Direct membership organizations account for 63 to 73 per cent of the associations in each system. The next common type is the mixed-membership group that is composed of associations and firms. Their share ranges from 20 to 30 per cent. In each system, relatively few groups serve as federations that unite different associations.

Even if the national interest group systems have these features in common, they display important differences that provide partial support for H 2. As expected, Germany has the highest share of federations. German groups appear to be joined together in 'complex pyramids of higher-order associations' (Streeck 1989: 268). But note that, in France, about 30 per cent of the associations organize both firms and associations whereas only a fifth of the German and British groups has a mixed membership. Given that mixed-membership groups may contribute as much to the vertical integration of the associational system as federations,[14] the

Table 3.4 Domain size by associational system and type of organization (per cent of type of organization in each national system)

Type of organization • Domain size	Associations		
	G (N = 303)	UK (N = 168)	F (N = 113)
Federation (per cent)			
• Cross-sectoral	7.9	12.5	25.0
• Sectoral	68.4	25.0	50.0
• Sub-sectoral	23.7	62.5	25.0
Mixed-membership (per cent)			
• Cross-sectoral	19.0	22.0	17.6
• Sectoral	44.8	29.3	50.0
• Sub-sectoral	36.2	48.8	32.4
Direct-membership (per cent)			
• Cross-sectoral	7.2	14.6	12.1
• Sectoral	58.0	37.2	51.5
• Sub-sectoral	34.8	48.2	36.4

Note: Germany Chi^2 10.360 (df 4) $p = .035$; UK Chi^2 2.252 (df 4) $p = .690$; France Chi^2 1.401 (df 4) $p = .844$.

French system may be as integrated as the German system, which is contrary to our expectations.

The next step is to analyse the association between domain site and type of organization. A closer inspection (see Table 3.4) reveals that the German pattern of vertical integration in higher associations is more pronounced than in France or the UK. In Germany, interest organizations that are placed at a higher layer of the associational system tend to have a larger domain size, indicating that the German interest group system is quite well ordered with higher-order associations taking on cross-sectoral coordinating functions. In particular, German federations integrate sub-sectoral groups into sectoral organizations for collective action so that there are comparatively few but quite encompassing cross-sectoral associations which unite these sectoral organizations. By contrast, in France and the UK, the domain size is not at all related to the position in the associational system. Many British and several French cross-sectoral organizations are built around specific tasks that range across sectors but the interest groups do not aggregate the interests of these sectors.

Finally, not all cross-sectoral associations are equally capable of overcoming the sectoral boundaries and inter-organizational demarcations. Here, the membership density serves as an important control variable. Corporatist theory (Lehmbruch 1977; Schmitter 1979; Schmitter and Streeck 1981) suggests that the associations can only fulfill an important coordinating role in the political economy if they organize large shares of their potential membership. A certain degree of 'comprehensiveness, integration and relative autonomy' is said to be needed 'to aggregate, process, and redefine the manifold interests of their members' (van Waarden 1991: 53).

Table 3.5 illustrates that the membership densities of business associations are quite high. The fragmentation of business into a variety of interests facilitates the

Table 3.5 Membership density of national associations (per cent of national associations)

Associations	Membership density (members as a percentage of potential members)			
	1–25%	26–50%	51–75%	76–100%
G (N = 306)	8.5	11.1	22.6	57.8
UK (N = 186)	12.4	22.6	22.6	42.5
F (N = 106)	6.6	15.2	22.7	52.7

Note: Chi^2 18.441 (df 6) p = .005.

formation of interest organizations because it reduces the group size (see Olson 1965) and makes for more homogeneous interests (van Waarden 1991). As a result, BIAs usually have higher membership densities than organizations representing more diffuse interests such as social interests, environmental interests or labour (see Streeck 1989: 265). Two-thirds or more of the groups in each country represent at least 50 per cent of their constituencies. Nonetheless, the membership densities differ systematically across countries. German and French associations display a great capacity for recruiting their constituencies into a formal membership: more than half of them organize at least three-quarters of their potential members, and another quarter of the groups represent 51 to 75 per cent of their potential members. British organizations recruit fewer of their potential members. Less than 50 per cent of them organize more than three-quarters of their constituencies. Not only does this undermine the capacity of the groups to act and speak on behalf of their members and be regarded as legitimate representatives of their domains, it also follows that fewer British firms are integrated into the associational system.

I use analyses of variance to check whether the membership density varies among different types of group. This procedure analyses whether there are differences among the mean values of an interval-scaled variable (here: the membership density) that are conditional upon the different groups of a nominally scaled variable (here: the national associations). It is quite robust if ordinal variables are treated as interval-scaled variables, which will be done in some of the following calculations. The procedure places the variance across the mean between the different groups (sum of squares (ss) between) in relation to the variance across the mean within each group (sum of squares (ss) in). The F-value is the ratio among the mean ss between the groups (ss between / df between) and the mean ss within the groups (ss in / df in). For the given degrees of freedom, the F-ratio specifies *whether* there is *a* significant difference among the group means. In addition, so-called post hoc comparisons can point out *which* group means vary.

This yields the following results.[15] British cross-sectoral associations find it particularly difficult to attract members and represent their collective interests. On average, the British groups represent only 48 per cent of their potential members thus organizing fewer segments of their potential members than the British associations with smaller domains. As a consequence, they can hardly help overcoming the fragmentation of the interest group system. In France and Germany, the membership densities range between 63 and 74 per cent in each domain size, indicating a fairly high and consistent degree of associational coordination within and across sectors. In none of these two countries do the membership densities of higher and lower order organizations differ significantly, showing a continuous integration across the different layers of each associational system.[16]

So far, the theoretical expectations about the extent of fragmentation and integration in the interest group systems have not been fully met. The findings do not correspond entirely with the predictions derived from major political economy theories. While the findings on the UK support the assumption that the interaction between a pluralistic mode of interest intermediation and a liberal market economy makes for a fragmented interest group system, unexpectedly, the French interest group system displays a lower degree of sectoral fragmentation and a higher level of vertical integration than was expected. While the German corporatist system is as fragmented as the French statist system, it displays a higher degree of vertical integration.

Cooperation and competition

It is important to bear in mind, though, that these findings do not allow us to jump to strong conclusions about the roles that higher order associations play within the interest group system. The patterns of cooperation and competition within the interest group systems as well as the resource endowment and the most important functions of the groups must be considered when assessing these roles. Many observers argue that the statist French and the pluralistic British systems of interest groups are less cooperative than the German system. Arguably, in these systems, different organizations compete for the same members and need to face rivals in their domains. Also pursuing narrowly defined interests, the organizations in the UK and France should cooperate less and also get less out of their cooperation than the German groups that are supposedly used to mutually beneficial exchanges in the corporatist associational order.

H 3 British and French associations cooperate less with other interest organizations and find that cooperation less useful than German groups.

Table 3.6 indicates how frequently the respondents cooperate with other interest organizations to represent their interests. The percentage of associations that never cooperates with other associations is very small. This is not surprising given that policy-making in advanced capitalist democracies evolves in interorganizational networks. The overwhelming majority of the groups cooperates occasionally or frequently with other organizations.

However, as expected, important cross-national differences remain. Being used to corporatist practices and long-term strategic interactions in the coordinated

Table 3.6 Do you cooperate with other organizations to represent your interests? (per cent of national associations)

Associations	Cooperation with other organizations		
	Never	Sometimes	Frequently
G (N = 313)	2.6	31.3	66.1
UK (N = 202)	1.0	49.0	50.0
F (N = 111)	2.7	46.0	51.4

Note: Chi^2 19.379 (df 4) p = .001.

market economy, German trade associations are highly collaborative: roughly two-thirds of them cooperate *frequently* with other organizations, and about 31 per cent collaborate *occasionally* with other actors. In both France and the UK, only half of the associations cooperate *frequently* with other organizations; the other half works *sometimes* with other groups in order to voice their political concerns. Hence, French and British groups collaborate less than German associations, which is evidence in support of H 3.

Presenting the respondents' cooperation partners and their assessments of the usefulness of their cooperation patterns, Tables 3.7 and 3.8 underscore that finding. Interestingly, the usefulness of the cooperation is independent of the domain size and the layer of the associational system at which the organizations operate.[17] Whereas the conventional interest group theory argues that collective action becomes more difficult with larger domain sizes and broader interests that are to be represented (Olson 1965), the findings put this perspective into question. They indicate that associational evaluations of their cooperation reflect some other organizational factors and national characteristics. Three empirical regularities emerge from the analysis. First, the respondents find the teamwork within their organization more rewarding than that with other interest organizations (Table 3.8). Second, business interest associations cooperate far more with other BIAs than with other kinds of organization (Table 3.7). Finally, nonetheless, they cooperate occasionally with firms, consultants, trade unions and diffuse interest groups when pushing their political interests (Table 3.7).

In general, business interest associations find their intra-organizational cooperation more useful than their inter-organizational relations. About four-fifths and more of the groups in each country testify that cooperation within their organization is 'very useful'. Putting the self-legitimizing components to these answers aside, three major reasons account for this pattern. First, deep conflicts of interests are limited because the variety of interests that is allowed to join in each group is small. It is quite common that the boundaries of these associations are deliberately 'determined by limits to the internal heterogeneity' that they 'can process' (Streeck 1989: 265). In turn, externalizing major conflicts of interests means that these become the subject of inter-organizational relations where they are more difficult to handle and to resolve. Moreover, many associations have

Table 3.7 Cooperation of trade associations with other organizations (per cent of national associations)

Cooperation with	National associations			
	G	UK	F	Sig.
National trade associations	96.7	97.4	99.0	.432
National umbrella associations	92.5	89.1	95.1	.183
Companies	83.0	90.4	87.5	.067
Consultants	66.4	74.0	72.7	.000
Scientific institutes	76.3	74.2	77.3	.810
Trade unions	53.8	55.1	67.7	.051
National environmental, social or consumer NGOs	69.0	79.3	65.3	.016

Note: Significance levels based on Chi^2 tests.

developed routine modes of cooperation in their committees, working groups and executive boards as well as procedures for resolving conflicts in the remaining areas of contention (Eising 1999: 225). Finally, the emphasis of state institutions on a unitary position of interest groups as well as the strength associations can derive from it in the political process vis-à-vis their opponents are important incentives to search for common positions.

Business interest associations cooperate more with each other than with other types of organization. It is indeed hard to find a German, French or British group that does not cooperate with other national BIAs (Table 3.7). Seventy-four per cent of the German organizations, 66 per cent of the British groups and 61 per cent of the French groups find that cooperation 'very useful' (Table 3.8, panel b). Far fewer groups specify that their cooperation with other interest organizations is equally useful. Institutional isomorphism (DiMaggio and Powell 1991) and the associational division of labour account for this pattern: most BIAs confront similar problems and have developed comparable organizational routines to handle them. These practices are extended to long-standing inter-organizational relations among BIAs such that routine relationships and a pronounced division of labour stretch across different sectors and layers of the associational setting.

Most BIAs find the cooperation with other types of actors less useful because it is not embedded in a functional division of labour. BIAs cooperate less with firms than with trade associations when representing political interests. Whereas the cooperation among BIAs serves to build coalitions and strengthen their case, which may also reinforce their status as interest intermediary among their members and state institutions, the political activities of firms can undermine that role and their organizational autonomy (see Chapter 2). Likewise, even though 70 per cent of the associations have already employed professional consultants, only a small minority finds that cooperation indispensable, although 45 to 49 per cent accord some use to employing these 'hired guns'. Evidently, the trade associations are not inclined to contract the representation of their members' interests out on a grand scale. They limit their use of consultants to specific tasks. Finally, about two-thirds of the associations collaborate with supposedly countervailing interests such as trade unions and social or environmental non-governmental organizations (NGOs). But only a small fraction considers this collaboration to be 'very useful'. In fact, convergent interests may sometimes lead to 'baptist and bootlegger' coalitions between industrial and, for instance, environmental groups (see Pollack 1997) but it is rather uncommon that they cooperate over the long term in dense and institutionalized policy communities.

In sum, business interest organizations have developed an important division of labour seeking to further the material benefit of their members and support their organizational autonomy. Even though there may be structural conflicts of interests among various BIAs, for instance on the issue of free trade versus market protection, these are embedded in the economic rationality of their members that can allow for package deals or agreements in which the differences are split. It is clearly more difficult for BIAs to come to common terms with organizations that pursue supposedly antagonistic goals (trade unions), engage strongly in value-loaded debates (environmental or social NGOs) or that might undermine their organizational status (consultants).

Despite these commonalities, the national settings continue to differ in three important respects. Thus, German associations find teamwork within their organizations more useful than French or British groups. They have become an important element in the collective representation of business interests and have to compete less with other formats of interest representation that are open to firms. In German associations, it is not uncommon that different sections of the membership are proportionally represented to assure an adequate representation of the associational constituency. In controversial questions, the neutral and conciliatory behaviour of the associational staff vis-à-vis different parts of the membership is called for. Similarly, the heads of committees that are recruited from firm members (in direct and mixed-membership groups) must act and speak for the overall interests of the membership and not privilege their own firm or sub-group (see Eising 1999: 225). In line with the theoretical expectations, it is more difficult in the more competitive pluralistic and statist regimes for associations to establish themselves as interest intermediaries.

As a corollary, higher order associations are more accepted as interest intermediaries in the German setting than elsewhere (Table 3.8, panel c). Two-thirds of the German groups find it very useful to design their political strategies in the context of national umbrella associations. In France and the UK, only 55 per cent and 48 per cent, respectively, of the associations find that their cooperation within higher-order associations is of great use. The greater scepticism of British groups is also evident from the fact that some 14 per cent of them regard cooperation within federations as ineffective. The score for German and French associations is only 7 per cent. Accordingly, the extent of associational coordination across the different levels of the system is greater in the German and, even if less so, French interest group systems than in the UK. All in all, higher order associations have a greater role to play in Germany than in the other countries. They are regarded as useful coordination devices making for a comparatively integrated associational

Table 3.8 Usefulness of organizational cooperation (per cent of national associations)

	Usefulness of cooperation		
	Not useful	Of some use	Very useful
Panel a) within the trade association (Chi^2 15.522 (df 4) p = .004)			
G (N = 275)	1.1	10.5	88.4
UK (N = 169)	4.7	17.8	77.5
F (N = 88)	0.0	18.2	81.8
Panel b) with national trade associations (Chi^2 9.043 (df 4) p = .060)			
G (N = 291)	3.1	22.7	74.2
UK (N = 185)	5.4	28.6	65.9
F (N = 104)	3.8	35.6	60.6
Panel c) in national umbrella associations (Chi^2 15.22 (df 4) p = .004)			
G (N = 259)	6.6	27.8	65.6
UK (N = 156)	13.5	38.5	48.1
F (N = 96)	7.1	37.8	55.1
Panel d) with consultants (Chi^2 3.945 (df 4) p = .413)			
G (N = 194)	41.8	44.8	13.4
UK (N = 158)	34.8	44.9	20.3
F (N = 72)	36.1	48.6	15.3
Panel e) with companies (Chi^2 9.606 (df 4) p = .048)			
G (N = 244)	21.7	38.5	39.8
UK (N = 169)	16.0	50.3	33.7
F (N = 84)	10.7	50.0	39.3
Panel f) with trade unions (Chi^2 8.725 (df 4) p = .068)			
G (N = 157)	49.0	37.6	13.4
UK (N = 103)	55.3	27.2	17.5
F (N = 65)	38.5	35.4	26.2
Panel g) with national consumer, social or environmental groups (Chi^2 6.249 (df 4) p = .181)			
G (N = 200)	46.0	41.0	13.0
UK (N = 149)	38.3	38.9	22.8
F (N = 64)	45.3	37.5	17.2

setting. The efforts of peak associations at coordinating the activities of their members and representing their interests are less likely to succeed in the fragmented British interest group system.

The third distinguishing trait is the teamwork of associations and companies. While the share of associations that collaborate with firms does not vary across nations, the perceptions of the usefulness of this cooperation do. British and French associations work more closely with companies when representing their interests than German associations (Tables 3.7, 3.8 panel e). In British pluralism, trade associations are accustomed to the political representation of interests by firms (Grant 2000), and in French statism, the bureaucracy has often consulted with firms rather than associations (Schmidt 1996). In both countries, firms may be able to provide the associations with an additional entrée to the political institutions or information about political processes. In contrast, in German corporatism, the political activities of firms pose a greater challenge to associations which have been able to act as interest intermediaries between their members and the state. Accordingly, German associations also work less with consultants than French or British associations.

These findings confirm that pluralistic modes of interest intermediation go hand in hand with less collaboration among associations and reduce their role as interest intermediaries. But they also modify some previous insights into the fragmentation and integration of the interest group systems. Notably, the French system is not as fragmented as expected. The French and German interest group systems display fairly similar degrees of fragmentation even though the patterns of integration and cooperation in these systems differ. In Germany, trade associations are more important coordination devices than in France. And higher-order associations play a more important part in the representation of interests in the corporatist regime than in the statist setting.

The resources and the functions of BIAs

Financial resources and sources of revenue

Associations depend for their economic and political activities on the resources that they can obtain from both their members and external sources. To secure their organizational survival and maintenance, they offer their (potential) members certain incentives in exchange, thus fulfilling a variety of functions for them (J. Wilson 1973: 30–55; see in more detail Chapter 2). In particular, associations depend on the financial contributions of their members. Studies on the national modes of interest intermediation and varieties of capitalism reason that German associations play a greater role in the national political economy than French or British groups. German associations should therefore be better endowed than French or British groups.

H 4 German associations are better endowed than French or British groups.

I test this proposition by comparing the average financial resources of the associations. According to Table 3.9, the average resource endowment of the associations does not vary much across countries. Roughly half of them has no more than 500,000 € at their disposal. Associations at the sub-sectoral or sectoral level, especially, are fairly small and have little staff. In all countries we find roughly equal shares of associations in the top three income categories. About 20 per cent of the groups command between 500,000 € and one million €, and about 21 to 25 per cent marshal between one million and five million €. The number of associations that is very well equipped is comparatively small: Only nine to ten per cent have an annual income of more than five million €.

Notwithstanding these similarities, a few cross-national differences remain. German associations have significantly more resources at their disposal than their British counterparts. Contrary to our expectations, the resources of French and German groups do not differ greatly, indicating further structural similarities of

Table 3.9 Financial resources of national associations (per cent of national associations)

Finance in 1,000 €	Associations		
	G associations (N = 296)	UK associations (N = 184)	F associations (N = 104)
0–100	12.8	31.0	8.7
101–500	32.8	22.8	41.3
501–1,000	18.9	16.3	17.5
1,001–5,000	25.0	21.2	24.1
More than 5,000	10.5	8.7	9.4

Note: Chi^2 35.3547 (df 8), p = .000. Deviations from 100% are due to rounding errors.

these systems. The most important cross-national difference consists in the share of very small associations with an income below 100,000 €: This share is far greater in the UK than it is in France or Germany, underscoring the fragmentation of the British interest group system.

Business associations have different ways of financing themselves. To various degrees, they derive their income from membership subscriptions, services they provide to their members, public finance and other sources of revenue. Many groups depend on the subscriptions of their members. Firms usually have sufficient resources at their disposal to finance their membership in organizations that represent their collective interests (see Chapter 2). Relative to the income of a firm, the membership subscription is not very costly (J. Wilson 1973: 144). In addition to the membership fees they raise, several associations derive their income from specific services such as legal counselling to their members, for which these need to pay. Moreover, associations may receive some form of public finance even though this way of obtaining organizational finance is more common among diffuse interests such as consumers or environmental groups that have greater difficulties organizing and sustaining themselves than it is among business interests.

The discussion of the modes of interest intermediation and the varieties of national capitalism in each country yields the expectation that the mix of financial sources varies systematically across the three countries. Given that they operate in a market-orientated environment, the relationship of British associations to their members should, to a greater extent than in the other countries, be governed by market relations. British associations should therefore obtain a greater share of their revenues from the services they deliver to their members than German and French associations. These should depend to a greater extent on membership subscriptions.

H 5 British associations depend to a greater extent on revenues derived from services than German and French associations. These finance themselves, relatively more, by membership subscriptions.

According to Table 3.10, on average, national business associations derive the bulk of their revenues – namely between 70 and 90 per cent – from membership

Table 3.10 Revenue sources of national associations (mean of revenue source in per cent of total income)

Source of revenue	Associations			Sig.
	G (N = 306)	UK (N = 193)	F (N = 108)	
Membership subscriptions	90.0	71.0	86.4	.000
Services	5.4	18.6	6.4	.000
Public finance	1.0	0.6	1.3	.559
Other	4.0	9.7	4.9	.000

Note: Deviations from 100% are due to rounding errors. Significance levels are based on analyses of variance.

subscriptions followed by a more or less substantial share of income they obtain from their services. The membership subscriptions are crucial not only because they are their largest source of income but also because they are usually not tied to specific tasks the associations are supposed to pursue. The associations can fairly autonomously dispose of these payments when defining and representing the collective interest of their members or producing more specific goods for them. By contrast, the income that is derived from services is more closely tied to the provision of these specific goods for their members. It is not uncommon for associations to face the competition of commercial providers of these services so that this source of income is also more insecure. Other sources of finance such as the revenues obtained through licensing agreements, marketing activities or donations are far less important to trade associations. Finally, as expected, earnings obtained through public finance amount only to a marginal share of their revenues.

The associations derive the bulk of their income for the collective goods they produce. This holds even for the British groups which operate in an environment that is structured to a greater extent by market relations than by other coordinating devices. However, British associations have a more diversified structure of revenues than French or German groups, which corresponds with H 5. As expected, they depend less on membership subscriptions, obtaining approximately 19 per cent of their income from the provision of services and roughly 10 per cent from other activities. The greater the budget of British groups, the more important become services as a source of income: Associations with an annual income of up to 500,000€ obtain, on average, only about 11 to 12 per cent of their income from services, but BIAs with a budget of more than five million€ derive 36 per cent of their financial means from services. In the UK, organizational growth and consolidation is highly dependent on the ability of associations to produce specific services for their members. This is in marked contrast with the situations in France and Germany where the total endowment is unrelated to specific sources of revenue.[18] In both countries, large and resourceful associations finance themselves as much through membership subscriptions as smaller and poorer associations. The conclusion is that market relations indeed play a much greater role for British associations than for French or German associations.

Specific exchanges govern the relationship between them and their members to a greater extent so that their expenditure is under tighter control than in the other countries. The implication is that British associations are less autonomous from their members than the French or German groups.

The functions of the national business associations

Business interest associations can serve a variety of purposes. They can serve as producer associations that represent the variety of the firms' interests pertaining to product markets, they can act as employer associations that represent the interests of firms in the labour market vis-à-vis state institutions and trade unions or they can serve as coordination devices in the market place, regulating market entry and behaviour or working towards education standards of the labour force or quality standards for products. The political economy literature predicts that business interest organizations in France, Germany and the UK assume different functions. From studies on the modes of interest intermediation it is reasonable to infer that the corporatist German and pluralistic British associations play a greater role in the representation of their members' interests in public policy-making than the statist French associations. Studies on the varieties of capitalism suggest that business interest associations in coordinated market economies play a greater role in setting standards and delivering services to members than those in Mediterranean or liberal market economies. Accordingly, German associations should be more involved in these tasks than British or French associations.

H 6 British and German associations are more involved in representing the interests of their members vis-à-vis the state than French associations.

H 7 German associations produce more services for their members and are more involved in coordinating markets than British or French organizations.

Table 3.11 groups the most important activities of BIAs in *three major functions* that may be performed for their members: To various degrees, they engage in the representation of interests, the provision of services and the coordination of markets. Within each dimension, the associations can provide a variety of tasks such as the monitoring of political activities, legal counselling or standard setting. Separately for each country, panel (a) indicates the mean percentage of resources that the associations devote to each function and panel (b) presents the percentage of associations that exert a specific task within each of these functions.

Prima facie, the functional profiles of the trade associations in each system resemble each other, highlighting important task contingencies that business interest associations must cope with. On average, the groups allocate between 42 and 50 per cent of their resources to the representation of interests and between 34 and 39 per cent to the provision of services to their members. Market coordination plays only a minor role. On average, the associations devote some 11 to 13 per cent of their resources to it. The setting of technical norms or quality standards takes up a

Table 3.11 Functions of national business associations

Function	Associations			
	G	UK	F	Sig.
Panel a) Mean financial resources spent on functions (per cent of total resources)				
Interest representation	49.8	42.1	44.9	.006
Services	33.9	38.5	39.2	.051
Market coordination	11.1	12.5	12.5	.481
Other functions	5.2	6.5	4.5	.353
Panel b) Do you provide the following functions? (per cent of associations)				
Interest representation				
Monitoring of political activities	68.9	88.1	53.3	.000
Informing members about political developments	82.4	89.2	39.1	.000
Political representation of members in committees and hearings	83.7	76.2	33.3	.000
Interest representation vis-à-vis other interest organizations	95.2	91.2	87.6	.024
Interest representation vis-à-vis trade unions	28.2	25.3	64.8	.000
Services				
Statistics and branch information	94.6	70.1	90.7	.000
Market research	60.1	52.6	75.7	.000
Legal and economic consulting	67.1	46.4	86.9	.000
Access to consultants	39.0	54.4	60.8	.000
Public affairs and advertisement	82.4	76.8	90.7	.001
Member education and qualification	64.2	61.9	54.2	.184
Market coordination				
Definition of technical norms and standards	63.3	73.4	67.6	.063
Definition of quality and education standards	55.4	58.9	59.3	.670
Coordination of research and development	44.3	48.4	42.6	.545
Regulation of market entrance	29.8	17.3	36.1	.001
Issuing of licenses and certificates	18.4	25.5	13.9	.035
Resolution of conflicts among members	47.9	54.7	47.2	.276

Note: Significance levels based on analyses of variance (Panel a) and Chi^2 tests (Panel b).

rather small share of their resources. Most trade associations do not regulate market entrance and behaviour because domestic and EC competition law usually stripped them of these functions (see van Waarden 1994). Finally, on average, the associations spend up to seven per cent of their income on residual activities.

In sum, the most important function of BIAs is the collective representation of business interests. Their vital task is to defend their members' interests in the policy-making process (Table 3.11, panel b). The production of specific goods or services for their members is only of secondary importance. Hence, the *collective representation of business interests* is *the raison d'être* of most organizations rather than a by-product of the services they provide to members. While a certain amount of these services may help to attach members closer to the associations they have only supplementary function. Given that this evidence applies exactly to those rational actors which Olson's logic of collective action (1965) purports to cover, it speaks against the importance of selective goods for the collective organization of business.

Nonetheless, there remain cross-national differences. Taking on an important role in corporatist interest intermediation, German trade associations allocate a greater portion of their revenues to the *representation of interests* than British associations. As expected (H 6), French associations are less active in representing business interests vis-à-vis state institutions than German or British groups (Table 3.11, panel b). Clearly, they take on a less political role: only little more than half of them monitor political developments and just a third represents their members in public committees or public hearings. These differences lessen when it comes to representing interests vis-à-vis other interest organizations. Interestingly, relatively more French than German or British groups assume the functions of employer associations. In Germany and the UK, the representation of employers' interests is concentrated on a smaller subset of BIAs that is organizationally distinct from that representing producer interests. As a result of their activities vis-à-vis other interest organizations, French associations devote as many resources to the representation of interests as British groups (panel a).

The differences between British and German associations are less obvious. However, a greater share of British than German groups monitors political developments, filtering and processing the incoming information to their members. The opposite is true for the representation of interests in formal meetings with policy-makers and for the representation of interests vis-à-vis other groups. The conclusion is that British associations serve to a greater extent than the German associations as listening posts. By contrast, the German groups are more frequently being delegated the task of representing the interests of their members than is the case in the UK, underpinning the differences between corporatist and pluralist regimes. It is important to reiterate, though, that these differences are a matter of degree when bringing the French associations into perspective.

The provision of *services* to their members is an important task of trade associations. While these services come nowhere close to being the raison d'être of the organizations, they can form selective incentives that tie their members closer to the associations (see Olson 1965) and ensure the flow of resources that associations need to operate. The production of statistics and branch information as well as engagement in public affairs and advertisement activities are the most common services that associations provide to their members. Nonetheless, there are significant differences in the service profiles of the associations across nations. Not all of these differences can be easily reconciled with the predictions derived from the literature on the varieties of capitalism. If one leaves out effects resulting from cross-national variations in the budget sizes of associations, the empirical evidence bears out the proposition (H 7) that German associations produce more services than British or French groups. It is only true that British associations provide fewer services to their members.[19] Having to compete to a greater extent with commercial service providers and being subjected to tighter budgetary pressures, their range of services is smaller than that of French or German associations.

Cross-national variations are least evident in the coordination of markets, which appears also to be the least important function of most associations. Otherwise than expected (H 7), German associations are not more involved in the coordination of markets than British or French organizations. The pattern of cross-national differences is quite varied: French organizations regulate market entry to a greater extent than British and German groups, and British organizations are more engaged in certifying their members' economic activities by issuing licenses than German or French groups. In other respects, there are no significant cross-national variations.

The functions that associations assume should not only vary cross-nationally but also across the different layers of the system. In general, higher-order associations should concern themselves more with the collective representation of business interests than lower-order associations. The latter are generally more concerned with delivering services to their members and coordinating market activities. Given the variations in the national modes interest intermediation, this division of labour should be more pronounced in corporatist regimes than in statist or pluralistic settings.

H 8 *German higher-order associations are more involved in the collective representation of interests than lower-order associations. In France and the UK, this division of labour is less pronounced.*

In line with this proposition, German federations concentrate more on the representation of political interests than mixed or direct membership groups: on average, German federations devote more than two-thirds of their resources to this task whereas the other groups allocate about 48 per cent to it. In France, the division of labour across the different associational layers is even more outspoken, which undermines H 8: French federations spend 83 per cent of their financial means on the representation of interests, whereas direct and membership groups allocate about 44 per cent and 40 per cent, respectively, to this task. By contrast, British federations do not spend significantly larger portions of their income on interest representation (54 per cent) than direct (43 per cent) or mixed-membership organizations (36 per cent), corroborating the evidence about their ineffective role as coordinating devices in the British political economy.[20]

Conclusion

Firms join interest organizations and enter into political exchanges with state institutions because business does not assume an unconditionally privileged position in the political economy of advanced capitalist democracies. Highlighting the importance of national ideas about state–economy and state–society relations as well as the relevance of political-economic institutions, two important strands of the political economy literature emphasize that these exchanges vary greatly across nations. Both the studies on the modes of interest intermediation and analyses of the varieties of national capitalism find that Germany, France and the UK fall into different camps. In essence, they suggest that business interest associations play a much greater role in the German political economy than in the French or British settings. The argument is that German BIAs are more important to the collective representation of business interests and also play a greater role in the coordination of the economy than their French or British counterparts.

Drawing on the EURLOB data, this chapter discussed these propositions. The empirical study confirmed some of these theoretical propositions but modified others. It must be stressed that the associational systems display important similarities across nations that can be traced to the task contingencies most business interest associations must cope with. However, the associational settings also display distinct national traits that have been identified in earlier studies even though the cross-national differences are less noticeable than is often asserted. In particular, the German and French interest group systems exhibit pronounced structural similarities.

In line with previous research, the British system of trade associations is more fragmented and less integrated than the German and French systems. The relations between British associations and their members are governed to a greater extent by the market than they are in France and Germany. British firms hold their associations on a tight budgetary leash and allow for associational growth only if they receive selective goods from them. The British pluralistic setting makes for less cooperation among associations and renders cooperation less useful than in a corporatist setting.

The surprising result of the comparison is that the French and German systems are not nearly as different as the comparative political economy literature suggests. Both systems of business interest groups resemble each other in terms of their sectoral fragmentation, their integration across different layers and their resource endowment. However, notwithstanding these structural similarities, the workings of the systems differ in important respects corresponding with political economy theories. The extent of associational cooperation is more pronounced in Germany than in France and so is the acceptance of higher-order associations as political interest intermediaries among the state and business. French associations are much less involved in the representation of interests vis-à-vis state institutions, underpinning the predominant characterization of France as statist. They mainly serve to promote their members' interests vis-à-vis other interest organizations and it is more common for them to provide a variety of services to their members.

In sum, the chapter verified important tenets of the political economy theories that were the basis for selecting the countries in which the national associations operate. However, highlighting the importance of the functional exigencies under which trade associations in all these systems operate and pointing to major cross-national similarities, the discussion also suggests that this literature is in need of being fine-tuned.

Part II
Multilevel governance and the Europeanization of domestic interest group systems

4 The evolution of the EU interest group system

To join or not to join?

This chapter gives an overview of the EU interest group system and analyses the reasons why firms and national associations join EU associations. The first section provides an account of the major trends in the evolution of the EU interest group system from the 1950s until 2001. It demonstrates that, over the course of the last 50 years, the European interest group system has co-evolved with the EU institutional setting (Eichener and Voelzkow 1994b). Ever more actors and types of organization have become active at the European level, and the interests represented at the EU level have also broadened considerably.

After presenting the EU interest group system, I subject different arguments about the logic of collective action in the EU to scrutiny, exploring two sets of factors that are held to be important for collective action: First, at the macro level, pluralist studies (see Truman 1951) have emphasized the importance of political contexts and socio-economic dynamics for the evolution of interest group systems. Drawing on the CONECCS data of the European Commission on EU associations and structural data on the EU member states, the impact of such factors will be studied in some detail. This analysis indicates that membership in EU associations by country is closely related to the size of a country, its level of economic prosperity and its patterns of interest intermediation.

Second, at the micro level, Mancur Olson (1965) has argued that actors make rational cost–benefit calculations when deciding to get organized in order to pursue collective goals. These calculations can impede collective action when individual costs exceed individual benefits even if the potential members of a group have parallel interests. In this situation, a collective good will not be provided or only a sub-optimal amount of it will be produced. Olson suggested that selective material incentives that are only available to the organizational members but not to non-members will increase the denominator of the cost–benefit ratio and make collective action therefore more attractive. Drawing on the EUROLOB data, the importance of the incentives that EU associations offer their members will be tested.

This analysis reveals that such selective material incentives are largely irrelevant for the decision of national groups to join an EU association. The findings support the argument that membership in EU associations is a second order collective action problem (see Jordan 1998): the decision to join EU associations is not one about *whether* to engage in collective action which has already been taken in the member states when national interest groups were formed but one about *how* to engage in it.

The evolution of the EU interest group system has been characterized by three general trends that parallel the development of national interest group systems: The *types of organization* that represent their interests vis-à-vis the EU institutions have diversified, and the *scope of the interests* that are being represented has widened. Correspondingly, the *number of interest groups* at the European level has increased over time.[1] The 'lobby-system in Brussels' is therefore no longer in its formative stages, as Sven S. Andersen and Kjell A. Eliassen (1991) still put it at the beginning of the 1990s. It is now highly differentiated, but still more dynamic than the associational systems in the Western European member states. The situation is different in the new Eastern European member states of the European Union in which liberal interest group systems have only emerged with the transition of these countries to democracy and capitalism.

EU level interest groups

The evolution of the EU level interest group system

Drawing on the European Commission's registry of civil society organizations (CONECCS),[2] Figure 4.1 displays the evolution of EU level interest groups. Associations that organize members from at least two EU member states are eligible to register. The Commission classifies the associations according to their own statements. Due to double countings and missing data on the foundation years of several Eurogroups, the number of associations that were reported in the database in May 2002 drops from 941 to 885. CONECCS includes only existing associations and thus does not provide information about population dynamics. It indicates the *net* increase or decrease in the number of Eurogroups that result from new foundations, mergers and dissolutions of interest groups in each year. CONECCS includes several international and European associations that do not concentrate on EU affairs. This explains the foundation years before 1951.

Building also on previous directories of the European Commission, and on the names and missions of the associations, Figure 4.1 groups the EU associations into seven general categories. The category *agriculture* denotes forestry, agriculture and nutrition. *Industry* covers various industrial sectors, products and employers. *Services* encompasses both commercial services such as finances and trade and many non-profit orientated services such as health or education. *Professions* includes mostly the liberal professions. *Regions* denotes the associations of localities and regions as well as of urban and rural planning. *Diffuse interests* stands for youth, religious, social, welfare, environmental, consumer and human rights associations as well as trade unions. *Various interests* is a residual category for those groups that cannot be assigned to any of the other categories.

Figure 4.1 highlights some general development trends and identifies the major cycles of organizational mobilization. Until the European Communities were set

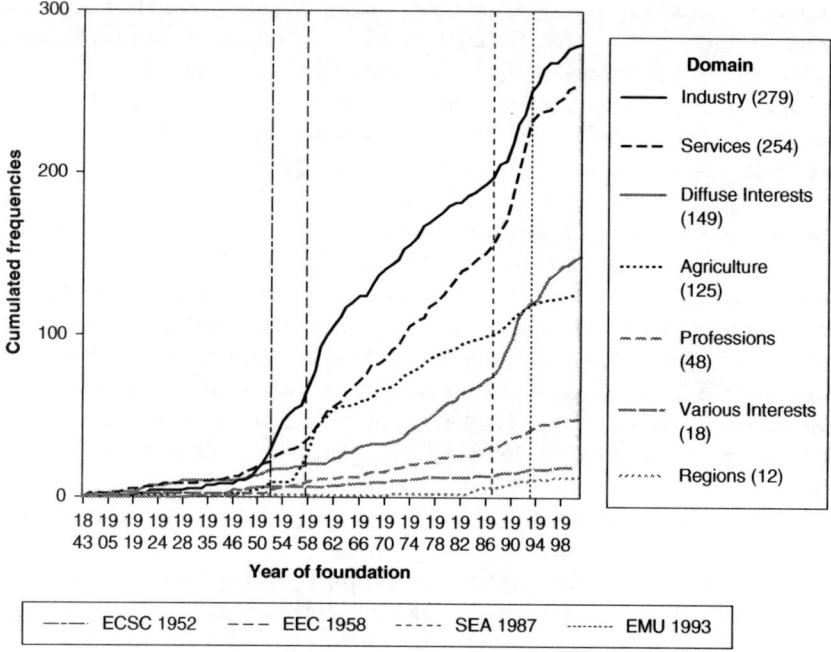

Figure 4.1 European associations according to domain and year of foundation from 1843 to 2001 (cumulated frequencies)

Source: General Secretariat of the European Commission. CONECCS data set, May 2002. Vertical lines denote the implementation of treaties or treaty changes.

up, the number of European associations was relatively small. After small beginnings, the number of European interest groups increased substantially over time: writing in 1958, Ernst Haas claimed that the formation of the European Community for Steal and Coal (ECSC) 'resulted in the formation of one peak association, two producers' groups, three consumers' groups and one organisation of dealers' (1958: 323). According to Leon Lindberg (1963: 97), the Commission already counted 222 European interest organizations in 1961, shortly after all three European Communities had been put in place.[3] The CONECCS data indicate that their number more than quadrupled over the course of the next 40 years. Clearly, the build-up of European institutions and the development of European policies led to a growing presence of EU level interest groups.

There are two major foundation waves. The first of them sets in with the foundation of the European Coal and Steel Community (ECSC) and loses pace in 1961/62, a few years after the foundation of the European Economic Community (EEC) and the European Atomic Energy Community (EURATOM). The second wave starts with the implementation of the Internal Market Programme (IMP) in the second half of the 1980s. It ebbs away after the Maastricht treaty on the Economic and Monetary

Union (EMU) comes into force in 1993. Between these high tides, the rate of increase in the number of EU associations is fairly constant in each domain, even though it differs across them. Thus, even during the long period of the so-called 'Eurosclerosis' from the mid-1960s to the early 1980s – also termed the 'dark ages' of European integration by prominent observers (Keohane and Hoffmann 1991: 8) – the number of groups did not decline but increased continuously.

Industry associations and trade unions organized early in response to the emergence of international organizations in Europe. Many of them set up European associations after the Organization for European Economic Cooperation (OEEC) and the European Community for Steel and Coal were founded in the early 1950s. Other kinds of domestic interest group hardly reacted to these developments by setting up European interest organizations. The establishment of the EEC sustained that momentum for a few more years until 1961. Between 1961 and 1985, the net growth rate of European associations dropped to an average of approximately four associations per year. In contrast to the employers and producers who agreed early on to set up a European federation of industry, the organization of European trade unions evolved differently. The formation of an encompassing European trade union organization was initially inhibited by ideological and organizational divisions among the national unions (Ebbinghaus and Visser 1994; Martin and Ross 1999: 321–2). Only with the founding of the European Trade Union Confederation (ETUC) in 1973, which was open to ideologically diverse national unions, was the organizational fragmentation of trade unions at the European level overcome.

The Internal Market Programme (IMP) and Economic and Monetary Union triggered the second wave of organizational mobilization that ebbed away in the second half of the 1990s. The agricultural sector organized comprehensively after the foundation of the EEC on the European level, that is, the national groups set up a large number of European organizations even before major decisions on the Common Agricultural Policy had been taken. Since then, the rate of increase in the number of European organizations has been fairly constant. Unlike in the other domains, neither the IMP nor EMU led to a more dynamic evolution in the sector's organization at the European level. As national economies in the 1950s were dominated by industries and not services, fewer European organizations for services accompanied the foundation of the European institutions. But from the early 1960s to the mid-1980s, the rate of increase in the number of service organizations was slightly higher than in industry. The number of service organizations increased dramatically during the implementation of the IMP and the move towards EMU. Hence, the growing importance of services in the economies of the member states did not show immediately in the organization of these sectors at the European level but was conditional upon the development of the European institutions. Non-occupational interests began to get more organized at the European level only in the 1970s. Their number increased during the implementation of the IMP and EMU because from then on, European competencies in non-economic affairs increased considerably. From the mid-1990s until 2001, the rate of increase in the number of EU organizations for diffuse interests exceeds those in other domains so that, by now, their number has come to surpass that of the agricultural associations.

Fifty-nine per cent of the organizations listed in CONECCS are located in Brussels, showcasing their focus on the EU institutions. Forty-one per cent are dispersed through the member states (N = 359). The founding members of the European Union and the United Kingdom host the large majority of these groups. Several Eurogroups that are not sited in Brussels are closely connected to or run by national associations. In several of these cases, the responsibility for managing the secretariat of the EU association changes every few years among their national members.

The functions and roles of Eurogroups

To different degrees, the Eurogroups serve to:

- acquire information about EU developments and process it to their members;
- open up linkages to the European institutions;
- provide a liaison among their members and develop common positions;
- represent their members in EU decision-making and vis-à-vis other actors; and
- participate in the formulation and implementation of EU policies.

More generally, an EU association can be an *actor* in its own right, an *instrument* for its members or a *forum* in which its members build their opinions. In general, EU associations are regarded as *fora* for their members rather than as autonomous actors. Several analyses point out that EU business associations find it difficult to acquire a status as actors. Frequently, these organizations manage to formulate a binding common position only when the interests of their members converge (Haas 1958: 320, 371; Lindberg 1963: 99; Caporaso 1974: 34). It is not unusual that it is not the staff of the Eurogroups who takes the lead in the internal negotiations but coalitions of national associations or firms (Kohler-Koch 1992: 97; Greenwood and Webster 2000; Lahusen and Jauß 2001: 76). Ernst Haas suggested in his classic study of the integration process in the coal and steel industries (1958: 318–54) that, because of the heterogeneous interests of their members and the complications arising from the need to aggregate interests at different levels, many European associations have substantial difficulties agreeing on a meaningful common position that would help them become relevant interlocutors of the European institutions. According to Haas, pragmatic bargaining is the dominant mode of interaction in these organizations:

> the type of agreement reached very seldom relates to a commonly held ideology or to fundamentally shared values. Consensus is 'tactical' in the sense that it relates to specific policy issues confronting the associations in question, giving rise to one pattern [of] cooperation in one instance and quite a different pattern in the next. Certainly this implies a high degree of functionally specific orientation on the part of the members. Not *Weltanschauung* but price 'extras' on wire rods or Grade 3 anthracite are focal issues.
>
> (Haas 1958: 353, emphasis in original)

For these reasons, several analyses put into question the capacity of these groups to steer the political activities of their members and to make them comply with the positions that have been taken (Greenwood and Webster 2000). Some EU associations are confined to being *instruments* of their members. It is most likely that they take on this role if one or a few large members dominate the association and use it as a collective cloak for the pursuit of their individual interests (Greenwood 2002a: 70–1). However, the fact that many national associations, firms and political consultants are now present in the European arena (see below) indicates that there are sincere limits to the amount of control any single member or group of members can exert over the EU associations. But note also that, according to some authors, EU associations can gain considerable autonomy from their members and devise strategies for their concerted political activities (Knill 2001).

Moreover, the role of a Eurogroup as a *forum* should not be underestimated. The EU associations put their members in permanent liaison and communication. Their associational structures and procedures provide means for both building consensus and resolving conflicts. Their members get to know the policies and structures in other member states and learn to empathize with different political positions (Platzer 1984: 165; Cram 1998: 76) even though they may continue to evaluate EU policy proposals primarily in terms of their organizational interests. This exchange of information about EU policy-making and the positions of other actors can affect their interest definitions, letting them sometimes converge with those of the other members (Eising and Jabko 2001). Ernst Haas' (1958: 337) assessment that different 'national ideological and structural factors' let 'no amount of discussion' succeed 'in persuading the members to a new and common view' may therefore be put into question. Their importance as a forum should increase when the EU associations are crucial channels for their members to the EU institutions – which many of them are (see Chapters 5–8).

The analysis of EU associations as fora, actors and instruments points to the scope conditions for each role. Empirical studies have highlighted several conditions that can support the role of an EU association as an *actor* rather than a *forum*. The increase in EU regulation and the switch from negative integration to positive integration pushed the value of EU associations for their members. It not only promoted the foundation of several new associations, but led also to changes within EU associations and widened their activities. Nonetheless, tighter EU regulation does not automatically enhance the autonomy of these groups. When the European industry federation UNICE (that is now BusinessEurope) sought to expand its competencies in response to the IMP, some of its members rejected these efforts, arguing that they would not let their organizational autonomy be reduced to such an extent that they could only be regarded as national parts of a unitary European industry.[4] Hence, the increase in the powers of the EU institutions has certainly enhanced UNICE's tasks and its workload,[5] but did not provide for a corresponding increase in its autonomy.

Corporatist theory has pointed out (Lehmbruch 1977; Schmitter 1979) that the delegation of decision-making and implementation rights to associations can enhance their organizational autonomy as well as their capacity to formulate binding positions for their members. The Social Dialogue gives such rights to the cross-sectoral social partners in a limited area of EU social policy. However, social policy experts (Falkner 1998; Martin and Ross 1999) are sceptical that the Social Dialogue has significantly increased the autonomy of UNICE, ETUC or CEEP (European Centre of Enterprises with Public Participation and of Enterprises of General Economic Interest) vis-á-vis their members. For example, the ETUC members:

> affirmed ETUC's negotiating role but confined it to intersectoral negotiations under the Social Protocol, only when given specific mandates, and subject to strict and continuous control by the national unions through national confederation and EIF [European Industry Federation] representatives on ETUC governing bodies.
> (Martin and Ross 1999: 339)

Hence, delegating political competencies to EU associations need not to enhance their organizational autonomy.

Moreover, the market structure in which firms are embedded can promote or impede their political cooperation at EU level. The research intensive pharmaceutical industry is said to match several conditions that support collective action and an autonomous role for its associations. The sector is heavily dependent on state regulation. Besides many small and medium sized firms, it consists of a limited number of large companies that can carry the burden of collective action. Competition among them is limited and, cross-nationally, the sector is marked by similar problems and a tradition of close cooperation with national state authorities (see Baumheier 1992; Kotzian 2003: 19–47). As a result of these features, the European pharmaceutical association EFPIA (European Federation of Pharmaceutical Industries and Associations) is held to be one of the best organized and most influential European associations (Greenwood and Ronit 1994) even though its capacities to shape EU regulation vary across issues (Greenwood 2003). Notably, as long as important regulatory competencies remain at the domestic level, it is not likely that EFPIA's activities will replace those of the national pharmaceutical associations.

Several other studies discuss the relation between the organizational characteristics of EU associations and their capacity to act and speak for their members. Konrad Schwaiger and Emil Kirchner (1981: 47–76) compared the organizational structure of 21 Eurogroups. Their index of organizational development stresses the resource mobilization of these groups (support, expertise, finance, personnel) as a major prerequisite for their capacity to fulfil their tasks and represent their members vis-à-vis the EU institutions. Justin Greenwood (2002a: 30) analysed the impact of 28 organizational features and members' characteristics on the ability of 49 Eurogroups to formulate common positions for their members and make them comply with these goals. Like other authors, he (2002a: 112) stresses that a narrow interest domain, a keen interest in EU regulation, economic overcapacities in conjunction with a high degree of sectoral concentration and organizational autonomy enhance the ability of EU associations to act and speak for their members. Chapters 7 and 8 test in detail the impact of such factors on the access of the interest organizations to the European Union institutions.

In sum, the role of EU associations in EU policy-making varies, partly depending on the market structures in which their members are embedded, on their organizational characteristics and on the issues that are at stake. Cross-sectoral EU level federations of national federations usually serve as fora but do not act and speak autonomously for their members. Several EU associations with narrower interest domains have proven to be more efficient actors. At the very least, the EU associations have evolved into information brokers among the EU institutions and their members. For many national associations, they remain the most important route to the EU institutions. Their involvement in EU politics and their increasing professionalism over the years provides them clearly with an advantage at the EU level over their national members.

National associations, firms and political consultants

Given the handicaps that restrict EU level groups' full representation of their constituencies, *national associations* have always been active at the EU level (Meynaud and Sidjanski 1971). Nowadays, approximately 170 national associations and 171 regions have set up bureaux in the Belgian capital to facilitate regular contacts with the EU institutions and provide a liaison with the EU associations (Greenwood 2003: 9). In addition, there is an unknown number of national actors that do not have an institutionalized presence in Brussels but are more or less regularly in touch with the EU institutions, particularly if they are located within a short travelling distance.

Only later, the role of large firms in the European Union came into focus. Today, about 250 of them maintain offices in Brussels in order to represent their interests (Greenwood 2003: 9). One important reason for their late appearance in Brussels is their traditional division of labour with associations, according to which they would act on the economic market while business associations would act as their representatives on the political market. For quite a long time, this division of labour also applied to European politics. Despite their substantial economic resources and their international mobility, even large firms concentrated on domestic political institutions in influencing EU policies (Feld 1970; Greenwood, Grote and Ronit 1992; MacLaughlin, Jordan and Maloney 1993; Eising and Kohler-Koch 1994; see Chapter 7). This was particularly so if they enjoyed privileged access to their national governments and parliaments, for instance because they were considered 'national champions' (Hayward 1995a, 1995b).

At the same time, they faced several difficulties in Brussels. Most European associations did not allow for the direct membership of firms. Furthermore, the European institutions were hesitant to consult large firms directly. Only the Commission's attempts at social regulation in the late 1970s and the new dynamics of the IMP in the 1980s led to greater efforts of large firms to influence European policy-making.[6] In particular, they responded to two regulatory initiatives: on the one hand, the initiative to introduce regulations for Works Councils in multinational firms (Vredeling directive) mobilized their resistance, and, on the other hand, the IMP led several large firms to support the Commission proposal. Since then, several studies have scrutinized the role of large firms in the re-organization of European sectoral and cross-sectoral associations, in the foundation of new EU interest groups that would allow for direct firm membership and in the establishment of the firms' lobby offices in Brussels (Coen 1997, 1998; Cowles 1997, 1998). According to these studies, large firms tend to pursue multiple strategies in the EU. They represent their interests directly vis-à-vis European and national institutions, they seek to cooperate with other firms in European producer clubs, they are active members in national and EU associations and they also hire professional consultants (see Chapter 7 for more detail).

Since the 1980s, the number of professional consultants has greatly increased. Most consultancies were set up after 1990 and have established themselves besides the EU associations and the offices of large firms. Even though numerous political consultants are now present in Brussels and have an ever larger number of contractors, only a few studies pay attention to their role in EU lobbying. Christian Lahusen (2002, 2003) has counted 285 consultancies, of which more than half are law firms (53 per cent) that advise and represent their clients in legal affairs such as EU competition policy, internal market or foreign trade issues. However, the borders to political interest representation are not always clear-cut. Many other consultants are occupied with economic affairs, management or public relations issues. Only 30 per cent concentrate fully on political interest representation. Almost all consultants (97.3 per cent) tend to work for private companies, and every other consultant is also hired by public authorities (59.1 per cent) or trade associations (51.6 per cent). Roughly a quarter of these commercial lobbyists is employed by non-governmental organizations that do not represent occupational interests (23.6 per cent) (Lahusen 2002: 708).

The increasing use of these organizations signals that lobbying in the EU has become more professional over time. The bulk of consultants monitor EU decision-making and process information about the evolution of EU policies or how to participate in EU funded projects. Many professional lobbyists advise their clients on how to organize public affairs strategies or media campaigns. Also offering guidance on how to apply for EU funds, they usually refuse 'to perform active lobbying, because they rather [see] this as a task for the client' (Michalowitz 2004: 135–6). However, some large firms have provided consultants with a mandate to represent them in EU affairs. Commercial lobbyists 'provide professional skills and services' to their clients that are 'above and beyond the specific interests or issues to be dealt with' (Lahusen 2002: 697). According to Lahusen (2002, 2003), commercial lobbyists partly complement the activities of business interest organizations, but also compete with them, as they are mostly working for private companies but also for trade associations. By contrast, Irina Michalowitz (2004: 135–6) emphasizes that these organizations complement the public affairs activities of large firms and trade associations, thus downplaying the potential competition with BIAs.

The EUROLOB data support the assessment that consultancies serve mostly as instruments and cannot be regarded as actors in their own right that compete with other interest organizations. According to almost uniform assessments of business associations and firms, they are the least important private actors in EU level interest representation (see Figure 4.2). These assessments are based on their prior experiences with commercial lobbyists: only 14.5 per cent of the EU level groups, 6.1 per cent of the large firms and between 16 and 34 per cent of the national associations have not hired professional consultants.[7] Like the national groups, EU associations and large firms tend to find that cooperation only of limited use. Just 9.7 per cent of the large firms and 21.5 per cent of the EU associations (EU) find it useful or very useful to employ commercial consultants, while 25.9 per cent of the firms and 32.3 per cent of the EU associations do not find it useful. Accordingly, the large majority of the large firms and business associations is not of the opinion that commercial lobbyists add significantly to their in-house lobbying capacities. The similarity of these assessments is surprising given that it is not uncommon for large companies to hire these lobbyists, whereas business associations have good reasons to think of them as competitors. In sum, the work of consultants serves to complement the activities of the other interest organizations to a limited extent.

In recent years, political science research has begun to pay greater attention to *non-occupational groups* (Pollack 1997; Young 1997; Balme, Chabanet and Wright 2002), that stand for specific policy ideas and causes such as human rights or environmental protection or that represent specific social groups such as women, the elderly or migrants. For a long time, these groups have not been very vocal in European politics: the 222 European interest groups that the Commission of the European Communities counted in 1961 were all occupational groups (Lindberg 1963: 9). According to Brian Harvey, well into the 1980s, welfare and social policy groups as well as human rights organizations were notably absent on the European level (Harvey 1993: 190). In 2002, however, approximately 20 per cent of EU associations represented non-occupational interests (Figure 4.1).

There are several reasons. One is that many of them have larger and more diffuse sets of supporters than occupational groups. According to Mancur Olson (1965: 12, 28), such large groups find it harder to organize and provide an optimal amount of a collective good than smaller groups because they face greater free rider problems. Their potential members may also attach less value to the benefits that might accrue to them from collective action than business interests, whose immediate economic survival can depend on EU regulation. Moreover, in the EU member states, many of these cause groups and social interest groups only came into being from the 1960s onwards, so that the national organizational context was not suitable for European political action. Furthermore, for a long time, European integration was about the dismantling of national economic borders and the creation of a common market rather than about common social policies and the taming of market forces. Hence, non-occupational interests faced sincere collective action problems, lacked an infrastructure of associative institutions in the member states, and had few incentives to get organized at the European level. Only a few organizations that could build on public support in the member states – such as the consumer groups, cooperatives and family organizations – organized early at the European level,[8] and to the extent that the measures for 'negative' integration

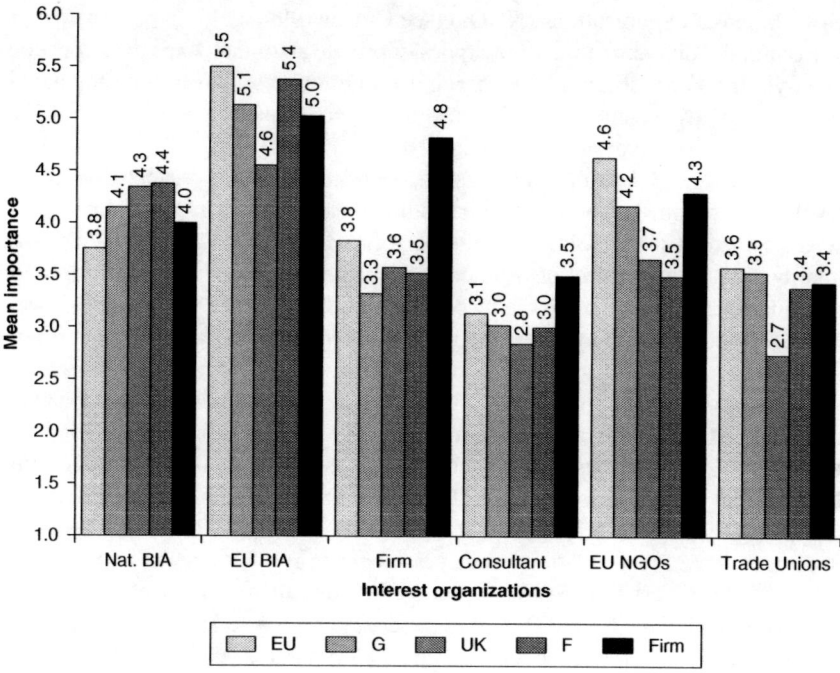

Figure 4.2 How important are the following interest organizations on the EU level?

Note: The scale ranges from (1) 'not important at all' to (6) 'very important'.

Analyses of variance for the importance of interest organizations by firms and associations:
- Nat. business associations: F 5.503, between 37.340 (df 4) in 1637.599 (df 790), p = .001.
- EU business associations: F 17.114, between 91.568 (df 4) in 1064.779 (df 796), p = .000.
- Firms: F 11.936, between 81.383 (df 4) in 1322.704 (df 776), p = .000.
- Consultants: F 2.354, between 15.938 (df 4) in 1301.809 (df 769), p = .052.
- EU NGOs: F 13.663, between 118.111 (df 4) in 1651.137 (df 764), p = .000.
- Trade Unions: F 1.557, between 2.715 (df 4) in 312.120 (df 716), p = .184.

were supplemented by 'positive' policies, more diffuse interests got organized at the European level.

The organization of environmental interests is a typical example. As the first environmental organization, the European Environmental Bureau (EEB) was formed in 1974. By then, environmental policy was already high on the international political agenda, and the European Community had decided upon its first environmental action programme. The cooperation of the national peak associations within the EEB was later followed by more specialized European environmental interest organizations. These responded to the growing importance of EU environmental policy since the mid-1980s (Hey and Brendle 1994). With the swing from negative to positive integration since the Maastricht treaty, a lot of groups representing diffuse interests have become more vocal at the European level, such as the nearly 40 members of the Platform for European Social Non-Governmental Organizations (NGOs) (see Cullen 1999).

In sum, the diversification of the types of private actor that voice their concerns vis-à-vis the EU institutions has brought important new players into the game. Nonetheless, EU business associations are still considered to be the most important actors in EU level interest representation.

The EUROLOB data allow us to assess the relevance of the organizations in EU level interest representation. Notwithstanding the difficulties in establishing themselves as actors in EU politics, EU associations are considered to be the primary interlocutors of EU institutions, underlining the importance of their role as fora for their members. According to the respondents in the EUROLOB survey, EU business associations are the most important private players in EU level interest representation. Asked to assess the importance of different types of interest organization on a scale from 1 (not important at all) to 6 (very important), EU business associations obtain average scores that range from 4.6 (by UK associations) to 5.5 (by EU level groups) (see Figure 4.2). EU business associations, large firms and national business associations all rank EU level BIAs first among the different types of interest organization that are present in Brussels. They find them very important to the representation of business interests at EU level. The ranking of all other players varies along EU BIAs, national groups and firms as well as along the national associations from different member states. On average, large firms score between 3.3 (by German associations) and 4.8 (by large firms), and national BIAs attain scores between 3.8 (by EU BIAs) and 4.4 (by French groups). Large companies rank them in between with a mean of 4.0. Note that both national associations, with the exception of the German groups, and firms are inclined to rank themselves second to the EU associations. Also, EU social and environmental NGOs are now accorded a prominent role in EU politics, scoring between 3.5 (by French groups) and 4.6 (by EU level BIAs). Usually, they are considered to form the second (by German and EU level groups) or third (by firms, UK and French associations) most important type of interest organization in EU politics. Trade unions and consultants tend to be accorded the least important places in EU level interest representation, scoring averages between 2.7 and 3.6.

The growing number of organizations that are present in the EU arena, the changes in the interests that are represented and the increasing professionalism of interest representation have important consequences. First, as the EU policy networks are typically permeable for new actors, they become more encompassing. This may aggravate the formation of lasting coalitions and the construction of closed policy communities as well as putting traditional patterns of alliance formation and the established division of labour under stress. In recent years, various case studies have underlined that the formation of ad hoc coalitions becomes more important and that several EU lobbying campaigns were targeted at specific issues (Aspinwall 1998; Pijnenburg 1998; Warleigh 2000). Interest organizations that could initially enjoy a monopoly in the representation of their domain – such as the European Environmental Bureau until the mid-1980s – must now compete with other groups in their domain when representing their cause or try to develop a reasonable division of labour among themselves. At the same time, access to the EU institutions becomes more difficult and the struggle for ear-time more intense. Concomitantly, insecurity about the evolution of the EU policy agenda grows.

Second, the increased representation of non-occupational interests reduces the bias in the EU interest group system that existed in favour of business interests. This does not imply that diffuse interests now have a greater impact on EU policy-making in line with their institutionalized presence in Brussels. Usually, their action capacity and sanctioning power are rated well below that of business interest groups (see Offe and Wiesenthal 1985; Imig and Tarrow 2001a; Balme and Chabanet 2008). Nonetheless, according to several observers, major societal cleavages now find their way into EU politics (Beyers and Kerremans 2005) and the presence of groups with strong value attachments and ideologies let value conflicts increase in importance so that European politics becomes far more politicized than it has been in the past (Marks and Steenbergen 2002; Eising and Kohler-Koch 2005b).

Third, the increasing professionalism of EU level interest representation has implications for both the internal organization of the groups and their inter-organizational relations. Increasingly, the associational staff belongs to a younger generation of professionals that is well acquainted with the European political process. To draw on the expertise of their members, important linkages between EU organizations and their members have been effected. Many EU business interest organizations have included the most powerful actors in their domain, namely large firms, both to draw on their resources and to allow that their opinion enters earlier in the process. Several organizations have also changed their decision-making procedures to allow for qualified majority voting and the presentation of dissenting opinions to the EU institutions.

Explaining membership in EU associations

Institutional contexts and socio-economic structures

What drives the evolution of the EU level interest group system? American pluralism related the development of interest group systems to political contexts and socio-economic dynamics.[9] Besides political regulation, 'technological changes, expanding markets and painfully sharp fluctuations in the trade cycle' were singled out as important factors that 'provided the stimulus' for the increasing number of trade associations and for the differentiation within the interest group system (Truman 1951: 75). The 'increasing division of labor within industry', 'rapid developments in transportation and communication', 'shifts in economic organization', 'market fluctuations' and the 'activities of competing groups' all contributed to the dynamic evolution of the American interest group system (Truman 1951: 106–7). Such disturbances of the interest group equilibrium were considered sufficient to give rise to the formation of associations. Neglecting political agency, for pluralists 'the mobilization of groups' in response to such problems 'was simply not a problem' (Baumgartner and Leech 1998: 65).

Even though taking into account political agency, several case studies on EU interest groups also stress *socio-economic and technological factors* because these reduce transaction costs or change the interest domains and interest definitions of actors: Volker Schneider (1992) traces the emergence of EU associations for the users of telecommunications services to the new opportunities embodied in these developments. Other studies illustrate that the technological convergence of telecommunications, information technology and the media triggered the reorganization of interest organizations along the newly formed sectoral boundaries (Bartle 1999: 369–70). For example, this process promoted the successive mergers of the European associations for telecommunications, information technology and consumer electronics within the EICTA[10] (Knill 2001; Blank 2002).

Beyond technologies and markets, the associational contexts at the national and international levels can leave an impact on the organization of interests at the European level. In general, national associational systems can facilitate collective action in the European Union because national interest groups need only to extend their activities to the European political layer. According to some scholars, the presence of national associations signals that the basic question whether to cooperate or not has already been answered affirmatively (Jordan 1998: 32). National collective action also bundles together the number of relevant national players and thereby facilitates collective action at the EU level. Of course, this does not rule out the need for political agency: in several instances, national associations and firms have acted as political entrepreneurs and taken the initiative to push collective action at the European level (Haas 1958; Cowles 1997). Furthermore, the wave-like evolution of the EU interest group system results partly from institutional and competitive isomorphism (DiMaggio and Powell 1991: 66). Observing the responses of other interest organizations to the evolution of the EU political system, several national associations acted accordingly and set up EU level groups. In some cases, groups reacted to the political mobilization of competing interests in their struggle for institutional legitimacy and political power. Furthermore, the cooperation in transnational associations can reduce transaction costs and ease the organization of interests at the EU level. For example, UNICE was initially set up within an interest organization of European industries vis-à-vis the OEEC (Haas 1958: 324). EURELECTRIC, the EU's encompassing electricity association grew out of prior cooperation within UNIPEDE, an international association of the electricity supply industry (Eising 2000: 205–6).[11]

In the remainder of this section I seek to explore the extent to which such socio-economic factors and institutional contexts account for the membership of national interest groups in EU associations. So far, there is no data available to analyse the role of these macro-level variables and at the same time control for micro-level organizational variables. Instead, I utilize the Commission's CONECCS data that provides information about the members of EU associations and data about the structural characteristics of the member states from which they stem. First, I give a brief account of the national membership pattern in EU associations. Then, I analyse the importance of the structural factors by means of regression analyses.

Three-hundred-and-ten EU associations that were listed in CONECCS indicated the nationality of their members. Table 4.1 presents the resulting membership pattern. On average, EU associations organized members from 11.8 of the

15 EU member states (SD 3.04) indicating a high geographical coverage of potential members. Associations from non-member states – and from the new member states following the Eastern enlargement in 2004 – were far less present in the EU interest organizations. On average, the EU level interest groups organized associations from 3.9 of the 13 accession candidates in 2002.

Note that there were also considerable variations along national lines both along the EU-15 countries and along the accession countries. Considering the former, associations from Portugal were present in merely 68.7 per cent of the EU associations whereas German associations joined 96.0 per cent of these groups. Malta's associations were members in only 17 per cent of the EU associations and Czech associations were represented in more than 50 per cent of them. Hence, interest groups from the new Eastern European member states were clearly less present in EU associations than interest organizations from the EU-15 countries. Accordingly, since the Eastern enlargement, the geographical coverage of EU associations has decreased even if a larger number of associations from the new member states may now have joined EU level groups. This is not just due to the fact that these countries joined the EU only recently. It is more important that these new member states are still in the process of building up the civil society infrastructure, which currently is still less differentiated than in the Western European member states. It still remains to be seen if membership in the EU will have major repercussions on the Eastern European interest group systems.

The subsequent analysis focuses on the EU-15 member states as comparative data is not yet available for the Eastern European states. The comparative literature on interest groups suggests that, inter alia, the number of groups is related to the size of a country, its economic prosperity and also its dependence on international markets (see Bischoff 2003; B. Wessels 2004). Furthermore, the mode of interest intermediation that is prevalent in a country and the duration of its membership in the European Union/European Community will be considered. These variables will be analysed in multiple regressions to test their separate effects on membership in EU associations.

Different theories raise different expectations about the effects of the *population size* on the number of interest groups in a society. On the one hand, pluralist theory suggests that a greater population should lead to greater socioeconomic differentiation and a greater number of interests in modern societies. At the same time, for a given variety of interests, an increase in the country size allows for the organizational representation of more specialized interests because the critical mass of members needed to support these organizations can be more easily reached than in smaller states (Lowery, Gray and Fellowes 2005: 52). Finally, cycles of political mobilization and counter-mobilization make for a growing number of interest groups. But as 'more specialized organizations are mobilized to represent ever more nuanced versions of the [population's] basic interest, issue niche space is exhausted' (Lowery *et al.* 2005: 52), thus lowering the collective organization of interests with each additional inhabitant so that a greater population should lead to a curvilinear increase in the number of memberships in EU associations.

Table 4.1 Membership in EU associations (N = 310) by country

	Country	Number of memberships in EU associations (%)
EU-15	Austria	240 (77.4)
	Belgium	288 (92.9)
	Denmark	243 (78.4)
	Finland	231 (74.5)
	France	293 (94.5)
	Germany	298 (96.0)
	Greece	169 (54.5)
	Ireland	200 (64.5)
	Italy	283 (91.3)
	Luxembourg	154 (49.7)
	Netherlands	275 (88.7)
	Portugal	213 (68.7)
	Sweden	244 (78.7)
	Spain	263 (84.8)
	United Kingdom	272 (87.7)
Non-EU member states (in 2002)	Bulgaria	79 (25.5)
	Cyprus	68 (21.9)
	Czech Republic	157 (50.6)
	Estonia	81 (26.1)
	Hungary	151 (48.7)
	Latvia	63 (20.3)
	Lithuania	69 (22.2)
	Malta	55 (17.7)
	Poland	141 (45.5)
	Romania	96 (31.0)
	Slovakia	107 (34.5)
	Slovenia	87 (28.0)
	Turkey	75 (24.2)

Note: Own calculations based on European Commission CONECCS data, May 2002.

On the other hand, Olson's logic of collective action (1965) suggests that bigger groups have more difficulties getting organized. As a consequence, 'a country with a large population should ... have less interest groups because the interest communities ... will be less likely to overcome free riding and form interest groups' (Bischoff 2003: 208). I assume that the former effect outweighs the difficulties getting organized in larger societies so that the population size should have a positive impact on the number of memberships in EU associations (see also Wessels 2004). Population size is measured as the log of the population in thousand inhabitants because I expect a non-linear increase in the number of associations with an increase in the population size.

Similar reasoning applies to the *size of the economy* which should therefore also have a positive impact on the number of memberships in EU associations. A greater economy is related to a greater differentiation of economic activities giving rise to a greater variety of producer, employer, labour and consumer interests as well as to manifold interdependencies among these interests. Given the importance of market integration in EU affairs, this is all the more important for the number of memberships in EU trade associations. Economic development also facilitates the organization of interests, reducing transaction costs through better communication and transport infrastructures. The size of the economy is measured as the log of the Gross Domestic Product (GDP) in billion US-Dollars (Purchasing Power Parities in 2001).

Furthermore, I expect that greater *economic prosperity* increases the number of memberships in EU associations: 'interest communities with a higher level of income and education can generate higher per capita contributions to support their common interest' (Bischoff 2003: 206). Several empirical studies have shown that a higher income is positively related to voluntary engagement in associations.[12] In addition, Ronald Inglehart reasoned that economic prosperity has given rise to post-material values and to new interests. The increasing number of groups for non-occupational interests in OECD countries since the 1960s provides some support for this claim (Baumgartner and Leech 1998). Hence, greater economic prosperity should give rise to a greater number of memberships in EU associations. Economic prosperity is measured as the GDP (in 1,000 USD PPP) per capita.

David Truman (1951) and others (e.g. Liefmann 1897) highlighted that market disturbances can give rise to the formation of new associations that serve to contain these fluctuations. Countries that depend greatly on foreign trade are more susceptible to the fluctuations of international markets than those that have low rates of foreign trade. Hence, the former should be more vulnerable to the impact of the international economy. Import competition 'increases the incentives' of some economic actors 'to found interest groups' in order to influence foreign trade policy and limit foreign competition (Bischoff 2003: 205), and of others to reduce market entry restrictions and benefit from better and cheaper import products. Peter Katzenstein's studies (1985) emphasize the positive relation between the high degree of foreign trade and corporatist interest intermediation in the smaller Northern European countries that aided in the flexible adjustment of these countries to world markets. As the European Union has acquired substantial powers in foreign trade policy and has also integrated the markets of its members, the number of national associations that join EU groups should increase with foreign trade dependence. The foreign trade ratio is measured as the percentage of exports and imports in the Gross Domestic Product.

Political structures and practices must not be neglected when accounting for the formation of interest group systems and patterns of membership. The previous chapter illustrated that the modes of interest intermediation differ among the large EU member states. I assume that these modes influence the political behaviour of interest groups and have therefore an effect on how many of them join EU associations. As associations play a greater role in corporatist countries than in pluralist countries and as they are also more used to cooperating within vertically integrated associational systems, I assume that associations from corporatist countries are more present in EU associations than those from pluralist countries. In order to compare the modes of interest intermediation in the 15 EU member states, I draw on Siaroff's index of corporatism (1999) that ranks countries on a scale from 1 (pluralism) to 5 (corporatism).[13]

Furthermore, the *duration of EU membership* should be related to the associational presence in EU level interest groups. The longer a country is a member of the EU, the longer national interest groups have been socialized into the European Union so that they will be used to representing their interests more or less regularly vis-à-vis the EU institutions and through EU associations. Therefore, the earlier a country has joined the EU, the more of its associations should be present in EU associations. The duration of EU membership is measured in years.

Finally, a control variable for *Belgian associations* is included because, being located in the same country as the majority of the EU associations they should find it easier to join them than associations from the other EU member states.

I test these hypotheses by means of multiple regressions. These assess the causal impact of each independent variable on the number of national associations in EU associations by country, controlling for the effect of all other variables included in the model. Table 4.2 presents the results of four different regression models. Raw coefficients indicate the change in the number of national memberships for a unit increase of the independent variables. Figures in brackets give the standard errors of the estimates and the beta coefficients. These fully standardized coefficients make the effects of different variables comparable, expressing both the changes in the number of memberships and the increases of the dependent variables in terms of standard deviations.

All four models elucidate the national membership pattern in EU associations well, accounting for 90 per cent and more of the variance in the dependent variable. The first model includes all independent variables except for the population size, which is highly correlated with the size of the economy. The second model omits those variables that do not bear significantly on the membership pattern in any of the analyses. These models support the argument that the size of the domestic economy has a positive effect on the membership of national interest groups in EU associations. The large number of business and also social interests, the critical mass of members that is needed to sustain associations and the dynamics of political mobilization that are present in large economies clearly outweigh the potentially harmful effects of large group sizes in such economies. The corporatist mode of interest intermediation has the expected positive effect on the number of memberships in EU associations. Groups from corporatist countries are more likely to be members of EU associations than groups that stem from pluralist member states. The control variable confirms that the location in Belgium matters: Belgian groups join between 51 to 64 EU associations more than do national associations from other member states.

Other than expected, the number of national interest groups that join EU associations is not conditional upon the foreign trade dependency of a member state, the duration of its membership in the EU or its economic prosperity when controlling for the other factors that are included in these models. Surprisingly, international economic activities do not stimulate national interest organizations to join EU level organizations. Those national groups whose members are less

Table 4.2 Membership of national interest groups in EU associations – regression analyses

Independent variables	Models			
	Model 1	Model 2	Model 3	Model 4
Constant	−538.133	−221.007	−971.976	−705.939
	(372.457)	(199.524)	(383.903)**	(226.027)**
Log of GDP in 1 bio USD PPP in 2001 (se)	30.967	34.720	–	–
	(6.315)***	(3.383)***		
[beta]	[.877]	[.984]		
Log of population in 1,000 inhabitants (se)	–	–	30.947	34.802
			(6.314)***	(3.400)***
[beta]			[.960]	[1.080]
Log of GDP per capita in 1,000 USD (se)	58.885	23.005	90.512	58.197
	(38.993)	(19.124)	(38.916)**	(20.705)**
[beta]	[.321]	[.125]	[.493]	[.317]
Foreign trade ratio (se)	−.183	–	−.186	–
	(.169)		(.168)	
[beta]	[−.264]		[−.269]	
Index corporatism (se)	7.403	9.716	7.319	9.634
	(4.261)	(3.330)**	(4.262)	(3.337)**
[beta]	[.215]	[.282]	[.212]	[.280]
Duration of EU membership (se)	−.051	–	−.047	–
	(.378)		(.377)	
[beta]	[−.021]		[−.019]	
Belgian associations (se)	63.690	51.477	63.890	51.583
	(19.218)**	(14.855)***	(19.220)***	(14.891)***
[beta]	[.370]	[.299]	[.371]	[.299]
R^2	.936	.926	.936	.925
(adj. R^2)	(.889)	(.896)	(.889)	(.896)
N	15	15	15	15

Notes: Two-tailed tests: * sig. at p = .1, ** sig. at p = .05, ***sig. at p = .01.
Data: OECD Main Economic Indicators 2001, European Commission CONECCS May 2002, Siaroff 1999.

affected by international competition are as likely to become members of EU associations as those that operate in international markets. An important reason may be that the EU institutions have acquired a wide range of policy competencies that also affect these actors. However, here a caveat is in order. The foreign trade ratio has very strong negative correlations with the size of the economy and with population size,[14] so that it is mostly small countries that have very high foreign trade ratios. This relation seems crucial to understanding the negative correlation of the foreign trade ratio with the number of memberships in EU associations (see Table A4.1) and its insignificant effect in the regression models. Contrary to expectations, economic prosperity does not affect the number of memberships in EU associations. The size of the economy is a more important predictor of these membership patterns than economic wealth. However, here it must be taken into account that the GDP per capita does not indicate the distribution of these resources in the population and among economic actors. While wealth may not matter across nations, it almost certainly matters within them. In the words of David Lowery and his collaborators (2005: 63): 'There are good reasons to expect that a larger and wealthier manufacturing firm is more likely to lobby than a smaller and less wealthy manufacturing firm' (see also Chapter 7). Finally, the duration of EU membership does not impact on the membership pattern. It seems that the actors adapt either very quickly to the new decision-making environment or retain their established ways of representing interests (on this topic, see also Chapters 5 and 6).

The third and the fourth regressions substitute the size of the population for the size of the economy. They explain the membership patterns as well as the first pair of analyses. Like the size of the economy, population size has a strong positive effect on the number of memberships in EU associations. More associations from the large member states have joined EU associations than from small member states. This outcome conforms to the results of studies that seek to explain the total number of associations in nation states. Interestingly, when the size of the population is taken into account rather than the size of the economy, economic prosperity also affects the membership pattern in EU associations. Only when the size of the economy is not controlled for, the economic wealth of a society has a positive effect on the number of memberships in EU associations. As in the first two models, corporatist interest intermediation and location in Belgium increase the number of memberships. In sum, the socio-economic structures and domestic modes of interest intermediation bear significantly on the membership pattern of EU associations. Notably, the size of a country and of its economy and a corporatist mode of interest intermediation have a positive impact on the number of national associations that become members in EU associations.

Organizational incentives and the decision to join

The previous section established that the coverage of members that EU associations reach is very high, particularly when taking into account their broad geographic reach that stretches from Finland to Portugal and from Ireland to Bulgaria. If one relates their membership density not to the geographic coverage but to the extent to which they organize their potential members, EU business associations also do quite well. According to the EUROLOB data, they organize more of their potential members than the national business associations:[15] on average, EU associations organize 79.2 per cent of their potential members, while German groups represent 70.4 per cent, British organizations cover 70.0 per cent, and French associations act for 61.8 per cent of their potential members. From another perspective, 87.4 per cent of the German business associations, 96.1 per cent of the French economic groups and 76 per cent of the British organizations have joined at least one EU association, and many of them are members in several EU groups. It seems that EU associations find it easy to recruit members. Even if fully conclusive evidence can only be reached in a study that covers all areas of associational activity and not just business associations, this evidence is

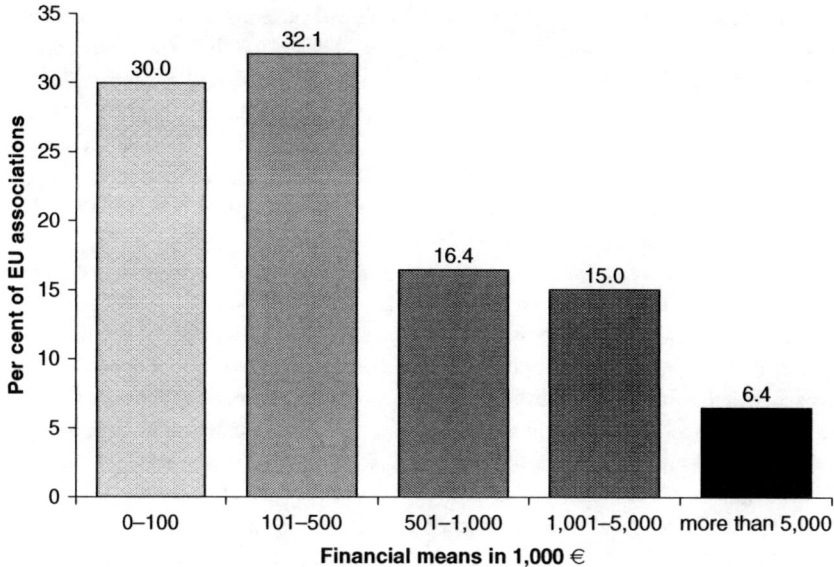

Figure 4.3 The financial resources of EU associations (in 1,000 €)

striking because the members of business associations are likely to make 'rational' cost–benefit assumptions.

Membership of EU associations differs systematically from that of national associations (cf. Table 3.3). The majority of national groups organize firms directly or together with other associations, whereas EU level groups tend to represent national associations, although increasingly in conjunction with firms: 43.8 per cent of EU business interest associations (N = 162) qualify as federations, 30.9 per cent organize both firms and associations, and roughly a quarter (25.3 per cent) represents firms, individuals or other organizations directly. While it is often said that European business associations are less well endowed than their national counterparts this is not generally true. When comparing their financial means (see Figure 4.3) with those of the national associations (Table 3.9), EU level groups (N = 140) have as many resources at their disposal as the British organizations but are less well equipped than the German and French associations.[16]

According to the logic of collective action, *organizational incentives* are the most important determinants of the decision to join an association. Borrowing from the classic studies by Olson (1965) and by Clark and Wilson (1961), two dimensions of incentives may be distinguished: On the one hand, *selective* incentives that are accessible only to associational members may be juxtaposed with *collective* incentives that can also be enjoyed by non-members. On the other hand, *material* and *social* incentives may be distinguished. Justin Greenwood and Mark Aspinwall (1998) have assessed the importance of these incentives and stressed the relevance of material incentives. Several EU business associations were asked to rate the importance of the incentives they offer to their members (Aspinwall and Greenwood 1998: 9–10). Most associations highlighted that two material incentives are of utmost importance. These are the *representation of interests for their members* as a collective material good and the *provision of information to their members* about European politics as a selective material good. Far fewer associations pointed out that other incentives such as the provision of services for their members were relevant. When Danish interest groups were asked to evaluate the incentives of the EU associations they had joined, a similar picture emerged (Sidenius 1998: 96–9).

These studies indicate that only a small number of collective and selective incentives that the EU associations have on offer are highly valued. However, this does not really tell us whether these incentives have a significant impact on the ability of EU associations to recruit their potential members. Analysis of the EUROLOB data gives a clear answer to that question: with the major exception of technical standard-setting, these incentives do not impact on the membership density of the Eurogroups. Specifically, I analyse whether the selective and collective material incentives that EU associations provide are related to their membership density. The first column in Table 4.3 lists these incentives. The second column presents the percentages of EU associations that provide them. The third column presents the significance levels of t-tests that indicate whether groups that provide these incentives have, on average, greater membership densities than groups that do not provide them.

According to Table 4.3, the overwhelming majority of the EU associations is engaged in monitoring EU political activities, providing information to their members about these developments and representing the interests of their members to the EU institutions and vis-à-vis other interest organizations. With respect to the representation of interests, their profiles resemble those of British or German associations (see Chapter 3). Clearly, EU associations tend to provide fewer services to their members than national associations. Furthermore, only a few of them are involved in the coordination of markets, the only exception being the technical standard setting in the EU standardization bodies. In short, EU associations have a narrow functional profile that concentrates heavily on the representation of interests (see also Greenwood 2002b: 11–12).

Surprisingly, almost none of the incentives that the EU associations provide is significantly associated with their membership density.[17] The only exception is the setting of technical standards. EU associations that define technical standards have a mean membership density of 81.2 per cent, whereas groups that do not define such standards tend to organize 75.5 per cent of their potential members. Note also that the number of incentives EU associations offer does not have an effect on the number of actors they can persuade to join (tests not reported). The conclusion is that the decision to join an EU association is largely independent of the variety and number of incentives that EU associations offer their members. Evidently, Olson's logic of collective action does not hold in EU business associations where collective action is not a by-product of associational services. However, future research might consider the quality and the amount of these incentives to a greater extent than could be done here.

Table 4.3 Impact of selective and collective material incentives of EU associations on membership density

Material incentives	Provided by per cent of EU associations	Sig. of t-tests
(a) Selective material goods		
Monitoring of political activities	85.4	.473
Informing members about political developments	88.6	.800
Statistics and branch information	82.2	.146
Market research	32.5	.283
Legal and economic consulting	37.6	.481
Access to consultants	31.8	.253
Coordination of research and development	45.5	.210
Regulation of market entrance	19.9	.313
Member education and qualification	34.0	.580
Resolution of conflicts among members	31.4	.502
Issuance of licenses and certificates	11.5	.329
(b) Collective material goods		
Public affairs and advertisement	56.1	.524
Definition of technical norms and standards	69.2	.020
Definition of quality and education standards	39.1	.632
Interest representation vis-à-vis other interest organizations	93.3	.717
Interest representation vis-à-vis trade unions	32.9	.840
Political representation of members in committees and hearings	76.6	.408

Note: The t-tests indicate whether EU-level groups that provide these incentives have a higher average membership density than groups that do not provide them.

On the basis of his interviews, Justin Greenwood arrives at even more radical conclusions: even if their members regard the activities of EU associations rather critically, 'collective trade association is seen as a must' (Greenwood 2002a: 230). The decision to join EU associations is not based on an explicit and detailed cost–benefit calculation, but is motivated by a more general consideration: collective interest representation by EU associations is part of the European political reality and indispensable in the dialogue with the EU institutions. Once the decision to join has been taken, membership is hardly ever again put into question (Greenwood 2002a: 242–9). That national associations and large firms consider EU interest organizations to be the most important private players in EU level interest representation (see Figure 4.2) supports this interpretation.

Conclusion

The European interest group system is no longer in its formative stages. It has co-evolved with the EU political system and become more pluralistic over time. When analysing the factors that shape the evolution of this system, institutional contexts and socio-economic dynamics have proven to be important. By contrast, selective incentives have not much to say about the logic of collective action in EU associations. EU associations are joined because they engage in the political representation of their members and process information about EU politics to their members. The decision of firms and national groups to join EU associations requires only a 'modest annual subscription' (Guéguen 2003: 50). The cost of their membership is quite small in relation to their incomes and in relation to the risks they incur if they remain outside the loop. The pooling of resources in EU associations saves them costs for the processing of information and the representation of interests. It can also enhance their political clout and make them aware of new political opportunities. By contrast, the opportunity costs of non-membership are unknown and may potentially threaten their organizational survival. Without joining EU interest organizations, national groups and firms are themselves forced to obtain information about EU political processes, assess the salience of these activities, build transnational coalitions and represent their interests vis-à-vis the EU institutions. Joining EU associations reduces the uncertainty about EU politics and has the character of an insurance premium (Jordan 1998: 48–9). In other words, it is a *sine qua non* for national interest organizations. Given that the basic decision to take collective action has already been taken in the member states and that the membership structure of EU associations differs from that of national associations, it is not surprising that the former achieve higher membership rates than the latter. As a result, EU associations channel the representation of domestic interests at the European level, provide national actors with a venue to the EU institutions and form both institutional constraints and opportunities for them.

Appendix

Table A4.1 Correlation matrix of variables included in the regression analyses

	Log GDP	Foreign trade ratio	Log GDP per capita	Log population	Corporatism	Duration EU membership
No. of memberships in EU associations	.848**	−.484	−.164	.802**	.109	.349
Log GDP		−.694**	−.434	.987**	−.242	.269
Foreign trade ratio			.777*	−.769**	.197	.318
Log GDP/capita				−.572	.450	.424
Log population					−.299	.168
Corporatism						−.135

Note: Pearson's r * significant at p = .05, ** significant at p = .01 (two-tailed tests).

5 Multilevel governance and business interests in the European Union

European integration has changed the political opportunity structures of interest groups (Marks and McAdam 1996), leading to the evolution of a European layer of interest organizations. It has also prompted domestic interests to promote their cases more readily before the EU institutions, as the previous chapter has shown. In this chapter, I investigate which interaction patterns between state and business the transformation of the European institutional context has brought about. The focus will be on the vertical dimension of the EU multilevel system.

I use the three major theories of European integration – neofunctionalism, intergovernmentalism and multilevel governance – as lenses to focus on this topic. Each of them lays out a very different scenario of how interest intermediation should be patterned following their conceptions as to where political authority resides in the EU institutional setting. Neofunctionalism claims that political authority shifts to the European level and makes a strong case for the centralization of interest group activities at that level. Intergovernmentalism posits that lobbying activities continue to focus on domestic institutions because it regards national governments as the dominant players in EU policy-making. Finally, multilevel governance suggests that political authority is dispersed across and shared between European and national institutions. It follows that interest groups interact with political institutions at both levels.

I argue that the concept of *multilevel governance* captures the essence of interest intermediation in the EU best. Accordingly, the *location of interest organizations in the EU multilevel system* shapes their political activities to a great extent. Being located at different levels of government gives rise to different strategies of interest representation and to a pronounced division of labour across these levels. Hence, EU associations concentrate on the EU level and national groups focus on the domestic context.

In the next section, the theories of European integration on which I draw are outlined and their implications for interest intermediation are explored. Thereafter, I describe the general responses of national interest groups to the integration process. Then, drawing on the EUROLOB survey, cluster analysis techniques are used to test the hypotheses put forward. The cluster analysis serves to identify a five-fold typology of interest organizations according to the scope of their political activities: niche organizations, occasional players, national players, EU players and multilevel players. The emergence of a significant share of multilevel players among the domestic groups serves as evidence in favour of the multilevel governance approach. Finally, I demonstrate that cluster membership differs significantly according to the location of interest groups in the institutional setting.

Theories of European integration and interest groups in the EU

In line with studies that highlight the impact of institutional contexts on the political behaviour of interest groups, the three predominant approaches to European integration – neofunctionalism, intergovernmentalism and multilevel governance – emphasize that interest organizations become politically active where political authority resides. As V. O. Key (1956: 168) has put it: 'Where power rests, there influence is brought to bear.' However, the theories differ clearly in their assessments of where political authority in the EU resides. This is the reason that they conceive differently of EU interest intermediation.

Thus, according to Ernst Haas' classic *neofunctional* definition, political integration is:

> the process whereby political actors in several distinct national settings are persuaded to shift their loyalties, expectations and political activities toward a new center, whose institutions possess or demand jurisdiction over the pre-existing national states. The end result of a process of political integration is a new political community, superimposed over the pre-existing ones.
> (Haas 1958: 16)

In other words: the progress of European integration lets political activities and values gravitate towards a new centre. Domestic interest groups turn 'to supranational institutions as devices for more effectively realizing demands at the national level' (Haas 1958: 221). The incremental spillover of supranational competencies into ever new policy areas leads these groups to form new expectations and put forward new demands to the European institutions. New alliances with the political institutions and interest organizations at the supranational level let 'their erstwhile ties with national friends undergo deterioration' (Haas 1958: 313). Hence, as Figure 5.1a illustrates, national interest groups re-orient towards EU institutions, and national systems of interest intermediation undergo significant change. When it comes to EU affairs, EU level activities gradually supersede national level activities. This leads to H 1.1:

H 1.1 The number of public–private interactions at the EU level and the importance of the EU institutions for interest organizations increase over time whereas interactions at the national level decrease and lose their significance.

According to *liberal intergovernmentalism*, the bargaining power of the member states and interstate bargains drive European integration. National governments are key to EU decision-making and serve as gatekeepers between domestic and European affairs. Their preferences are shaped in discussions with domestic interest organizations and are not influenced by EU level developments (Moravcsik 1998: 24). Domestic interests influence policy through their peak associations (Moravcsik 1998: 36). Because European integration is not assumed to create a new political space for societal actors, according to intergovernmentalism, interest groups remain largely inactive at the EU level. They lobby only very occasionally at the supranational level to complement their national efforts or 'to recover ground lost in national policy domains' (Butt-Philipp 2000: 6). National interest organizations remain rooted in their domestic contexts because political authority continues to reside in the national governments (see Figure 5.1b). This results in H 1.2:

H 1.2 With the advance of European integration, the interactions among national interest groups and national institutions increase in numbers and gain in importance. Interactions with the EU institutions do not have much relevance for domestic groups, and their number increases only to a very limited extent.

The notion that a *multilevel system* has emerged in the European Union gained wide acceptance (Jachtenfuchs and Kohler-Koch 1996; Benz 1998; Grande 2000; Marks and Hooghe 2001; Hooghe and Marks 2003) even though the concept remains elusive. Different authors highlight different aspects of *multilevel governance* (MLG). Some authors emphasize that national institutions must now share important powers with EU institutions and have lost some of their autonomy (Marks and Hooghe 2001); others point out that a multitude of public and private actors are involved in the process of governing (Jachtenfuchs and Kohler-Koch 1996; Kohler-Koch and Eising 1999), highlighting the importance of interface actors among the different levels of EU policy-making (Grande 2000; Knill 2001). Still others refer to the complexity of the network-like institutional configuration and the linkages among different arenas in this setting (Benz 1998; Ansell 2000; Peterson 2003); and yet others draw attention to the variety of interaction patterns that are characteristic of EU policy-making (Scharpf 2000). The following paragraphs present those ingredients of multilevel governance that are necessary to understanding its effects on domestic interest groups.

First, multilevel governance has a *statist and institutional core*: public actors from at least two different levels of government *share* political authority in formal institutional arrangements. While public actors at the upper level are to some extent autonomous, lower level units 'are not subordinate' (Mayntz 1999: 101) and participate in higher-level decision-making. This may not separate multilevel governance from international organizations or federal polities, but it helps to distinguish multilevel governance from any intra-organizational division of labour and from private governance arrangements. As described in Chapter 4, several institutions with autonomous political powers have been set up at the upper (supranational) level in the European Union: the European Commission, the European Parliament and the European Court of Justice. Lower level units have

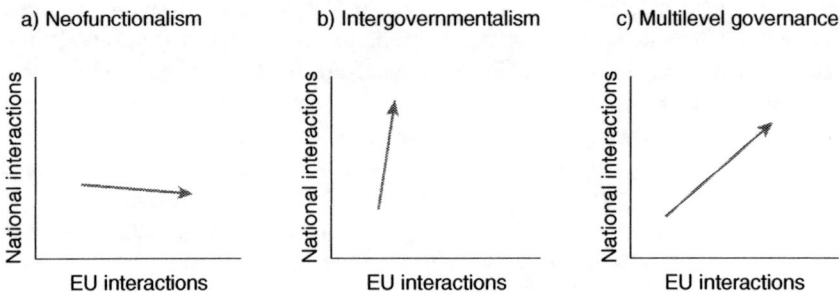

Figure 5.1 Theories of integration: presumed evolution of national and EU interaction patterns with the advance of European integration

very strong participatory and decision-making rights. The member states of the EU are represented in the Council of the European Union and in the European Council. The Council of the EU shares executive functions with the European Commission and legislative functions with the European Parliament. In general, a qualified majority, if not all of the member states, must agree to decisions taken at the EU level. A notable exception is EU competition policy, where the Commission can decide autonomously. Judicial functions have been allocated to the European Court of Justice as well as to national courts. For the most part, subnational regions and societal interests have only been granted a formal consultative status such as in the Committee of the Regions and in the Economic and Social Committee. Only the social dialogue allows the peak associations of labour and employers to take EU policy decisions and to implement them (for detailed analyses, see Falkner 1998; Martin and Ross 1999). EU structural policy also makes provisions to include the social partners in these programmes.

Second, *functional tasks do not coincide with territorial competencies* (see Bartolini 1998). Rather, the former cut across the latter. The allocation of functional responsibilities to different levels of government can be decided for the short term or the long term, it can cover few or many policies and policy instruments and it can lead to the separation or to the sharing of responsibilities among the governmental institutions. While federal systems are usually marked by a quite stable allocation of competencies, multilevel governance is very dynamic and evolves continuously in the European Union (see also Hooghe and Marks 2003). After fifty years of European integration, it covers a great range of issue areas and builds largely on regulatory policies to create, police and complement the common market. In several of these issue areas, the member states cannot take autonomous decisions any more, be it on *de jure* or de facto grounds. As the public actors at EU level and in the member states share responsibilities in many issue areas and as they face many interdependencies with private actors, the need for cooperation and coordination across levels of government and types of actor is particularly high. Finally, institutional authority varies across and within issue areas and also along the policy-making cycle.

Third, multilevel governance combines *various modes of interaction*: competition, bargaining based on self interests, negotiations to build consensus, majority decisions and hierarchical imposition (see Scharpf 2000). In heterogeneous settings such as the EU, which consists of formally equal territorial units without a hegemon, the sharing of political authority makes consensus a *sine qua non* of long-term cooperation. It is certainly true that negotiations in the different EU pillars vary in the degree to which supranational and intergovernmental institutions are involved and that they can take place in the shadow of judicial hierarchy and majority decisions. But, in general, the Commission, the Council of the EU and the European Parliament prefer to build consensus among all actors involved to bridge heterogeneity and ensure compliance with EU law (Hayes-Renshaw and Wallace 1997; Katzenstein 1997; Kohler-Koch and Eising 1999). Consensus formation is facilitated by the fact that, in general, party competition plays a lesser role in the political system of the EU than in the parliamentary democracies of its member states.

This institutional set-up has important consequences for interest groups: the scope and salience of EU decision-making attract a multitude of private actors, and the complex multilevel setting offers many points of access. Some authors conclude that it is indispensable for interest organizations to have a 'dual strategy' (Andersen and Eliassen 1991: 181–2; Kohler-Koch 1997: 3; Mazey and Richardson 2002: 135) and to be present at both the EU and the national level (and possibly even at the regional level) in order to monitor and influence EU programmes along the entire policy cycle. As a result, actor constellations at different levels of government can overlap considerably. But none of the public or private actors is omnipresent, because the multilayered negotiations are interconnected and sequential rather than multilateral (see Benz 1998; Ansell 2000; Marks and Hooghe 2001). Discussions and negotiations take place in different arenas (i.e. European Commission committees, European Parliament intergroups, Council working groups, EU inter-institutional working groups), at each level of government, and also across these levels. In general, they are loosely rather than tightly coupled: policy debates at one level and in one arena do not necessarily trigger changes at another level or in another arena (see Benz 1998).

This leads to H 1.3 that is illustrated in Figure 5.1c:

H 1.3 Multilevel governance implies manifold interactions among private and public actors both at the national and the EU level and an increase in the importance of institutions at both levels for the representation of interests.

In multilevel governance, 'interest groups at any territorial level are free to lobby government at any number of levels' (Constantelos 1996: 30). However, it is unlikely that domestic groups will be evenly represented at both the EU and the national level of government. Even if interest representation is the *raison d'être* that forces them to respond to changes in the political environment, they are tied to their national members and to the national context in which they emerged. They are embedded in social relations (see Granovetter 1992) and depend on the routine exchanges with established domestic partners from whom they extract resources (see J. Wilson 1973). Hence, it can reasonably be expected that their *location at a specific level in the multilevel system* shapes their political activities as well as their access to the political institutions.

H 2 In the model of multilevel governance, most national associations concentrate on domestic institutions whereas most EU associations focus their political activities on EU institutions.

Only if EU regulation has an important impact on the national groups and on their members, if the division of labour between them and those EU associations which represent them vis-à-vis the EU institutions appears to be unsatisfactory, or if the terms of EU policy implementation at the national level must be worked out, will these groups extend their activities to the EU level.

The following sections test the hypotheses that have been laid out. Based on the propositions on how domestic interest groups assess the importance of EU political institutions and how they act in the EU multilevel system, the cluster analysis may be expected to yield three clusters of interest organizations. According to neofunctionalism, there should be a strong cluster of EU players. Consistent with intergovernmentalism, there should be a dominant cluster of national players and, in line with multilevel governance, there ought to be a cluster of multilevel players. Table 5.1 presents the criteria chosen as a test for each theory respectively. Of four potential criteria that indicate the density of interactions at each governmental level to assess the evidence from the cluster analysis, I leave aside both the most comprehensive criterion as a very rigid test and the single case criterion as a very loose yardstick. Since both intergovernmentalism and neofunctionalism have formulated unconditional propositions about the evolution of national interest group activities, the strategies these theories outline should dominate:[1] an absolute or simple majority of all interest groups should follow the expected strategy. In the case of intergovernmentalism, an additional criterion needs to be met. There must not be an important share of multilevel players because this invalidates the expectation that national interest organizations focus exclusively on domestic institutions. To assess multilevel governance, the location of interest groups in the institutional setting must be taken into account. Multilevel interest representation need not be the dominant strategy of domestic interest organizations because many of them are still embedded in the domestic political contexts. However, to confirm H 2, at least an important share of the national associations and firms should represent their interests routinely at both levels of government.

Interest organizations in multilevel governance

Interest group perceptions of political authority in the European Union

The changes in the allocation of political authorities to different levels of government suggest that European integration has altered the perceptions of both EU and national institutions by national interest organizations. In general, national business associations find that EU institutions have become more important for the representation of their interests since the Single European Act (SEA) in 1986 (see Figure 5.2). This holds particularly for the European Commission: almost 69 per cent of these

Table 5.1 Test criteria for theories of European integration

Theoretical proposition	Comprehensive strategy	Dominant strategy	Important strategy	Idiosyncratic strategy
Neofunctionalism National interest organizations become EU players	All national interest organizations	*Absolute or simple majority*	Important share	One
Intergovernmentalism National interest organizations remain national players	All national interest organizations	*Absolute or simple majority*	Important share	One
Multilevel governance National interest organizations become multilevel players	All national interest organizations	Absolute or simple majority	*Important share*	One

Note: The decisive criterion for each theory has been marked in italics.

organizations attribute a greater relevance to the supranational bureaucracy. A clear majority also maintains that the European Parliament and the EU regulatory authorities have gained in importance. Forty-three per cent of the groups believe that the Council of the European Union has become more significant.

However, these reassessments of the EU institutions are not matched by equivalent decreases in the relevance of national institutions. For more than 60 per cent of the national associations, domestic institutions are as important as they were in the mid-1980s. About one-sixth of the interest organizations think that these institutions have lost their political weight. However, between 15 per cent (for the national parliament) and 25 per cent (for the national regulatory authorities) find that their relevance has even increased. Hence, EU institutions have clearly gained in importance, and domestic institutions remain as significant as they were in the mid-1980s. The firms and BIAs do not associate the delegation of political authority to the EU institutions with a corresponding loss of authority at the national level because national governments are represented in the most important decision-making body of the EU, the Council of the EU, and govern the implementation of EU policies on domestic grounds.

As a consequence, the domestic groups began to include EU institutions in their strategies of interest representation. In general, they combine five strategies in one way or the other: they have formed or joined EU interest organizations as the previous chapter indicated; they present their interests directly to EU institutions; they rely on national institutions to promote their causes; they coalesce with other national, transnational or EU interest organizations; and some organizations hire professional consultants to promote their cause. In fact, it seems that today many national actors do indeed follow a dual strategy to promote their interests (Kohler-Koch 1997; Mazey and Richardson 2002). All but one of the 34 firms and about two-thirds of the national

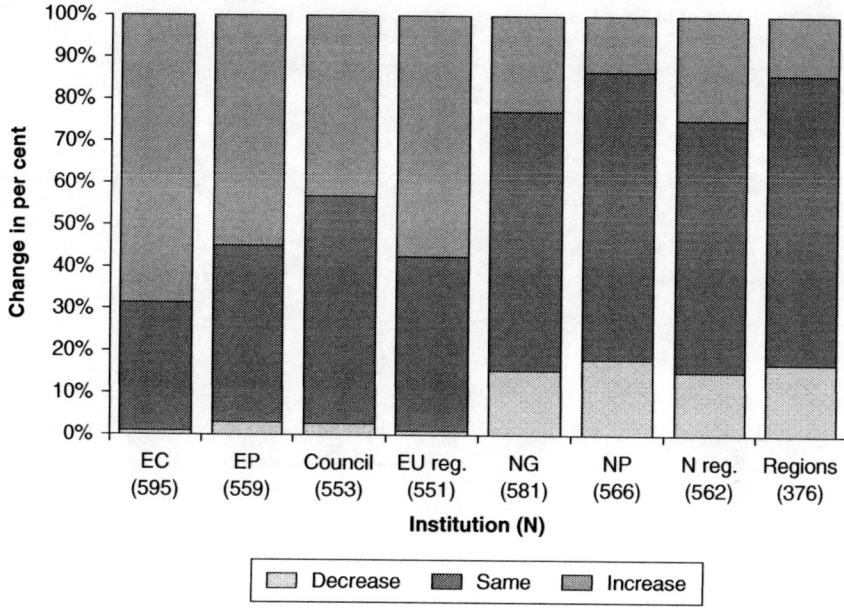

Figure 5.2 Change in the importance of EU institutions and national institutions for the representation of interests since the mid-1980s

Note: EC = European Commission, EP = European Parliament, Council = Council of the EU, EU reg. = EU regulatory and standardization authorities, NG = National Government, NP = National Parliament, N reg. = National regulatory and standardization authorities, Regions = Regional political authorities (this applies only to France (conseils régionaux) and Germany (Bundesländer and Bundesrat)).

associations are in contact with both EU and national institutions (see Table 5.2) and even more have joined EU associations (see Chapter 4). Clearly, only a minority of them relies on just one political route. As a consequence of their strategic adaptation, a plethora of interest organizations is now present at the EU level and a multitiered system of associations has emerged in the European Union.

These perceptual, organizational and strategic developments already indicate that national interest organizations 'are no longer nested exclusively within' national arenas (Marks and Hooghe 2001: 89). Taken together, the changes in the perceptions of EU institutions, the organization of EU and national interest groups and the endurance of national level interest intermediation in EU affairs appear to support the multilevel governance approach.

Clusters of interest organizations in multilevel governance

The preceding section paints a broad picture. It does not show nuances in the pattern of interest organization reaction to multilevel policy-making. Therefore, a cluster analysis serves to construct empirical types of interest organization to

Table 5.2 Share of business associations and firms maintaining contacts with national and EU institutions

Contact with	EU associations	German associations	British associations	French associations	Large firms
EU institutions	98.1% (158 of 161)	76.6% (246 of 321)	66.7% (132 of 198)	75.2% (85 of 113)	97.1% (33 of 34)
National institutions	65.4% (106 of 162)	87.0% (275 of 316)	86.5% (173 of 200)	86.4% (95 of 110)	97.1% (33 of 34)
At national *and* EU level	64.2% (104 of 162)	71.7% (230 of 321)	61.0% (122 of 200)	68.1% (77 of 113)	97.1% (33 of 34)

Note: Figures in brackets present the number of cases for each data cell.

identify systematic variation among the groups. Cluster analysis is a technique that devises an empirical classification scheme for a number of cases (or variables), each of which is described by a set of numerical measures. It sorts the objects into a number of classes such that the objects within classes are similar in some respect (Everitt 1980; Bacher 2001). The cluster analysis in this chapter is based on an analysis of the interest organizations'

- contact patterns with the EU and the national institutions;
- lobbying activities throughout the policy cycle; and
- access to information from the political institutions.

Interestingly, the analysis does not lead to the expected three clusters of national, EU and multilevel players but yields instead five clusters of interest groups.[2] In addition to the three clusters that were expected on the basis of the three integration theories (*multilevel players*, *EU-players* and *national players*), there are two additional clusters of *niche organizations* and *occasional players* that are little involved in political interest representation. The reason for the emergence of these clusters is the associational division of labour which is not satisfactorily covered by the three integration theories (see below).

Table 5.3 presents the centres (means) of each cluster on the standardized variables that entered the analysis. It illustrates that *multilevel players* are clearly more active and present throughout the entire policy cycle at each level of government than the average interest organization and the members of the other clusters. They have far more than average contacts with each national and EU institution, their activities throughout the policy cycle exceed those of the average association and they find it easier than the average association to obtain information from political institutions. They maintain as many contacts with national institutions as with the equivalent EU institutions. It is therefore safe to conclude that interest representation in the EU multilevel system has become a matter of routine for them. Their high level of EU activities and contacts sets them apart from those associations concentrating on the national level, while their activities at the national level clearly distinguish them from the EU players.

Overall, the multilevel players may be regarded as the most important business interest organizations in EU policy-making and implementation.

National players have a more specialized profile. They maintain only very occasional contacts at the EU level to supplement their national activities, and they have more difficulties obtaining relevant information from the EU institutions than from national institutions. Occasionally, they are active when the political agenda is set. But, mostly, they get involved when national institutions develop their positions on EU policy and when EU Directives are transposed into national law and implemented. Their activities on the EU level concentrate on these last two stages of the policy cycle. At the national level, their level of contacts, activities and information does not differ much from that of the multilevel players. But in contrast to the latter, their contacts concentrate on the national governments and rarely extend to the national parliaments. Thus, these groups are still firmly rooted in the national political settings and are 'policy-takers' at the EU level.

Occasional players resemble national players by concentrating on the national level, except that almost all their activities, their contacts and the information they obtain are clearly on a lower level. They are only rarely involved in national policy-making and implementation because they pay more attention to providing services than to representing interests (see also Chapter 6).

EU players are very active at the EU level and entertain manifold contacts with the EU institutions. Even though they do not have fewer contacts with the EU institutions, they find it more difficult to obtain relevant information than multilevel players. During the policy cycle, they concentrate mainly on the agenda-setting and policy formulation stages rather than on the transposition and implementation of EU Directives. In addition, they are hardly involved in national political processes about EU policies. Hence, these organizations are specialized in representing interests at the EU level during the early stages of the policy-making process.

Finally, *niche organizations* are hardly active at all during the policy cycle. Their contacts with both national and EU institutions are well below average, as are their activities during all phases of the policy cycle. These actors depend almost entirely on other interest organizations in the associational division of labour when it comes to monitoring political developments and advocating their political interests. Nevertheless, the estimates of their access to information from national and EU institutions are above and about average, respectively. Taking into account that only a minority of these organizations is in touch with political institutions and has access to information from them (see appendix Table A5.1), their overall degree of information must be considered below that of the other clusters. Even though they maintain fewer than average contacts with regulatory and standardization authorities, these authorities, rather than the executives or parliaments, are their most frequent contact partners.

Theories of European integration and clusters of interest organizations

Table 5.4 presents the cluster membership. All five clusters include national associations, EU associations and, with the exception of the niche organizations, also

Table 5.3 Clusters of interest organizations in the EU multilevel system

	Niche players	National players	Occasional players	EU players	Multilevel players
EU level agenda setting	*−.89*	−.17	−.12	.36	**.70**
European Commission contacts	*−.99*	−.28	−.37	**1.02**	**.84**
European Commission information	−.03	.01	*−1.12*	.24	.44
EP contacts	*−.90*	−.39	*−.52*	**.97**	**1.01**
EP information	.02	−.17	*−1.08*	.05	**.59**
Council of the EU contacts	*−.74*	−.42	−.46	**.76**	**1.00**
Council of the EU information	.21	.00	*−.98*	−.29	**.56**
EU regulatory and standardizatio authorities	*−.60*	−.12	.13	.31	.38
EU level transposition	*−1.03*	**.57**	−.04	*−.88*	**.51**
EU level implementation	*−.91*	**.57**	−.02	*−.97*	.45
National level agenda setting	*−.62*	.15	−.02	*−.97*	**.65**
National government contacts	*−1.09*	.43	−.07	*−.65*	**.74**
National government information	.22	.47	*−1.27*	*−.61*	.29
National parliament contacts	*−.85*	.24	−.34	*−.71*	**.95**
National parliament information	.35	.32	−1.13	*−.74*	.32
National level position formulation	*−.98*	.42	.01	*−.91*	**.57**
National regulatory and standardization authorities	*−.69*	.35	.25	*−.79*	.44
National level implementation	*−.88*	**.60**	.18	*−1.36*	.33
National level transposition	*−1.02*	**.59**	.20	*−1.41*	.45
N	158	227	142	104	203

Notes: Since they had different scales, the variables have been standardized so that they have approximately means of zero and standard deviations of one. Positive cluster means equal to or larger than half a standard deviation were considered as strong systematic deviations from the total mean and have been marked in **bold**, and negative cluster means of that size have been marked in **bold** and *italics*. Table A5.1 in the appendix to this chapter presents the corresponding values on the original variables.

Table 5.4 Cluster membership of firms, national associations and EU associations (per cent of associations and firms)

	Firms and associations			
	EU associations	National associations	Large firms	Total (N)
Niche organizations	11.1	21.9	.0	18.9 (158)
Occasional players	10.5	19.3	5.9	17.0 (142)
National players	11.1	32.1	11.8	27.2 (227)
EU players	52.5	2.5	8.8	12.5 (104)
Multilevel players	14.8	24.1	73.5	24.3 (203)
Total	100.0 (162)	100.0 (638)	100.0 (34)	100.0 (834)

Note: Chi^2 346.078 (df 8) p = .000, Cramer-V .456.

large firms. The table illustrates that national business associations pursue various strategies of interest representation whereas the overwhelming majority of large firms have evolved into multilevel players. Applying the criteria laid out earlier, neofunctionalism seems to be invalidated by the evidence about national interest group activities in the European Union. Only 2.5 per cent of these organizations are EU players and disregard national political institutions almost entirely. This minority is either heavily affected by EU regulation, shut out from domestic political processes or runs EU associations from domestic grounds. After more than 40 years of European integration, these groups are an exception rather than the rule which invalidates H 1.1.

Intergovernmentalism fares better. In each of the three member states, most national associations continue to represent their interests occasionally or routinely vis-à-vis national political institutions but act only rarely at the EU level. Of the domestic organizations 51.4 per cent are either occasional players (19.3 per cent) or national players (32.1 per cent). Hence, even if a significant number of national business associations have extended their political activities to the EU level, the majority remains rooted in the domestic political context.

While intergovernmentalism predicts the dominant strategy of national business interests correctly, it cannot cope with those organizations that represent their interests routinely at both levels of government, however. Almost a quarter, namely 24.1 per cent of the French, British and German associations, has evolved into multilevel players.[3] Even though multilevel interest representation comes nowhere close to being a dominant strategy it must be regarded as an important one, which is empirical support for the multilevel governance approach and for H 1.3. This becomes even more evident when singling out those national associations that act routinely as interest intermediaries among their members and state institutions, namely the national players and the multilevel players: roughly 43 per cent of these organizations have evolved into multilevel players whereas some 57 per cent continue to concentrate their efforts on the domestic level and remain embedded in domestic policy networks.

In support of H 2, the composition of the clusters indicates that the *location* of interest organizations in the multilevel setting exerts a strong influence on their strategy of interest representation but does not determine it. On the whole, contacts between private and public actors located at the same level of government have a greater density than contacts between actors located at different levels (for details, see Table A5.2). Most EU associations concentrate on the EU institutions, and most national associations focus on the national institutions. This territorial division of labour extends to the different stages of the policy cycle. As EU players, the majority of the Eurogroups concentrates on the agenda-setting and policy-formulation stages of the policy cycle whereas national associations allocate their attention more evenly across the different phases. Only those national associations that are multilevel players reach the contact density between EU associations with EU institutions. Some 15 per cent of the EU associations are multilevel players that are regularly in touch with political institutions in the member states. However, as these groups are in touch with institutions in several member states, their contact densities with specific national institutions can be assumed to be below those of national groups that are national players or multilevel players.

The central position of EU interest organizations in the early stages of the EU policy cycle (see also Bennett 1997d: 87) casts some doubt on analyses that question their ability 'to be routine governance partners with the [EU] institutions' (Greenwood and Webster 2000: 13). As interest intermediaries, the Eurogroups are both constraints and aids to the representation of national business interests. They may be able to modify their members' perceptions of EU issues and channel their lobbying behaviour. At least some of them have turned into important interlocutors between EU institutions and national members and may be regarded as actors rather than fora or instruments of their members (see Chapter 4). The resources they can offer to the EU institutions are expertise, support and compliance of members with EU law. Delivering these goods does not always require an autonomous associational leadership as neocorporatist writings suggest (Schmitter and Streeck 1981), but only agreement amongst the (dominant) members of the association.

The majority of national associations concentrates on the national level, and many of their activities extend into the latter phases of the EU policy cycle because the EU institutions have developed a considerable body of policies and important rights to check domestic implementation. In view of the fact that many EU Directives have a framework character (Héritier 1996) and contain several flexibility clauses to allow for their appropriate implementation (Eising 2002), their transposition into national law and implementation by national authorities often lead to subsequent negotiations with EU institutions. During these stages, national associations have more context-specific expertise to offer than the EU groups. A more concerted effort at EU level will only evolve if a greater need for a European 'level-playing field' arises. The European electricity regulation forum is a good example. In this body, delegates from EU trade associations, from national bureaucracies and national regulatory bodies as well as from the European Commission try to develop a harmonized framework of cross-border electricity trading in order to implement the internal energy market. Those organizations that limit their attention to the national level and to the final stages of the EU policy process must rely on other groups to promote their cases elsewhere – that is, they depend on the multilevel players and on the EU players. Thus, they will often have to accept EU policy as a *fait accompli*. These findings imply that multilevel players assume crucial positions in the EU policy networks. They are the nodal points that link their members with both the domestic and the EU institutions. Linking the domestic with the European arena, they are the interface actors (Grande 2000; Knill 2001) of business in multilevel interest representation. They tend to control and regulate the transfer of information between the different levels and political arenas, represent their members in committees and negotiations at another level and provide for their access to these settings (Grande 2000: 18–19).

Unsurprisingly, multilevel players show greater *institutionalized* presence in Brussels than the other types of interest organization: 41.8 per cent of those national associations that are multilevel players maintain an office in Brussels. This holds only for significantly smaller shares of niche organizations (11.4 percent), occasional players (22.5 per cent) and national players (19.7 per cent).[4] Among the EU associations, all of the multilevel players, 83.8 per cent of the EU players and 82.4 per cent of occasional players are located in Brussels whereas niche organizations and national players are more likely to operate from a member state: only 53.3 per cent of the former and 42.9 per cent of the latter keep an office in Brussels. These liaison offices serve to regularize contacts with the EU institutions and other interest organizations as well as to participate in the work of the EU associations.

Analysing the patterns of cooperation and alliance formation corroborates the central position of multilevel players in EU politics. These organizations do not only maintain more contacts with the political institutions than associations in the other clusters but also cooperate more often with other private actors. Table 5.5 illustrates that firms, EU associations and national organizations are embedded in manifold interorganizational relations and that these relations differ significantly along the clusters. First, almost all economic actors are used to cooperating with national BIAs, indicating the importance of these organizations in domestic interest intermediation and market economies. In this respect, associations working in the niches of the systems have fewer relations than other groups, but the differences are small. Only the EU players that consist largely of EU interest groups are less involved in the domestic policy networks. Note also that a pronounced cooperation of the economic actors across borders has emerged, including involvement in international business associations, with niche organizations and occasional players focusing more on the domestic context than national or multilevel players. Second, multilevel players and EU players rely to a greater extent on external advice by consultants and scientific organizations than other types of group, pointing to the need for professionalism and specialized policy information in the European Union context. Third, the least frequent form of cooperation involves diffuse interests such as trade unions or environmental groups. Again, multilevel players and EU players are more inclined to join coalitions with these groups than other actors. This means that such coalitions do not strengthen niche organizations vis-à-vis other actors, but involve the central interest intermediaries of business.

Conclusion

The delegation of political authority to EU institutions has profound effects on the political behaviour of business interests associations and firms. A cluster analysis served to identify five types of interest organizations that respond in different ways to the transformation of governance in the European Union: niche organizations, occasional players, national players, EU players and multilevel players. This empirical study qualifies both neofunctionalism that expected the centralization of interaction patterns at the European level and intergovernmentalism that considers decentralized interactions in the member states as characteristic. Rather, the delegation of political authority to different levels of government has brought about a multilevel system of interest representation. The effect of the multilevel setting on interest representation is mediated by the division of labour in the associational

100   *Multilevel governance and Europeanization*

Table 5.5 Lobbying cooperation with private organizations by cluster (percentage 'Yes')

Cooperation with	Niche organizations	Occasional players	National players	EU players	Multilevel players
National BIAs (N = 775)	87.2	94.9	97.7	72.0	96.4
Foreign BIAs (N = 769)	69.3	85.3	88.1	84.6	93.9
EU BIAs (N = 785)	81.1	92.0	93.6	99.0	97.0
International BIAs (N = 765)	65.0	76.3	81.7	90.3	89.8
Firms (N = 760)	78.2	84.2	89.4	86.0	94.3
Consultants (N = 764)	65.0	69.6	75.9	84.4	85.6
Science organizations (N = 758)	62.1	74.6	80.3	83.9	89.7
Trade unions (N = 756)	44.8	53.4	55.1	69.9	72.6
National diffuse interests (N = 754)	58.3	72.2	71.7	73.6	82.7
EU diffuse interests (N = 749)	52.0	63.8	64.0	81.1	80.3

Note: According to Chi^2 tests, all differences are highly significant at p = .01.

systems and by the location of interest groups at a specific level of government. Accordingly, niche organizations and occasional players are less vocal than the other types of organization, and national and EU players have established a pronounced division of labour among them. EU players focus on the EU level and also on the agenda-setting and policy-formulation stages of the policy cycle. Due to their frequent interactions with EU institutions during these stages, they have evolved into important negotiation arenas and interlocuters between the EU institutions and their national members. National players centre their attention on national governments. Unlike the Europlayers, they not only cover the early stages of the policy cycle but also the transposition of EU Directives into national law and their implementation.

An important share of multilevel players has also emerged, representing their interests routinely at both EU and national levels of government. While supporting the multilevel governance approach empirically, multilevel interest representation is not common. Nonetheless, when only considering those national associations in the analysis that represent their interests regularly vis-à-vis political institutions, some 44 per cent of domestic interest organizations and 75 per cent of large firms have evolved into multilevel players, indicating how profound the EU impact on the behaviour of these actors is.

As a corollary, the patterns of alliance formation in the EU multilevel system vary along the clusters: whereas niche organizations, occasional players and national players focus on cooperation with firms and business interest associations, EU players and multilevel players have a broader repertoire of coalitions. They also pull in more advice from consultants and from scientific organizations, indicating the high need for expertise and professionalism as well as the scope of actors that is now relevant in the EU multilevel system.

Appendix

Table A5.1 Cluster statistics

Cluster statistics	Cluster k									
	1	2	3	4	5	6	7	8	9	10
ETA	.00	.22	.29	.22	.32	.37	.28	.35	.40	.31
PRE	−99	.22	.09	−.10	.13	.07	−.14	.10	.07	−.14
F-MAX	−99	232.5	171.4	78.0	96.8	96.6	53.0	64.4	67.8	41.6

Note: ETA is the explained variance of a k-cluster solution. F-MAX is the explained variance of the k-cluster solution that is adjusted for by the number of clusters. PRE indicates the proportional reduction of error of the k-cluster solution.

$ETA = 1 - Sq_{in}(k)/Sq_{total} = 1 - Sq_{in}(k)/Sq_{in}(1)$
$PRE = 1 - Sq_{in}(k)/Sq_{in}(k-1)$
$F\text{-Max}_k = (Sq_{between}(k)/k - 1) / (Sq_{total}/n - k)$.

N denotes the number of cases, k denotes the number of clusters, Sq_{total} denotes the total sum of squared Euclidean distances, $Sq_{in}(k)$ stands for the sum of squares within the k clusters ('error sum of squares') and $Sq_{between}(k)$ indicates the sum of squares between the k clusters ('explained sum of squares') (see Bacher 2001).

Table A5.2 Number of contacts with political institutions, level of activity during the policy cycle and access to information by clusters (means)

	Niche organizations	Occasional players	National players	EU players	Multilevel players	Total
EU level agenda setting	1.46 (.58) [134]	2.03 (.70) [131]	1.99 (.67) [207]	2.38 (.66) [94]	2.64 (.53) [193]	2.12 (.74) [759]
European Commission contacts	1.66 (1.08) [155]	2.77 (1.57) [140]	2.92 (1.37) [218]	5.25 (.93) [102]	4.92 (.98) [194]	3.43 (1.79) [809]
European Commission information	4.44 (1.34) [55]	2.97 (1.19) [100]	4.49 (1.28) [174]	4.81 (1.12) [103]	5.08 (.97) [198]	4.48 (1.35) [630]
EP contacts	1.29 (.68) [150]	1.93 (1.25) [135]	2.16 (1.08) [215]	4.44 (1.17) [95]	4.52 (1.10) [194]	2.81 (1.69) [789]
EP information	4.37 (1.36) [41]	2.83 (1.24) [87]	4.10 (1.26) [159]	4.40 (1.22) [100]	5.16 (.98) [192]	4.33 (1.40) [579]
Council of the EU contacts	1.09 (.33) [149]	1.53 (.97) [132]	1.59 (.96) [204]	3.41 (1.43) [95]	3.79 (1.46) [184]	2.24 (1.55) [764]
Council of the EU information	4.17 (1.50) [36]	2.37 (1.10) [84]	3.86 (1.40) [142]	3.42 (1.37) [92]	4.69 (1.20) [182]	3.85 (1.51) [536]

(Continued)

Table A5.2 (Continued)

	Niche organizations	Occasional players	National players	EU players	Multilevel players	Total
EU regulatory and standardization authorities	1.42 (1.00) [153]	2.65 (1.82) [133]	2.23 (1.58) [203]	2.96 (1.67) [96]	3.08 (1.74) [181]	2.43 (1.69) [766]
EU level transposition	1.43 (.53) [129]	2.20 (.70) [132]	2.68 (.57) [218]	1.55 (.58) [95]	2.64 (.57) [192]	2.24 (.78) [753]
EU level implementation	1.49 (.58) [125]	2.18 (.69) [132]	2.64 (.59) [218]	1.44 (.56) [93]	2.55 (.61) [185]	2.20 (.78) [753]
National level agenda setting	1.83 (.66) [132]	2.26 (.67) [136]	2.38 (.67) [214]	1.57 (.66) [77]	2.75 (.44) [194]	2.27 (.72) [753]
National government contacts	1.88 (1.23) [147]	3.66 (1.56) [136]	4.55 (1.14) [221]	2.66 (1.77) [102]	5.09 (.98) [191]	3.79 (1.76) [797]
National government information	4.94 (.92) [71]	2.99 (1.12) [111]	5.27 (.86) [210]	3.86 (1.31) [49]	5.04 (1.03) [193]	4.65 (1.31) [634]
National parliament contacts	1.44 (.89) [142]	2.29 (1.39) [128]	3.25 (1.36) [214]	1.67 (1.27) [96]	4.45 (1.18) [190]	2.86 (1.67) [770]
National parliament information	5.04 (.91) [57]	3.21 (1.17) [100]	5.01 (.91) [195]	3.69 (1.24) [39]	5.01 (.98) [185]	4.61 (1.23) [576]
National level position formulation	1.93 (.63) [135]	2.56 (.55) [139]	2.82 (.41) [219]	1.97 (.75) [79]	2.92 (.28) [195]	2.56 (.64) [767]
National regulatory and standardization authorities	1.90 (1.34) [137]	3.60 (1.79) [125]	3.78 (1.59) [191]	1.71 (1.26) [96]	3.93 (1.66) [166]	3.15 (1.81) [715]
National level transposition	1.72 (.51) [132]	2.57 (.51) [136]	2.84 (.38) [219]	1.45 (.53) [77]	2.74 (.46) [194]	2.43 (.69) [758]
National level implementation	1.74 (.58) [131]	2.50 (.60) [134]	2.81 (.42) [217]	1.39 (.49) [76]	2.61 (.57) [188]	2.37 (.72) [746]

Note: The figures in each cell present the mean, (the standard deviation), and [the number of cases]. Contacts have been measured on a 6-point scale: 1 (no contacts), 2 (yearly), 3 (half-yearly), 4 (quarterly), 5 (monthly), 6 (weekly). Activities to represent interests throughout the policy-making cycle have been measured on a 3-point scale 1 (never), 2 (sometimes), 3 (often). Access to information has been measured on a 6-point scale from 1 (very difficult) to 6 (not difficult at all).

6 The Europeanization of interest groups and interest intermediation

The patterns of interaction between state and business are conditional upon the structure of the EU multilevel system. So far, I have accounted for these patterns by general references to the transformation of the state in capitalist democracies and to the dynamics of socio-economic sub-systems. To advance a more detailed explanation of the EU impact on domestic interest organizations and modes of interest intermediation, I draw on the Europeanization concept that has come to guide the analysis of the EU consequences for its member states in recent years. An important analytical tool often linked to this concept is the so-called degree of fit (Knill and Lenschow 1998; Cowles, Caporaso and Risse 2001) among the EU and its member states. This concept is supposed to explain a large part of the national adaptation to European integration. After discussing this concept, I also put competing propositions about the EU impact on domestic interest intermediation and domestic interest groups to the test.

This chapter proceeds in the following way: first, I present major elements of the Europeanization literature and discuss its proposition that the degree of fit matters most when explaining the EU impact on its member states. Next, I analyse the domestic modes of interest intermediation that have emerged in response to EU policy-making. Finally, I analyse the adaptation of domestic interest groups to multilevel policy-making, drawing on the cluster analysis that was developed in Chapter 5. Here, I argue that organizational characteristics matter more than the degree of fit when explaining the adaptation of business interests to the European Union. More generally, the empirical analysis indicates that the division of labour and the power structure in the domestic interest group systems are by and large transferred to EU politics.

The Europeanization concept

It is now widely accepted that the term Europeanization has come to connote the consequences of European integration – the build-up of European institutions and the development of European policies – for national actors, structures and processes.[1] The Europeanization literature has pointed out that degree of fit can be an important variable when seeking to explain the impact of European integration. The congruence among the situations at the EU level and at the domestic level is at the heart of this proposition. Europeanization studies tend to proceed in three steps. First, they identify the degree of fit among the EU and the national situations. Second, their general argument is that a low (high) degree of fit will lead to a high (low) degree of adaptational pressure at the national level. Finally, they test this proposition by analysing domestic change, taking into account additional independent or intervening explanatory variables that may facilitate change or stand in its way (see Cowles, Caporaso and Risse 2001).

However, frequently, measuring the degree of fit is easier said than done: sometimes, this congruence is hard to establish. Not all units of observation are equally well suited to that task. The less formalized and the more abstract the units of analysis are and the more dimensions they have, the more difficult it is to establish the degree of fit among the EU and its member states. The congruence of informal rules of the game or established practices cannot be as easily recognized as the degree of fit between the codified substance of EU Directives and national laws. Furthermore, European integration may not necessitate congruence at the domestic level but require merely some form of compatibility: while EU Directives require legal congruence because they need to be transposed into domestic law, informal patterns of interest intermediation at the different levels need not be congruent. It is not required to transfer the EU mode of interest intermediation into all member states, and their modes must only be compatible with it. As a consequence, different modes of interest intermediation at the two levels need not mount up to adaptational pressure in the member states.

It is also important to note that the degree of fit gives no clear-cut indication about the scope of changes at the domestic level that follow from it (Figure 6.1). Thus, if the patterns of interest intermediation at the EU level and in the member state are perfectly compatible, no change is to be expected because the national groups should be perfectly adapted to representing their interests in the EU policymaking process (*similarity*). In the case of a poor degree of fit, two scenarios that depend on the reform capacity at the domestic level are possible: on the one hand, interest organizations may find it difficult to respond to European integration pressures because the EU situation differs too much from the domestic situation (*immobility*). Hence, they are unable to extend interest representation to the EU level. Quite paradoxically, despite very different degrees of fit, immobility and similarity may have the same consequences, namely no domestic change at all (see also Knill and Lehmkuhl 1999).

On the other hand, a low degree of fit may trigger changes that reach from limited *adaptation* to the *transformation* of the domestic situation. Assuming that each actor has the will and sufficient capacities to respond to European integration – and that no further impediments stand in his or her way – adaptation to the EU will always be perfect. In the case of fully fledged incompatibility, this 'perfect elasticity' would lead to a fundamental transformation of the domestic situation. Tremendous adaptation pressures would trigger a restructuring of the landscape of interest groups, including the foundation of new domestic interest organizations that cover EU affairs. This would reshuffle the domestic power structure and division of labour of the established groups.

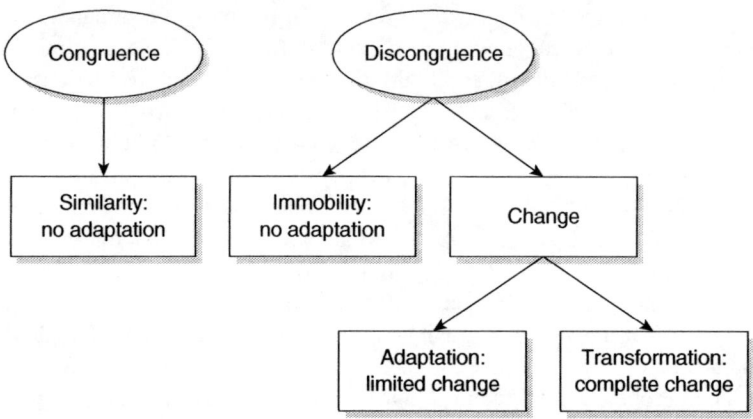

Figure 6.1 Congruence and discongruence – consequences for national interest intermediation

But assuming that the capacity and the will to change are not unlimited and that the latter depends also on the degree of fit, it is unlikely that domestic change will ever be so radical. It is likely to be more limited because several domestic actors will continue to follow tried and tested routines and others will seek to defend their vested interests in order to resist a loss of status or the redistribution of resources (see Aspinwall 1999 on the transport sector). To overcome such resistance, other powerful domestic actors would need to support the EU policies or the EU institutions would need to enforce domestic compliance. In cases of weak or modest incompatibility, the adaptational pressure is more limited. In these circumstances, it is plausible to assume that the resistance to domestic change will be less and that domestic change will correspond more to the European situation. Given these impediments to domestic change and fully fledged convergence of the member states on a European model, it is of little wonder then that most Europeanization studies find that adaptation to Europe occurs in national colours (Haverland 1999; Eising 2000; Héritier *et al.* 2001; Falkner, Trieb, *et al.* 2005). The following sections explore in detail the implications of the degree of fit hypothesis for domestic interest intermediation.

The EU and domestic modes of interest intermediation

The modes of interest intermediation revisited

What is the precise impact of European integration on 'the' domestic modes of interest intermediation? Answering this question requires outlining the modes of interest intermediation that are prevalent in the EU and in each national system as well as determining the extent of adaptational pressure emanating from these constellations before analysing domestic change. As discussed in Chapter 3, the literature on state–society relations distinguishes among three major modes: pluralism, corporatism and statism. Network governance is a more recent conceptualization, reflecting socio-economic dynamics and institutional changes currently occurring within Western Europe, and highlighting the multilevel interactions in the European Union (Kohler-Koch and Eising 1999; Ansell 2000; Peterson 2003). The European Union is frequently portrayed as a variety of pluralism or as the embodiment of the network mode of governance. In the network mode, the state is said to be vertically and horizontally segmented, with its role being that of an 'activator'. Due to the high degree of organizational segmentation, the dispersion of powers and the need to legitimize policies in the heterogeneous member states, it is often said that state actors in the European Union strive for consensus rather than imposing political solutions upon societal actors (Lijphart 1999). The processes of governing evolve in loosely coupled inter-organizational networks. The European Commission is highly active in involving interest organizations into EU policy-making and drawing actors into European networks. However, while acknowledging the consultative functions of interest groups, EU institutions are wary to allocate self-regulatory competencies to them, because they fear an uneven implementation of EU policies in the member states (Commission 2001). As examined in Chapter 3, the UK is frequently held to be pluralist, Germany is often regarded as an instance of weak corporatism and France represents statism. When conceiving of the EU as quasi-pluralist, the expectation would be that the UK faces less adaptational pressure than either France or Germany (Cowles 2001).

However, it is not easy to identify the extent of adaptational pressure in the member states. First, the EU affects domestic interest organizations through a variety of causal mechanisms. These do not necessarily pull them in the same direction. As shown in Chapter 5, the EU operates as an institutional opportunity structure opening up new channels for interest representation. By definition, opportunity structures provide the actors with incentives that encourage certain modes of behaviour, but they also leave them a lot of discretion in making strategic choices. For instance, the interest organizations may opt out of their domestic systems, reinforce ties with national policy-makers or stick to their domestic routines in order to cope with European integration. The outcome of the cluster analysis in Chapter 5 yielded quite varied responses by domestic interest organizations. Furthermore, modes of interest intermediation are rather informal practices and ways of doing things. Even though they may be nested in institutionalized rule systems, they affect the actors mostly by socializing them into certain modes of behaviour. Obviously, the incentives to adapt to the EU mode of interest intermediation are higher at the EU level than in the member states, so that domestic patterns may well be resilient to change.

Second, the typological analysis of interest intermediation is fraught with problems when determining the degree of fit and its implications. Sometimes, the definitions of these types of interest intermediation vary profoundly because they are based on different elements. Moreover, the different elements of these definitions do not always co-vary empirically in the ways foreseen, so that the cases match the types only incompletely. Finally, a focus on different units of observation (countries, sectors, issues, time-periods) may lead to dissimilar characterizations of a case. As a result, the EU, Germany, France and the UK have all been characterized in different ways.[2] This makes it difficult to establish the exact degree of fit between the EU mode and any national mode of interest intermediation.

I illustrate these points by discussing the dissimilar outcomes of two earlier studies. Both look at the same countries and have in common the assumption that the degree of fit between the EU and the member states explains domestic change and continuity to a great extent. Vivien Schmidt (1999, 2006) analyses the repercussions of EU interest intermediation on the domestic modes in France, Germany, the United Kingdom and Italy. She finds that quasi-pluralistic patterns are prevalent at EU level and characterizes Germany as corporatist. In her line of reasoning, German corporatism fits European pluralism better than the statism that she identifies in the UK, Italy and France. Hence, adaptation pressures should be greater in this group of countries than in Germany.

Maria Green Cowles (2001) follows a similar line of reasoning in her study of the EU effects on the national industry federations in France, Germany and the UK. However, despite looking at the same countries (omitting Italy) and presenting a similar argument, she arrives at fundamentally different results to Vivien Schmidt in her study of the impact which the Transatlantic Business Dialogue (TABD) has on national industry federations. She characterizes the EU mode as a form of 'elite pluralism' because, in the context of the TABD, large firms have a direct say in the formulation of EU foreign economic policy. She argues that this elite pluralism poses a greater challenge for German corporatism and French statism than for British pluralism. Notably, she (2001: 161) finds that the direct involvement of large German firms in the TABD erodes the 'authoritative voice' of the Federation of German Industry (BDI) vis-à-vis the German government.[3] Cowles finds empirical support for her argument in the German and British cases and contends that the French industry association has actually been empowered on the domestic level due to its involvement in the TABD negotiations.

To some extent, the contradictory results are an outcome of *varying definitions of the same concept*. They owe much to the fact that Schmidt and Cowles conceive differently of pluralism. In her definition, Schmidt (1999: 157–62) paints a broad picture of the EU policy-making process, dividing it into the twin phases of policy formulation and implementation. She notes that the EU institutions are open to interest group influence in policy formulation and used to cooperative decision-making. However, she also finds that EU institutions are partly insulated from undue influence because the politics of party and money are not as important in the EU as they are in the United States or in the member states, respectively, and because they exclude interest groups temporarily from the policy-making process and tie themselves to specific policy positions (Grande 1994) in order to reject unwelcome interest group demands. By contrast, Cowles focuses on a narrower observation: she highlights the fact that large firms are more involved in EU foreign trade policy-making than are industry federations. Hence, these authors stress quite different elements of 'pluralism', which is one of the reasons why their conclusions vary so much.

Second, and partly as a consequence of their different concepts, they also study *different empirical objects*. While Schmidt (1999, 2006) analyses cross-sectoral patterns of policy-formulation and implementation in the EU and its member states which averages out sectoral differences, Cowles (2001) generalizes from the patterns of decision-making she finds in a specific institutional forum of EU trade policy-making. As a result, the contradictory findings may accord well with the authors' objects of study but not with other issue areas, levels of analysis or time-periods.

Finally, the *characterization* of *the cases* in these two studies varies. Both Schmidt and Cowles characterize the EU mode as some form of pluralism, the German mode as corporatist and the French mode as statist, but they disagree on the United Kingdom. Emphasizing the capacity of the British state to act single handedly, Schmidt groups the UK among the statist countries whereas, for Cowles, it falls in the pluralistic camp because of its fragmented interest group structure and the characteristic relations that interest organizations have built up with the British government. Accordingly, they have contradictory expectations about the EU impact on the UK and Germany. While Schmidt finds a poor degree of fit between the EU mode and the British mode, she stresses that German corporatism matches the consensual mode of policy-formation in the European Union quite well. In contrast, Cowles identifies an excellent degree of fit between European and British pluralism, whereas she foresees much greater adaptation pressures for German interest organizations. In sum, the greater part of the discrepancy in the results of these authors stems from problems built into typological analysis.

Modes of interest intermediation and empirical interactions

Let us now look in more detail at the relations among the state and business associations in the three countries to check whether European integration affects them differently. In this section, I concentrate on the domestic modes of interest intermediation, and in the next section I highlight the adaptation of French, German and British groups to multilevel policy-making. Chapter 3 already characterized the three countries as corporatist (Germany), pluralist (United Kingdom) and statist (France), but suggested also that the cross-national differences are less pronounced than expected. French associations deviate from German groups mostly in functional terms, by concentrating less on the representation of interests in public policy-making, and the British interest group system differs from the French and German systems mostly in structural terms by being more fragmented and less integrated. Nonetheless, the starting assumption remains that we should witness substantial variations in the national responses to European integration. Therefore, I seek now to tease out the crucial implications of the literature on the varieties of capitalism and modes of interest intermediation for the adaptation of interest intermediation to the EU. I expect that the following aspects of state–business relations vary in regard to EU policy-making:

H 1 The density of contacts between state institutions and trade associations is greater in Germany and the UK than in France because corporatist and pluralist relations make for a greater political role of associations in public policy-making.

The Europeanization of interest groups   109

H 2 German associations find it easier than British or French groups to obtain information from government and parliament about EU policy-making because they are more involved in the political process.

H 3 German associations are more present throughout the EU policy-making cycle than French or British groups: in French statism, groups enter the game only once public policies have been decided, and in British pluralism, groups lack the governance capacities to play an important role during the implementation of public policies.

H 4 Due to the corporatist mode of interest intermediation, German state actors include business interest associations more frequently into EU policy-making processes than British or French state actors.

Domestic contacts among interest organizations and state institutions

According to Figure 6.2, the domestic contact patterns that have emerged between business interest organizations and state institutions in response to EU policy-making do not differ greatly across the three nations. They have been measured on a six-fold scale covering no contacts, annual contacts, half-yearly contacts, quarter-yearly contacts, monthly contacts and weekly contacts. With respect to the national governments, contacts with the working level of the institution are distinguished from those with its political leaders, and, with regard to the parliaments, I separate meetings with Members of the Parliament from parliamentary committee work.

For the most part, this analysis demonstrates important cross-national similarities undermining H 1. In all three countries, the contacts that large firms maintain with political institutions outnumber those between business associations and state institutions. This not only applies to the pluralist United Kingdom where firms are said to act quite independently of the industry associations, or to France where the state has nurtured the build-up national champions in its 'grands projets' (Cohen 1995), but also to the supposedly corporatist Germany. Arguably, business associations are of only limited importance as intermediaries between large firms and the state. Even though they may make use of these intermediaries, several French and British large firms regard this only 'as a second choice compared to direct contacts' with policy-makers (Fairbrass 2003: 326). Note also that the contacts the interest organizations maintain with the executives clearly outnumber those with the parliaments. This discrepancy is more pronounced among associations than among firms. The interest organizations are more frequently in touch with bureaucrats at the working level than with the political leadership of the institutions. Regarding the parliaments, they seek access to the Members of Parliament (MPs) rather than the parliamentary committees.

Government departments and public administration are the central contact partners of interest organizations. The allocation of competencies to these public actors is crucial to their lobbying efforts. With regard to Germany, Renate Mayntz and Fritz W. Scharpf point out that 'it is the ministries and not parliament or the political parties to which organized interests turn first, where they argue their demands in detail, and to whom they present information in support of their claims' (1975: 132). Previous studies of German senior administrators have indeed revealed that these 'see specialized interest groups as their main source of information' and that interest groups are 'the organizations with which they have the most contact' (von Beyme 1993: 172). The same pattern holds for the UK, where interest organizations place civil servants and ministers first and second in their list of important channels for influencing public policy (Jordan and Maloney 2001: 39). Given the German federal structure in which the Länder are mostly responsible for implementing public policies and have a say in federal legislation via the Bundesrat, German BIAs also find it more relevant to address regional public actors than British or French BIAs.[4]

In this context, it is important to note that the government departments are more involved in EU policy-making than the national parliaments. Andrew Moravcsik (1998) argues that national executives obtain substantial resources from their involvement in EU politics which may enhance their autonomy from domestic parliaments and interest organizations. It appears that European integration strengthens their capacity to set the domestic political agenda, control the flow of policy information, legitimize their political actions, and contain the ability of opposing actors to veto their political initiatives. In short, the national executives are supposed to be the gatekeepers to the European Union at the domestic level. Even though the analysis of EU multilevel politics in Chapter 5 qualified this assertion to some extent, it is certainly true that their decision-making powers in the European Council, in the Council of the EU and in its administrative sub-structure, as well as their task to implement European Directives and Regulations, make them the most valued domestic contact partners. On average, the national interest groups meet government officials four times a year regarding EU issues. While access to the government institutions does not differ greatly *across* the three countries, there is large variance *within* the national interest group populations. In all three countries, some 16 to 18 per cent of national associations are not at all in touch with their governments, whereas in the UK about 21 per cent, in Germany about 23 per cent and in France about 13 per cent of the groups maintain weekly contacts with the national executives.

Unsurprisingly, relations with the government departments *concentrate on the working level* rather than on the top level. This pattern is indicative of the specialization and segmentation of these institutions and is also characteristic of the difficulty of getting access to the top layer of decision-makers. A large proportion of public rule-making consists of or includes specific technical matters, where the interest organizations can bring in their specialized expertise about products, markets, and technologies. Their contact with political leaders, who are rather remote from the nitty-gritty of policy-making is far more selective: between 34 per cent (France) and 37 per cent of the associations (Germany) in each country do not have access to the secretaries of state, the national ministers or the heads of government. Only between two per cent (France) and four per cent (UK) of the organizations have weekly contacts with the national political leaders. Lobbying at the highest level of government and ensuing interventions

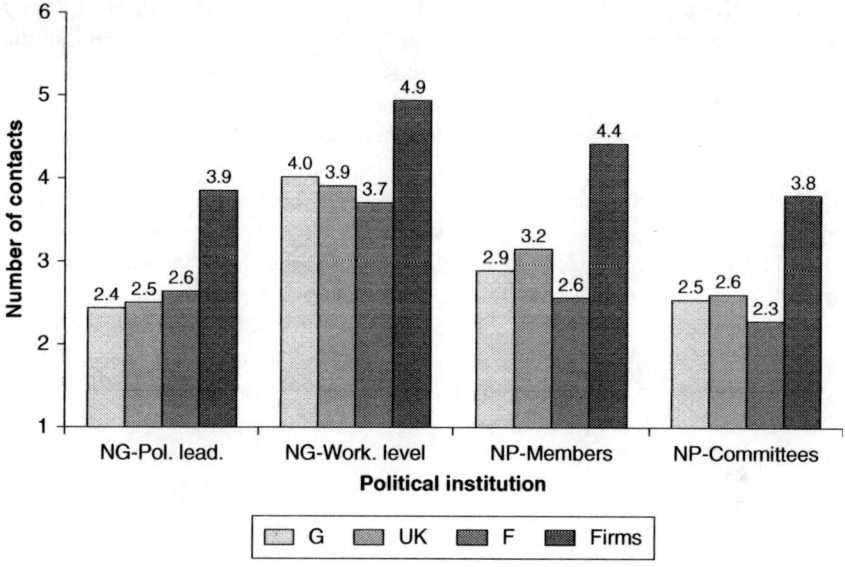

Figure 6.2 Domestic contacts among state and business (means)

Notes: 1 (no contacts), 2 (annual contacts), 3 (half-yearly contacts), 4 (quarter-yearly contacts), 5 (monthly contacts), 6 (weekly contacts). Analyses of variance: National government political leadership 60.40 (df between 3) 1,284.10 (df in 593). F 9.30 p = .000; National government working level 40.78 (dfb 3) 1,814.99 (df in 632). F 4.73 p = .003; National members of parliament 92.20 (dfb 3) in 1,611.77 (df in 605). F 11.54 p = .000; National parliamentary committees 58.58 (dfb 3) in 1,307.73 (df in 588). F 8.78 p = .000.

such as Chancellor Schröder's reversal of the German position on the end-of-life-cycle Directive for automobiles are rare phenomena.

Even though interest organizations dedicate most of their attention to the bureaucracies, they don't neglect the *parliamentary bodies* (see Hayward 1996: 245). Business associations maintain, on average, between annual and half-yearly contacts with the MPs, the parliamentary parties and the parliamentary committees. The rather low level of contact is a consequence of the lower standing of the parliaments compared to the executives. By implication, the electoral parties are even less relevant than the parliamentary parties. In the semi-presidential France of the Fifth Republic, the powers of the National Assembly and the Senate were heavily curtailed to establish 'a strong executive relatively free from parliamentary harassment and interference' (Rizzutto 1996: 46). In the two parliamentary democracies, the 'functional unity' of the executives and their supporting majorities in the legislative chambers only let parliaments come in once a detailed Bill has already been drafted by the executives. In the UK, the 'majority of government Bills clear parliament without substantial amendment. Once policy is presented to parliament, the policy is likely to prevail' (G. Wilson 1990: 81). The hegemony of the British government is underlined by the traditional understanding that 'governmental responsibility is exercised collectively by a single party through the processes of the Cabinet and the co-ordination of policy between departments' (Wallace 1996: 62). In Germany, it is more usual that the *Bundestag* makes amendments to government bills during the legislative process than it is for the *House of Commons* in Great Britain or the *Assemblée Nationale* in France. The reasons are the differences between the parliamentary parties that form the coalition government, the detailed scrutiny of government bills in the specialized committees that mirror the government departments and the ability of opposing parties in the Bundestag that have a majority in the Federal Council (Bundesrat) to impact on federal legislation (see Döring 1992; Saalfeld 1996: 14). In France and the United Kingdom, the legislative bodies affect the policy-making process more by factorizing into it 'a requirement to consider wider partisan/parliamentary/public concerns – even if only in the limited sense of seeking to anticipate or to forestall possible future public criticism in Parliament' (Judge 1990: 32 on the British parliament).

In all three countries, the parliamentary influence on EU legislation would seem to be even more limited than it is in domestic politics. Even if, in recent years, the national parliaments underwent some organizational changes, secured themselves better access to information about EU level developments and gained more rights with respect to the negotiating stance of their national governments (Hix and Raunio 2000), it is generally felt that such changes 'have not greatly enhanced' their ability to scrutinize and influence 'the Government in European affairs' (Rizzutto 1996: 57 on the French parliament).[5] The parliamentary majorities take into consideration that they are constitutive of the national governments and cannot, in general, undermine their position, and the parliamentary opposition does not have the same access to EU information that the majority enjoys via government. Moreover, the opposition forces sometimes restrain the use of their information and decision rights in order not to tie the hands of the national government too much in its supposed defence of national interests (Auel and Benz 2004).

Accordingly, the cross-national variance is once more very limited, undermining H1. However, British groups have slightly more contact with Members of Parliament than French groups, with German groups being in between. The MPs are the most important addressees of interest group demands. A closer look illustrates again the large variance within each country: 26 per cent of the British associations, 30 per cent of the German groups and 36 per cent of the French associations are not in touch with their MPs. In France and Germany, between four per cent and five per cent of the groups discuss matters that are of concern to them with the MEPs on a weekly basis, and this holds for an even larger share (11 per cent) of the British associations.

All in all, these domestic contact patterns do not support the assumption that national interest intermediation varies immensely with respect to EU policies. A closer inspection of the access to information from the state institutions, the timing of lobbying during the policy-making cycle and the activities to initiate contacts between state and business allows for more fine-grained distinctions.

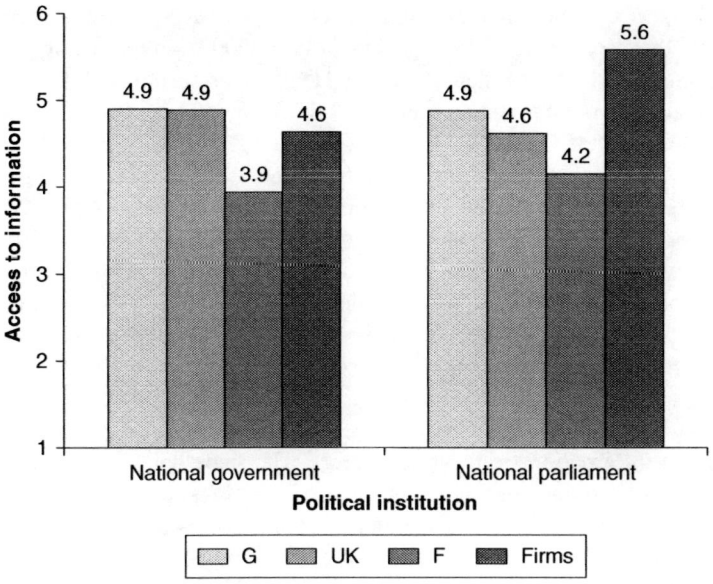

Figure 6.3 Access to information from domestic political institutions (means)

Notes: (1) very difficult–(6) not difficult at all. Analyses of variance: National government: 65.60 (df between 3) 810.78 (df in 534). F 14.40 p = .000. National parliament: 31.31 (dfb 3) 675.35 (df in 491). F 7.59 p = .000.

Domestic state–business relations: a closer look

The exchange of *information* is a crucial element in the relationship between state institutions and business interests. The extent to which business is able to obtain salient information from politicians and bureaucrats is an important indicator of the quality of state–business relations. In general, poor access to information suggests that state actors make strategic use of the information that is available to them and withhold it from associations. This implies that they tend to develop public policies quite autonomously and shut private organizations out from public policy-making. This pattern is most likely to occur in a statist regime and least likely to happen when corporatist patterns of interest intermediation prevail and interest organizations are co-equal with state institutions, with pluralist systems assuming an intermediate position.

The ease of access to information from policy-makers has been measured on a six-fold scale ranging from 1, 'very difficult' to 6, 'not difficult at all'. Figure 6.3 illustrates the mean access to information from the national governments and parliaments. In general, the associations find it rather easy to obtain relevant information from these institutions, so that both the cross-national and the inter-institutional differences are quite limited. In general, the decision-making routines with which the governments handle EU legislation at the domestic level seem cooperative and conducive to good working relations with business interests.

Nonetheless, some cross-national variations support observations that have been made in earlier studies of national state–business relations (Katzenstein 1987; Wilson 1987; Kohler-Koch 1993; Schmidt 1996, 2002). In particular, the French associations find it harder than British and German groups to obtain information from their government and parliament. Only five per cent of the German groups and six per cent of the British organizations have difficulties (lowest two categories of the scale) obtaining information from domestic policy-makers, but 21 per cent of the French groups have that impression. In that vein, 71 per cent of the British associations and 74 per cent of the German groups have no difficulties (upper two categories of the scale) obtaining useful governmental information. This holds only for 37 per cent of the French organizations. In other words, roughly two-thirds of the French business associations perceive moderate to great difficulties when entering into the exchange of information about EU policies with their government and administration.

With regard to the parliaments, just one per cent of the German groups finds it difficult to attain information from the legislators. The same applies to six per cent of the British groups and ten per cent of the French organizations. Correspondingly, 67 per cent of the German associations do not find it difficult to get information from the Bundestag. This share drops slightly to 61 per cent in Britain and falls sharply to 45 per cent in France. In sum, British and German groups have established better working relationships with government and parliament than French associations. Other than expected in H 2, the differences between the corporatist and the pluralist modes are trivial. Both allow interest organizations better access to information than the statist mode.

Figure 6.4 presents the evidence on the *timing of the lobbying activities*. The interest organizations were asked to indicate how frequently (never, sometimes, often) they represent their interests during four phases of the EU policy-making cycle at the domestic level: agenda setting, national position formation, transposition and implementation. Again, this analysis yields considerable similarities: the majority of the organizations often represents the interests of their members to the political institutions when national positions are being formed, EU legislation is transposed into national law or administered by the national institutions. Obviously, they feel the need to leave an imprint on EU legislation through the domestic governments in order to minimize their adaptation costs and to affect the transposition and implementation of EU policies, which often grant a lot of discretion and flexibility to the national implementers.

Note, however, that German associations and large firms are markedly earlier involved in this process than are their colleagues from the United Kingdom and France. About 60 per cent of the former try to set the EU political agenda or respond immediately to early political initiatives that have been taken by other actors. This applies only to 42 per cent of the British organizations and far less (26 per cent) of the French groups. British groups are slightly less active than French and German organizations when the national government forms its position with respect to EU policy-making. Hence, we witness notable differences during the initial stages of the policy-making process. In contrast, cross-national differences

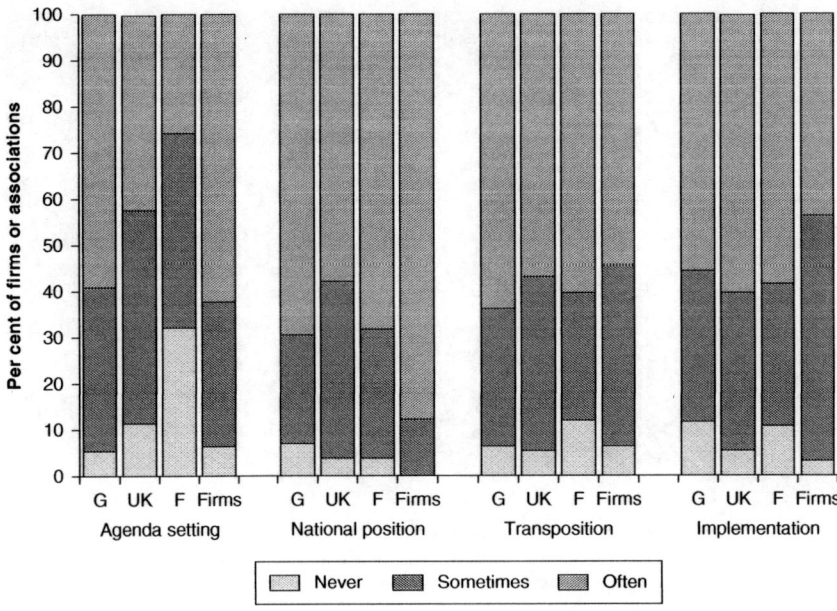

Figure 6.4 Timing of interest representation at the domestic level (per cent of associations and firms)

Note: Chi^2-tests: Agenda setting: Chi^2 71.129 (df 6) p = .000; National position formation Chi^2 21.638 (df 6) p = .001; National transposition Chi^2 8.940 (df 6) p = .177; National implementation Chi^2 11.890 (df 6) p = .064.

during the later phases of the policy-making cycle can be neglected. In all three countries, the associations assume important functions for their members when EU policies are transposed in domestic law and implemented on domestic grounds. By way of comparison, the firms concentrate their activities more on the early periods of the political process than on the implementation of EU policies. The associational activities conform well to the expectation that corporatism promotes close relations between state and business throughout the policy-making cycle whereas groups socialized in statism would only come in once the basic policy contours have been outlined (H 3). However, British groups fit neither the assumption that pluralist groups are quite active during the initial stages of the policy-making cycle and less involved in policy-implementation, nor the opposite expectation that they only come in once the government has elaborated its position. Rather, they devote their attention evenly to the formation of the national position, the transposition of EU Directives into domestic law and their implementation.

Finally, the actors who start these contacts should vary across the political systems (H 4). In a corporatist regime, state institutions draw interest organizations quite regularly into the policy-making process, whereas this should be less common in pluralism and statism. In pluralism, relations between the state and interest

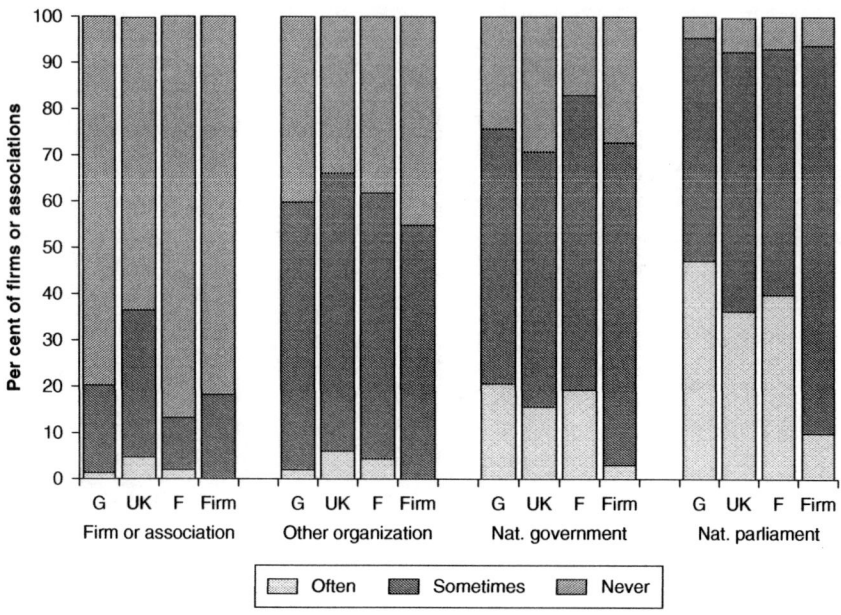

Figure 6.5 Contact initiatives at the domestic level (per cent of firms and associations)

Note: Chi^2-tests: Own initiatives of firms or associations Chi^2 28.845 (df 6) p = .000; Other interest organizations Chi^2 9.401 (df 6) p = .152; National government Chi^2 12.262 (df 6) p = .056; National parliament Chi^2 20.259 (df 6) p = .002.

groups are supposed to emerge from bottom-up initiatives of the associations and firms. In a statist regime, these initiatives should also play a role. But as state institutions enjoy a lot of discretion in their decision whom to consult, the initiatives of interest organizations should play a lesser role than in pluralism. Figure 6.5 illustrates which actors initiate the contacts between state and business.

First, in all three countries, it is far more common for firms and associations to approach the political institutions than to rely on other organizations or wait for an invitation from the state institutions. In that sense, state–business relations are bottom-up rather than top-down processes. It is important to bear in mind, though, that many interest organizations seek contact with government officials and politicians only in response to public policy initiatives and not in order to shape the political agenda. Second, even though most organizations prefer to take their own actions, a cooperative division of labour has emerged at the domestic level. The majority of the firms and associations relies at least occasionally, and some 40 per cent even frequently, on other organizations to provide an entrée to the state institutions or to represent their interests. Third, it is quite common for government departments to draw interest organizations into the political process: they consult the majority of the associations and firms occasionally and more than 20 per cent frequently on their own initiative. But unexpectedly (H 4), there are no significant cross-national differences. The active consultation of business is a common phenomenon in all advanced capitalist democracies, regardless of the mode of interest intermediation or the variety of capitalism.

Finally, business interests are less frequently included in parliamentary debates than in bureaucratic interest intermediation. The MPs limit their attention to a restricted number of business interests because their resources are more thinly spread than those of the government departments. Only a very small minority of firms and associations is frequently invited to present their opinions in parliamentary committees or hearings. The legislative bodies also make a greater distinction between firms and associations in their consultation patterns than the bureaucracies. While the legislators consult some 48 per cent (Germany) to 56 per cent (UK) of the associations occasionally, this applies to roughly 84 per cent of the large firms. Hence, surprisingly, those policy-makers that are directly legitimized by democratic vote display the most biased consultation patterns. Two mutually reinforcing factors account for this pattern. On the one side, MPs with scarce resources focus their attention on those actors whom they consider to be most important in their quest for expertise and re-election. On the other side, the parliaments are very much considered as institutions that are only of secondary importance in public policy-making. As a consequence, they are approached mostly by those organizations that control a sufficient amount of resources to allow them to also deal with these 'secondary' institutions.

Within the context of these broad similarities, some cross-national differences can be noted: the inclination of the interest organizations to start political initiatives varies along countries. Four-fifths and more of the German groups, French associations and firms, but only 64 per cent of the British associations frequently start contact initiatives. This is surprising given that pluralism is usually associated to a greater extent than corporatism and statism with political processes that are bottom-up driven (H 4). This feature of pluralistic policy-making seems to be outweighed by the fragmented structure of the interest group system and the scarcity of resources that many British associations must cope with (see Chapter 3). The small British groups are not in a position to start contacts with political institutions.

In sum, the detailed comparison of the interaction patterns that emerged in France, Germany and the UK with respect to EU policy-making yielded many similarities and just a few differences. Executives rather than parliaments are the centre of interest group attention, and, in general, large firms seem to play a greater role than associations. However, some national differences persist. French statism shows in the relatively poor access that French groups have to information from government and parliament and in their late arrival on the political scene during the policy-making process. British pluralism and the fragmentation of the British interest group system are evident in the greater inability of British groups to initiate contacts with state institutions. However, the extent of cross-national similarities does not correspond well with the prevailing assumptions about statism, corporatism and pluralism.

Partly, this is due to the fact that these modes hardly ever exist in their pure form and that the differences among these countries are less pronounced than is posited by political-economy theories (see also Chapter 3). Since the early 1980s, the three large EU member states have embarked on major liberalization and privatization programmes and divested themselves of important policy instruments to steer the economy. As all three countries are long-standing members of the EU, their interest organizations have long been socialized into the European setting. Even if many of them may have not been affected by the early EEC policies, the completion of the internal market programme, the economic and monetary union and the extension of EU policies to non-market areas have certainly contributed to levelling out some of the national differences.

Europeanization and governance capacities of interest organizations

Governance capacities and cluster membership

The first sections in this chapter indicated that it is difficult to infer immediate consequences from the degree of fit among the EU and its member states for domestic interest intermediation. In this section, I discuss the alternative proposition that it is their organizational capacity to change that is crucial for the responses of domestic interest groups to European integration. Earlier studies highlighted that domestic interest organizations need substantial material resources and negotiation capacities to adapt to European integration. In her case study of the Irish agricultural sector, Maura Adshead (1996) illustrates that only well-established national agricultural associations were able to use the political opportunities of the EU multilevel system and to reaffirm their position in the domestic political arena. In their analyses of EU regional and structural policy, Beate Kohler-Koch et al (1988) and Liesbet Hooghe (2002) came to the conclusion that only those regions that had a firm status in domestic politics – such as the German Länder – were able to represent their interests effectively in the EU multilevel setting. Finally, Doug Imig and Sid Tarrow (2001b, 2001c) trace some of the difficulties of social movements to act in the EU multilevel system to the lack and the specificity of the resources of these collective actors.

In this section, the emphasis will be put on the *governance capacities* of interest groups. I define the governance capacity of an association as its ability to represent its members' interests and mediate between them and the interests of the state institutions (see also Schmitter and Streeck 1981; Greenwood and Webster 2000). I distinguish between two major elements of such capacities: *negotiation capacities* and *organizational resources*. The ability to recognize the needs of state actors in decision-making processes, to mediate between the competing demands of state institutions and their own members and to contribute to the compliance with, and the implementation of, public policies by interest group self-regulation is crucial. In correspondence with the discussion in Chapter 3, I assume that these negotiation capacities are affected by the domestic contexts. Notably, they are shaped by the mode of interest intermediation that is prevalent in a political setting. Moreover, the specialization of business interest associations in the representation of interests and the resources the organizations devote to this function should affect their negotiation capacities.

Assuming that the modes of interest intermediation affect the organizational responses to multilevel policy-making even though they have been subject to convergence pressures, I argue that corporatism supports the development of negotiation skills more than pluralism and statism because, in the corporatist mode, interest organizations are regular interlocuters of state institutions. Correspondingly, German BIAs should have greater negotiation capacities than the French or British groups.

H 5 German interest organizations adapt more easily to multilevel policy-making than the French and the British groups.

The modes of interest intermediation can socialize interest organizations into certain modes of behaviour and leave an imprint on their negotiation capacities, but evidently, as goal-orientated actors, the associations and firms can also develop these capacities themselves by specializing in the representation of interests.

H 6 The interest organizations that specialize in the representation of interests find it easier to adapt to multilevel policy-making.

These negotiation capacities are but one element of governance capacities. *Organizational resources* – such as time, money, staff and the support of its members – are widely regarded as preconditions for an effective representation of interests (Truman 1951; J. Wilson 1973; Knoke 1990). In the complex European multilevel setting, actors need profound organizational resources to keep track of policy developments and to represent their interests continuously at the different levels of government and throughout the policy cycle. Thus, a larger amount of financial resources allows them not only to hire specialized staff and acquire the relevant expertise for their task domains more easily, but also to devise and implement adequate strategies of political communication, to cooperate with other associations and to ensure regular access to both national and EU institutions.

H 7 Organizations that have a greater amount of financial resources at their disposal find it easier to act in the EU multilevel setting.

An important implication of these hypotheses is that, by and large, the power structure within the domestic interest group system and its established division of labour will be extended to the EU context. Thus, I expect that European integration leads to extensions and modifications of established domestic practices and settings that reaffirm, to a large extent, the domestic situation.

The next sections test the proposition that interest groups with greater governance capacities find it easier to adapt to multilevel governance than groups with fewer capacities. First, I analyse whether groups with greater negotiation capacities find it easier to act in the EU multilevel system than those with few of these capacities. Second, I test the hypothesis that groups with greater organizational resources adapt more easily to European integration.

Negotiation capacities and cluster membership

I assume that corporatism equips associations with greater capacities to negotiate with state actors than pluralism or statism. Accordingly, I expect that corporatism produces a higher share of multilevel players than statist or pluralist modes (H 5). Hence, German associations should find it easier to adapt to the European Union than French or British associations. If the competing proposition of the Europeanization literature were true, a better degree of fit should turn a greater share of pluralist British associations into multilevel players than German or French groups whose domestic modes of interest intermediation are supposed to fit that of the EU less well (see Cowles 2001). At the level of the interest organizations, a greater specialization in interest representation also makes for greater negotiation skills (H 6), but does not invalidate the hypothesis derived from the Europeanization concept.

To analyse these propositions, I study the composition of the clusters that were developed in Chapter 5 (see Table 6.1). About a fifth of the German interest organizations fall among the *niche organizations*, and this holds for about one fourth of the British and French associations. British and German groups are more likely to become routine interlocuters of their national institutions (*national players*) than only *occasional players* like the French associations.[6] Hence, associations from a pluralist or a corporatist setting find it easier to act in the EU multilevel setting than associations from a statist regime. The differences between corporatism and pluralism are less important than was suspected and is claimed in other analyses (Schmidt 1999; Cowles 2001). This invalidates H 5, which postulated that corporatism promotes the development of greater negotiation capacities than both pluralism and statism. Unsurprisingly, 82 per cent of the EU players are EU associations. As documented in Chapter 5, only a small minority of national associations from each country is included in this cluster and exits from the domestic political systems. Finally, almost three quarters of the large firms are *multilevel players*. This holds for 29 per cent of the German business interest organizations, 22 per cent of the British associations and only 14 per cent of the French groups. When focusing on the interaction patterns between state and business in the European Union, corporatist and pluralist backgrounds provide associations with better means to act in the EU multilevel system than the statist tradition. In that respect, it seems that the functional similarities between British and German groups are more important than the structural similarities between German and French groups (see Chapter 3).

Domestic modes of interest intermediation have only an indirect effect on organizational negotiation capacities by socializing the interest organizations in certain practices. It is therefore easily possible that the functional specialization of the interest groups matters more for these capacities. Associations that specialize in the representation of interests are in a better position to reconcile the conflicting demands of state actors and members and to act in a multilevel setting than those that specialize in other tasks. I test this proposition in two steps. First I single out the core tasks of the business interest associations. These are the

Table 6.1 Cluster membership of large firms and associations by political system (per cent)

Clusters	Associations and firms					
	EU associations	German associations	British associations	French associations	Large firms	N (%)
Niche organizations	11.1	19.3	24.0	25.7	0.0	158 (18.9)
Occasional players	10.5	17.8	16.2	29.2	5.9	142 (17.0)
National players	11.1	32.7	35.3	24.8	11.8	227 (27.2)
EU players	52.5	1.2	2.5	6.2	8.8	104 (12.5)
Multilevel players	14.8	29.0	22.1	14.2	73.5	203 (24.3)
N (%)	162 (100.0)	321 (100.0)	204 (100.0)	113 (100.0)	34 (100.0)	834 (100.0)

representation of interests, the coordination of market activities, the provision of services, the issuance of licenses and resolution of disputes and the provision of market information. These basic tasks have been obtained by means of a factor analysis that reduces the various activities and the resource allocation of the interest organizations (that were presented in Chapter 3) to this set of five underlying dimensions. The five factors resulted from a principal components analysis with an orthogonal (varimax) rotation. Following the Kaiser criterion, each factor has an Eigenvalue that is larger than one. Together, the five factors extract 66 per cent of the variance of the 13 variables that entered this analysis.[7] Figure 6.6 presents the mean factor scores of the national cluster members on each task in order to illustrate their functional profiles. Since factor scores are standardized, positive deviations from the mean indicate specialization on a function relative to the average association whereas negative deviations indicate less than average activities.

In the United Kingdom and in Germany, the routine interlocutors of the political institutions, namely the national players and the multilevel players, concentrate more on the representation of interests than the members of the other clusters.[8] With regard to the other functions, no further significant distinctions emerge among the German clusters while, in the UK, multilevel players are also more engaged in providing market information than other kinds of association. The pattern in France is quite different: there is no significant functional difference at all

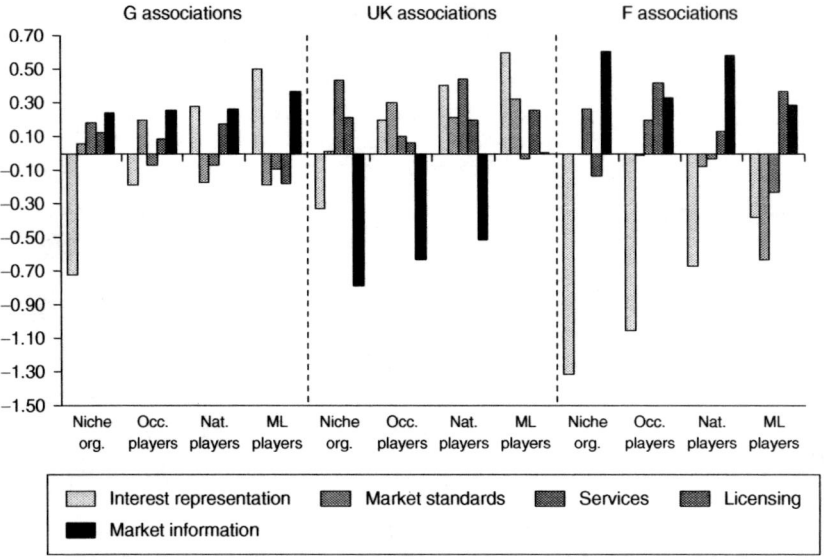

Figure 6.6 Functions of national associations by cluster (mean factor scores)

among the clusters. The findings underscore that, apart from the French associations, multilevel players have built up substantial negotiation capacities and concentrate on representing their members' interests (H 6). Beyond that, there are a few differences among the clusters when it comes to setting standards or to issuing licenses but these variations are not very pronounced. In short, the associational division of labour among the clusters centres on interest representation.

These findings support the proposition that the functional division of labour among the associations is not transformed but extended and only partially modified by the European integration process. Those organizations responsible for the representation of interests vis-à-vis domestic political institutions are also the voices of their constituencies vis-à-vis the respective EU institutions (multilevel players). Associations that are not or are only occasionally involved in national policy-making and implementation (niche organizations, occasional players) are not very active at the European level. Only very few domestic associations chose to exit from the national political arenas in order to pursue their interests rigorously at the European level (EU players). The only exceptions to this pattern are the national players that are well involved in national policy-making but not in EU policy-making. More generally, domestic interest organizations transfer domestic practices and the domestic division of labour onto the European level of governance. Of course, this extension of domestic activities to the European level is less than perfect given that the EU institutions do not fully replace the functions of domestic institutions.

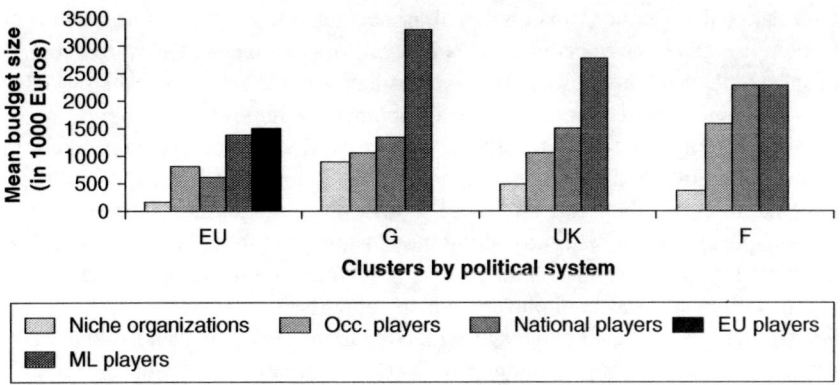

Figure 6.7 Budget size of associations by cluster (means)

Note: National associations that are EU players have been omitted because of their small numbers.

Organizational resources and cluster membership

According to the capacity hypothesis, organizational resources are important prerequisites for the representation of interests vis-à-vis institutions at different levels of government (H 7). I use a two-fold test to investigate this hypothesis. First, I analyse the share of large firms in the different clusters because these are considered to be particularly resourceful actors (see Chapter 2). Accordingly, they should find it easy to adapt to multilevel policy-making. Second, I discuss the financial resources that are at the disposal of business associations, expecting that multilevel players control more resources than other interest organizations. These analyses suggest that organizational resources support the capacity to act in the EU multilevel system (see Figure 6.7).

As well-endowed corporate actors, large firms are more likely to become multilevel players than associations. These corporations may not be as 'footloose' as they are often projected (see also Coen 1997, 1998), but several of them have internationalized their economic activities. Their public affairs activities are closely associated with their widespread economic enterprises. When regulation shifts to the EU or international level, they need to respond quickly by adapting their public affairs activities. Accordingly, almost three-quarters of the large firms represent their interests routinely at the EU and the national levels of government (see Table 6.1). It is therefore safe to conclude that these highly mobile and well resourced actors adapted well to the changes in the institutional setting. While many of them lobbied the European Community via national governments and via European federations well into the 1980s (see Cowles 1997), nowadays their lobbying strategies mirror the politics of multilevel governance. Several of them developed 'sophisticated peak level co-ordination over their subdivisions, cross-border holdings and subsidiaries' (Coen 1998: 80) in order to coordinate their lobbying efforts in the member states and at the EU level. On average, these firms maintain more contacts with national institutions than national associations and more contacts with EU institutions than EU associations. At both levels of government, their direct control of substantial economic resources as well as their market and technical knowledge turn them into important interlocuters for political institutions.

Furthermore, business associations that are well equipped are more likely to evolve into multilevel players than those that are not. Controlling for the political systems, in which the associations are rooted, the average financial resources at their disposal vary significantly along the clusters.[9] Figure 6.7 demonstrates that multilevel players are in command of significantly more resources than niche organizations or occasional players, which supports H 7. In the United Kingdom and Germany, multilevel players also marshal more resources than national players. To illustrate, the sum of money an average German multilevel player spends on interest representation exceeds the mean budgets of German niche organizations, occasional players or national players. In general, associations operating in the niches of the associational systems command significantly fewer resources than the organizations in the other clusters (except occasional players) whereas the differences between the occasional players and the national players are insignificant. In France, the pattern is somewhat different: associations that promote their interests regularly in the domestic arena or in both the domestic and European arena – the national players and the multilevel players – are better endowed than other types of organization. To conclude, in general, actors pursuing a multilevel strategy of interest representation tend to be well endowed. Accordingly, multilevel players are for more likely to maintain an office in Brussels than any other type of interest group (see panel a in Table 6.2).

To validate these findings, I consider now the position of the associations in the population of interest organizations (see panel b of Table 6.2). To some extent, the clusters differ with regard to the type of members they organize. In general, German multilevel players and national players are located at the higher echelons of the associational system: 38 to 43 per cent of them are either federations or mixed membership organizations. Niche organizations and occasional players are far more likely to organize firms directly. Only 20 per cent of the associations in these clusters are higher-order organizations. By contrast, in France and the UK, there is no significant relation among the cluster membership and the position of BIAs in the associational setting. Apparently, in Germany, contacts with the political institutions are channelled through higher-order associations confirming the findings on their functions and roles in Chapter 2. This pattern conforms to the characteristics of the corporatist mode of interest intermediation, whereas the patterns in the statist and pluralistic modes are more unordered. In that respect, the established national patterns appear to prevail in each country.

Conclusion

This chapter analysed competing propositions about the factors that shape the adaptation of domestic interests to European integration. The empirical analysis

Table 6.2 National interest groups by cluster: a) offices in Brussels and b) federation or mixed-membership association (per cent)

	Clusters					
	Niche organizations	Occasional players	National players	Multilevel players	Cramer's-V	N
Panel a) Office in Brussels (per cent)						
G (%)	12.1	22.0	21.1	45.1	.286*	294
UK (%)	7.9	13.8	12.3	30.0	.223*	172
F (%)	14.8	31.3	32.1	53.3	.260	102
Panel b) Federations or mixed-membership associations						
G (%)	20.0	19.6	38.4	42.9	.217*	306
UK (%)	25.6	25.0	20.0	38.6	.161	189
F (%)	34.5	42.4	32.1	46.7	.112	105

Note: *Chi^2 test asymptotically significant at p = .05.

indicates that the way interest groups adapt to European integration depends not so much on the degree of fit among the EU and the member states but on the governance capacities of the interest organizations and on some characteristics of the domestic modes of interest intermediation. In particular, multilevel players need to possess substantial governance capacities: large firms that are highly mobile and well resourced are most likely to represent their interests routinely at both levels of government. For business associations a well established status in the interest group system, profound negotiation capacities and financial resources, and specialization in the representation of their members' interests seem crucial if they want to establish themselves as relevant actors vis-à-vis national *and* EU institutions.

The changes in the institutional setting have not led to a major reshuffling of the domestic interest group systems. For the most part, European integration stimulated extensions and modifications of established practices. In general, it reaffirmed the positions of those organizations that had already developed capacities to articulate, aggregate, organize and represent the interests of their members. This tendency is more pronounced in corporatist settings that channel political representation through peak associations than it is in pluralist or statist settings. The EU institutions tend to include those national associations and firms into the making and implementation of EU policies that are well established in the domestic political settings. Only those domestic associations that rely strongly on their traditional communication channels with national institutions tend to lose substantial political ground because they must rely on the EU players and the multilevel players when it comes to representing their interests vis-à-vis the EU institutions.

In sum, it appears that the Europeanization of interest intermediation has an inbuilt tendency to work to the disadvantage of less resourceful interests even though each and every policy decision does not need to reflect this asymmetry (see Pollack 1997). While this general finding has been derived from the empirical analysis of a large number of business interest organizations in three large member states it may well hold for other contexts and types of actor, as the studies on agricultural interests in Ireland, European regions and social movements have demonstrated.

Part III
The access of business interests to the EU institutions

7 The politics of access in the European Union I
Towards elite pluralism?

Relations among the EU institutions and business interest groups have become a major element in the governance of the European Union. Many scholars consider the access of interest groups to the EU institutions as important because systematic variations in these access patterns can result in biased politics. Thus, finding an elitist bias in these contact patterns, Thomas Hueglin (1999: 260) transferred Ernst E. Schattschneider's well-known comment on the political process in the United States to the European Union: 'the heavenly chorus sings with a strong upper class accent'. David Coen (1997, 1998) arrives at the same conclusion when characterizing the EU patterns of interest intermediation as a form of 'elite pluralism' (see also Cowles 2001). Analysis of these access patterns is all the more important because European Commission officials maintain almost as many contacts with interest organizations as with Members of the European Parliament (MEPs) or with officials in the Council of the EU. The Commission officials are more frequently in exchange with interest organizations than with position holders in the Committee of Regions or the Economic and Social Committee. In fact, they are only more often in touch with national civil servants than with *business* interest groups. Among interest organizations, the Commission maintains more contacts with firms and business associations than with trade unions or environmental and consumer groups (Hooghe 2001: 64–5).

It is therefore puzzling that comprehensive studies of these interactions are rare (but see Beyers 2002; Bouwen 2002a, 2002b; Mahoney 2004, 2008). In their seminal study of European interest group politics at the beginning of the 1970s, Jean Meynaud and Dusan Sidjanski (1971: 491–638) outlined the contours of a '*morphologie d'accès*' to the European institutions that expressed what has become the conventional wisdom about these interactions. Among the various routes that the interest organizations could take to influence the institutions of the early European Communities, they highlighted the importance of the Commission and pointed out that access to the Council of the EC occurs for the most part indirectly, with national interest organizations via those national departments that are in charge of the policy dossier and send their experts to the Council working groups. Interest groups would rarely seek and obtain access to the Council as a collective decision-making body. Given that the European Parliament then had only a consultative status in the formulation of European policies and was composed of national parliamentarians, Meynaud and Sidjanski (1971: 577–86) ranked it, together with the

Economic and Social Committee, as an institution of secondary importance to interest organizations. As in the case of the Council, many contacts with MEPs were initiated by national associations rather than by Eurogroups.

In recent years Pieter Bouwen (2002a, 2002b) has put forward an elegant and systematic explanation of these access patterns. He suggests that the 'access goods' of interest groups account for the access patterns. He compares the access of three forms of organizations: firms, EU associations and national associations,[1] claiming that these organizations deliver different 'access goods'. The argument centres on the information that interest organizations can provide to EU politicians and officials (Bouwen 2002b: 11–12; see also Crombez 2002): supposedly, firms are best at delivering expert knowledge about markets and technologies, EU associations control information about the so-called 'encompassing European interest' of their members and national associations command information about the 'encompassing national interest' of their members. However, he does not analyse empirically whether the organizations are in control of these access goods. Instead, he takes the contacts that EU politicians and officials maintain with these three forms of organization as indicators to test these propositions. The assumption is that the contact patterns result from the exchange goods that the organizations presumably control. The empirical data about these contacts derived from interviews with the representatives of the EU institutions.

This study is important, but also piecemeal. It draws only on evidence provided by the demand-side (EU politicians and bureaucrats) about the financial sector, it disregards variations among the firms and among the associations and it neglects explanatory factors beyond the information of the interest organizations. It also aggregates contacts at different levels of an EU institution. In Chapters 7 and 8, I intend to broaden the study of the access patterns by drawing on the EUROLOB data from the supply-side. In these chapters, I bring several themes of this book together. I adapt the resource dependency perspective to the EU level context and argue that access is shaped by resource dependencies, the EU institutional context, and the forms, structures and strategies of business interest organizations. In Chapter 7, I discuss the impact of organizational forms, comparing the strategies and the access of large firms, EU associations and national groups, separately for the working level and the political leadership of the EU institutions. In Chapter 8, I deepen the explanation of the access patterns, focusing on business interest associations. This empirical analysis corroborates that institutional context, resource dependencies as well as organizational factors need to be taken into account when analysing access to EU policy-makers. Focusing on just one of these dimensions leaves out important facets of the access patterns.

Chapter 7 is set up as follows. First, I outline the access concept and adapt the resource dependency perspective to the EU institutional context, arguing that large firms, EU associations and national groups bring different exchange goods into EU politics. Seeking to identify their preferred strategies of interest representation, I distinguish among insider, outsider and nationalistic strategies. Second, I compare the access of these types of organization to the EU institutions. Then, I validate the outcome of the access study by focusing in detail on the relations that have emerged between state and business in the EU. The results indicate that different forms of organization employ a different mix of lobbying strategies and cast into doubt the proposition that elite pluralism is characteristic of EU interest intermediation.

The politics of access in the European Union

I define access as the frequency of contacts between interest organizations and EU institutions. These contacts range from informal meetings with EU officials and politicians to institutionalized committee proceedings. This definition emphasizes that the organizations actually acquire contacts and do not just aspire to them or forgo their access opportunities. Obviously, this access concept excludes indirect ways and means to exert influence on policy-makers via the public or the media. Nonetheless, it is well suited to study the representation of interests by business, which is said to pursue insider strategies and seek face-to-face negotiations with policy-makers (J. Wilson 1973; Walker 1991; see also below). Access implies either a successful attempt of an interest group to approach the EU institutions or the incorporation of an interest group into EU policy-making by these institutions. I argue that political access results from resource dependencies among the interest groups and the political institutions, political opportunities enshrined in the EU *institutional structure*, and, finally, from the *form of interest organizations* because this is linked to the resources they control.

Resource dependencies and policy information

Resource dependencies matter because neither state institutions nor interest groups can autonomously pursue and achieve their political goals (see Chapter 2). Hence, access cannot be fully understood without an exchange paradigm. On the one hand, owing to their regulatory tasks, the EU institutions depend on interest groups for their information, their consent to EU policies or their active cooperation (see Meynaud and Sidjanski 1971: 523; Majone 1989: 163). Some authors maintain that political money in the EU is information (see Bouwen 2002a, 2002b; Crombez 2002) because their organizational features make for the dependence of the EU institutions on external advice: they have only limited resources at their disposal and are detached from the implementation of EU policies on domestic grounds. Accordingly, they are in need of information that enables them to devise policy proposals that solve the problems at hand, can be administered in the member states and win a sufficient political majority (Meynaud and Sidjanski 1971: 552; Mazey and Richardson 2002: 148).

The EU institutions have recourse to several sources of information. International organizations, member state administrations, think tanks, interest organizations and scientific experts all give important policy advice. Legal information is needed to make sure that the plans do not contravene EU law or are not incompatible with national constitutional law. Economic information is indispensable when the allocative efficiency of the proposals and their distributive consequences are to be evaluated. Knowledge about the administrative implications is required to ensure that the proposals do not run into the resistance of national implementers and can be managed by member state bureaucracies. Technical information is crucial in the detailed regulation of markets or the harmonization of products in order to assess the problem-solving capacity of the proposals.

The multiple sources of information that are available to them reduce the dependence of the EU institutions on any single source of supply and decrease the amount of truly private information. The corresponding ability to check its reliability decreases the risk that actors withhold or manipulate information. The incentives to provide false or incomplete information are further reduced by the fact that the EU has acquired substantial policy-making competencies so that the actors are involved in a series of exchanges in which their reputation and political standing suffers if they have proven to be unreliable. Thus, business interest organizations are by no means the only actors that give advice to the EU institutions and they do not have a monopoly on the information they feed into the political process. However, firms and business interest associations are particularly important – and sometimes exclusive – sources of information in the areas of market integration, standard setting and external commercial policy.

As a result, the European institutions consider interest group involvement essential in the development of EU policies. The Commission has emphasized this point in various communications (Commission 1992, 1999, 2001). The contacts of the EU institutions with interest organizations range from informal, ad hoc meetings to more formal arrangements in committees, expert groups or public hearings. They vary in different parts of EU institutions even though the institutionalization of interest intermediation has increased over time (Mazey and Richardson 2002: 124). So far, efforts at regulating EU-level interest intermediation have not sought to restrict access, but to improve transparency and establish minimum standards. In 1992, the Commission emphasized that it wanted an open and structured dialogue with interest organizations. In its 2001 White Paper on European Governance, it envisaged more extensive partnership arrangements and a stronger role for some groups (under restrictive conditions) as co-regulators (Commission 2001: 17, 21). As a result of the follow-up process to the White Paper, it has adopted general principles and minimum standards for the consultation of interest groups (Commission 2002) that were implemented in a legally non-binding form in 2003. In May 2008, it agreed to a voluntary register and a code of conduct for interest groups. The debate about the democratic deficit has also brought the Economic and Social Committee, as a promoter of civil society involvement in EU politics, more into focus (ESC 2004). And the Lisbon treaty includes provisions for greater civil society involvement in EU policy-making that is meant to strengthen the legitimacy of EU politics.

On the other hand, business interests seek access for a variety of reasons. The resource dependency relationships with their members and with EU institutions impact on the access patterns. Seeking to survive as organizations, EU lobbying serves to maintain or expand their membership and financial status, secure the attention and support of EU policy-makers or obtain a favourable public opinion climate (see Lowery 2007: 48). As discussed in Chapter 2, business interest organizations cannot be sure that the EU institutions anticipate their interests when devising policy proposals, so they seek information about EU policies and attempt to influence their development. After all, they carry the costs of or obtain benefits from EU regulation (see J. Wilson 1980; Majone 1996). In order to secure a final policy outcome, they also need to inform the institutions about their policy preferences and about the merits and drawbacks of alternative courses of action. Hence, whenever EU politicians and officials do not take into account business interests because they do not know them, are unaware of the consequences of their policies for business or pursue other goals than business, interest groups need access to these decision-makers in order to reduce the burden that may follow from EU policies or enhance their benefits.

Insider, outsider and nationalistic strategies

Interest organizations have a variety of options to represent their interests vis-à-vis the EU institutions. By now, it is common to distinguish between insider and outsider strategies (J. Wilson 1973; Walker 1991; Mahoney 2008). An insider strategy involves close consultation with political and administrative leaders and staff and the exchange of substantive expertise. An outsider strategy is based upon appeals to the public through the media and the grass-roots mobilization of citizens (Walker 1991: 9).

Panel (a) in Table 7.1 illustrates how useful business interest organizations find different ways and means of representing their political interests to EU policy-makers. The panel indicates whether they find personal contacts, presence in EU committees, the tabling of position papers and scientific evidence and the mobilization of the media and public useful to their causes. Firms, EU associations and national groups rank these alternative courses of action in quite similar ways. At first glance, the interest organizations prefer an insider strategy to an outsider strategy. There is broad agreement that personal contacts with EU officials and politicians are very useful when representing business interests. On a scale from 1 (not useful at all) to 6 (very useful), the mean scores range between 4.8 (British groups) and 5.7 (EU associations). The second most useful instrument is the tabling of political position papers with average scores between 4.1 (UK associations) and 5.2 (EU associations and large firms). With average scores between 3.5 (German associations) and 4.0 (French associations), the mobilization of the public and the media ranks below all other options (with the exception of the British groups). The criteria that the interest organizations have when selecting their contact partners in the EU corroborate this evidence (see Table 7.1, panel (b)). On a scale from 1 (not important at all) to 6 (very important), the allocation of administrative responsibilities is of primary importance, ranking higher than any other criterion. The average scores are between 4.5 (British groups) and 5.4 (large firms). With mean scores between 2.2 (EU associations: nationality) and 3.6 (British associations: language), language and nationality are of much less relevance even though they might become more important in a political system

Table 7.1 Usefulness of lobbying instruments and importance of criteria for selecting contact partners in the EU (means and standard deviations)

Instruments and criteria	Associations and firms				Firms	ANOVA
	EU associations	G associations	UK associations	F associations		
Panel (a) *Usefulness* of lobbying instruments						
Personal contacts	5.7 (.6)	5.1 (1.3)	4.8 (1.3)	5.3 (1.1)	5.6 (.7)	.000
Regular contacts	5.4 (.8)	4.8 (1.4)	4.6 (1.3)	5.2 (1.0)	5.6 (.6)	.000
Targeted contacts	5.3 (1.0)	5.0 (1.2)	4.6 (1.4)	5.1 (1.0)	5.5 (.7)	.000
Position papers	5.2 (1.1)	4.6 (1.4)	4.1 (1.6)	5.4 (1.0)	5.2 (.9)	.000
Committee presence	4.7 (1.2)	4.1 (1.5)	3.5 (1.6)	4.4 (1.3)	4.4 (1.2)	.000
Scientific evidence	4.5 (1.4)	3.4 (1.5)	3.3 (1.7)	4.1 (1.5)	4.3 (1.1)	.000
Public and media	3.7 (1.5)	3.5 (1.8)	3.6 (1.7)	4.0 (1.7)	3.7 (1.5)	.259
Panel (b) *Importance* of selection criteria for contact partners						
Administrative responsibilities	5.1 (1.3)	5.3 (1.2)	4.5 (1.5)	5.2 (1.1)	5.4 (1.0)	.000
Nationality	2.2 (1.5)	2.8 (1.7)	2.7 (1.7)	3.1 (1.8)	3.4 (1.9)	.000
Language	2.3 (1.5)	3.0 (1.7)	3.6 (1.8)	3.5 (1.8)	3.1 (1.5)	.000
Party membership	1.9 (1.4)	1.8 (1.2)	1.7 (1.2)	2.0 (1.3)	2.2 (1.4)	.057

Note: In panel (a), the scale ranges from 1 (not useful at all) to 6 (very useful). In panel (b), the scale ranges from 1 (not important at all) to 6 (very important).

that consists now of 27 member states. Note that even the national associations ascribe only little relevance to nationality and language when selecting contact partners in the EU institutions. However, all forms of organization agree that the least important criterion for selecting contact partners is party membership. Average scores between 1.7 (British associations) and 2.2 (large firms) signal a diminished role for political parties in EU level interest group politics and put into question that EU politics is politicized along party political lines.

All forms of organization consider not only their regular contacts with EU policy-makers and the provision of background information as very useful but also more targeted contacts and position papers that are related to specific policy issues (see Table 7.1, panel (a)). Apparently, establishing continuous relations with EU policy-makers and more focused lobbying efforts are not mutually exclusive. The organizations seek both to build up and maintain close relations with EU institutions and focus their efforts on the politicians and bureaucrats who are in charge of specific issues. Maintaining close ties helps to establish trustworthy relations with EU policy-makers. These enduring relations can also ease the identification of and access to specific addressees of their political demands. Hence, specific political exchanges are often embedded in relations that are marked by a more diffuse reciprocity (see Keohane 1984). It is therefore not surprising that the business interest organizations find their informal relations with EU bureaucrats and politicians more valuable than the formal contacts in the EU committee system or parliamentary hearings. Note that EU associations and large firms find their contacts with the EU politicians and officials more important than the national associations, indicating a preference of the EU institutions to deal with the former rather than the latter (see below).

I use analyses of variance to compare the mean usefulness and importance of these instruments across the different organizational forms. The results indicate that there remain significant differences among firms, EU associations and national associations when choosing instruments to represent their political interests and selecting contact partners in the EU. The location of the organizations at different layers of the EU multilevel system and their control of different exchange goods contribute to these variations. The only exceptions are the usefulness of media campaigns and the importance of party membership. All forms of organization rate these two strategic instruments in fairly similar ways.

However, I do not discuss these outcomes in detail because the presented 11 variables do not correspond to 11 different strategies. Rather, I explore whether these observations can be explained by a set of hypothetical factors that stand for the basic insider and outsider strategies. A principal component analysis shall serve the purpose to reduce these variables to a smaller set of latent underlying factors. To interpret the outcome I inspect the matrix with the factor loadings. This matrix indicates the correlations between the underlying factors and the observed variables. The higher these loadings, the more an underlying factor is associated with an observed variable. In using factor analysis it is often assumed that the resulting factors are uncorrelated (orthogonal) to each other. I depart from this assumption because various lobbying instruments might be used in both insider and outsider strategies, for example public statements in EU committees or the organization of conferences in which policy-makers take part. Therefore, I have chosen an oblique rotation instead of an orthogonal structure. This allows me to explore whether and to what degree the resulting interest group strategies are independent from each other. I determine the number of resulting factors by relying on the Kaiser criterion which posits that the Eigenvalues of the factors should have a minimum value of 1.0. This yardstick ensures that each factor contains at least as much information as one of the original variables that enter into the factor analysis.

Contrary to expectations, the analysis yields three strategy factors. In addition to the expected two factors for insider and outsider strategies, it produces a third that I label 'nationalistic strategy'. These three factors account for 62 per cent of the variance of the 11 variables. 'Insider strategy' has an Eigenvalue of 4.0 and extracts 36 per cent of the variance, 'outsider strategy' has an Eigenvalue of 1.0 and extracts 9 per cent and 'nationalistic strategy' has an Eigenvalue of 1.7 and extracts 16 per cent.

According to the factor loadings in Table 7.2, personal contacts, the tabling of position papers and attention to administrative responsibilities are characteristic of the insider strategy. Organizations leaning towards the nationalistic strategy find language, nationality and party membership important to the representation

Table 7.2 Strategies of interest representation in the EU (matrix of factor loadings)

Variable	Strategy		
	Insider strategy	Nationalistic strategy	Outsider strategy
Personal contacts	**.73**	−.05	−.00
Regular contacts	**.77**	.05	.09
Targeted contacts	**.75**	−.01	.15
Position papers	**.83**	.00	.11
Committee presence	.32	−.10	**.59**
Scientific evidence	.19	−.11	**.71**
Public and media	−.08	.12	**.79**
Admin. responsibility	**.76**	.12	−.24
Language	−.03	**.79**	−.06
Nationality	.10	**.85**	−.06
Party membership	−.06	**.58**	.29
Explained variance	36%	16%	9%

Note: Factor loadings larger than 0.5 are marked in **bold** to illustrate the resulting factors. Interfactor correlations: insider strategy – outsider strategy 0.40 (Pearson's r), insider strategy – nationalistic strategy not significant, outsider strategy – nationalistic strategy 0.13 (Pearson's r).

Table 7.3 Factor scores by form of organization (means and standard deviations)

Strategy	Associations and firms					
	EU associations	G associations	UK associations	F associations	Firms	ANOVA
Insider strategy	.37 (0.58)	−.04 (1.01)	−.47 (1.09)	.24 (0.68)	.49 (0.46)	.000
Outsider strategy	.40 (0.85)	−.20 (1.00)	−.22 (1.05)	.30 (0.90)	.21 (0.78)	.000
Nationalistic strategy	−.37 (0.96)	.02 (1.01)	.11 (0.94)	.26 (0.99)	.33 (0.90)	.000

Note: By way of calculation, factor scores have a mean of 0 and a standard deviation of 1.

of their interests. The outsider strategy is pursued by those organizations that focus on the mobilization of the public and the media, bring in scientific evidence, and pay attention to their public visibility in the EU committee structure. Note that the insider and the outsider strategies are moderately associated with each other (Pearson's r .40). Associations seeking an insider status seek also to be present in EU committees and bring in scientific expertise. The outsider strategy and the nationalistic strategy are also significantly associated with each other, even though this correlation is weak.

The use of these strategies should vary by organizational format given that the interest organizations are located at different levels of the EU multilevel system and provide different exchange goods. As EU associations concentrate on their relations with EU institutions, they should have less recourse to a nationalistic strategy than firms or national groups that are nested in domestic contexts. For the same reason EU associations should be more inclined than national groups to employ an insider strategy when targeting the EU institutions. Given that large firms are resourceful corporate actors that can exit from domestic settings and on whose technical and economic information the EU institutions depend, these actors are also more likely to employ an insider strategy at EU level than national groups. Finally, I assume that EU associations and firms are more inclined to enhance their public visibility at EU level through an outsider strategy than national groups.

H 1 EU associations are less inclined to employ a nationalistic strategy than firms or national associations.

H 2 EU associations and large firms are more likely to use an insider strategy at EU level than national interest groups.

H 3 EU associations and large firms are more likely to employ an outsider strategy at EU level than national interest groups.

The average factor scores in Table 7.3 illustrate what use EU associations, national business interest groups, and large firms make of these strategies. Confirming H 1, EU associations tend to have far less recourse to a nationalistic strategy than the other forms of interest organizations. National associations and firms do not differ significantly in their use of this strategic option. H 2 finds only limited support. Firms and EU associations, but also French groups rely to a greater extent on an insider strategy than German groups, and these have more recourse to it than British associations. Hence, there are significant differences among national groups when employing an insider strategy. Finally, EU level groups, firms, and also French groups, rely considerably on an outsider strategy, thus disconfirming H 3. Being present in EU committees, tabling scientific evidence and engaging the media and the public is less common among the German and British groups.

In sum, the interest organizations combine these strategic options in different ways. Whereas EU associations rely strongly on insider and outsider strategies, French associations and large firms employ all three strategies. German groups tend to combine an insider strategy with a nationalistic proceeding. Finally, British groups seem most limited in their strategic choices. They rely greatly on a nationalistic strategy and pay relatively little attention to insider and outsider strategies. Hence, the form of organizations explains some of these strategic choices but the similarities among French groups and large firms, on the one hand, and the dissimilarities among national associations, on the other hand, illustrate that other factors need to be taken into account when explaining interest group strategies.

Access and influence

It is now clear that many business interest organizations pursue an insider strategy to obtain access to the EU institutions. However, having access to the EU institutions does not imply that these contacts have an effect on EU policies (Meynaud and Sidjanski 1971: 465; Beyers 2002). Even many discussions with EU policy-makers may not bring about the desired results. In fact, the more groups are present in the European policy space, the less likely it is that any of them will have a significant impact on political outcomes. In crowded policy arenas, policy-makers may be able to play off interest groups against each another. More generally, EU policy-makers may prefer to decide against business interests and pursue their own policy agenda. EURELECTRIC, the association for European electricity utilities, learned this when the sector was liberalized in the mid-1990s. In order to forestall that reform, the association was closely in touch with all EU institutions, but it proved unable to prevent the liberalization of the sector (see Eising and Jabko 2001; Eising 2002). The European Commission, a liberalization coalition in the Council of the EU and large parts of the European Parliament proceeded with the regulatory reform against the resistance of many European utilities.

Even in those cases in which EU politicians take business concerns into consideration in EU legislation, this is not necessarily a consequence of their interactions with business organizations. It may simply be the result of convergent policy preferences. Thus, firms that operate in international markets tend to prefer liberal trade regimes that support their commercial activities. Being enshrined in the European Union treaty, this idea is central to the *acquis communautaire* and part and parcel of the Internal Market Program, whose beneficial economic impact is almost taken for granted and which enjoys broad political and business support in the member states. What is more, EU institutions might co-opt interest organizations to pursue their own policy preferences. In the case of electricity liberalization, a rather small European interest group of regional electricity suppliers that operate mostly in Spain and France, GEODE, enjoyed exceptionally good access to the Commission because its members were among the few market players who supported the plans for the liberalization of the sector from the outset (Eising 1999).

In short, access is not equal to influence in the sense that the input of interest organizations shapes the substance of EU policies. Nonetheless, many groups find their contacts with EU policy-makers necessary in their efforts to have a say in EU policies, given that these tend to require a lot of detailed policy input and are frequently the outcome of lengthy debates between EU bureaucrats and politicians, national executives and administrations as well as interest organizations. It is therefore hardly surprising that interest groups complain when they are shut out from EU decision-making. Edgar Grande (1996) suggests that the temporary closure of decision-making processes to interest organizations can enable EU policy-makers to fence off societal demands. In sum, those organizations regularly in touch with EU officials and politicians are better informed about EU policy-making and better able to voice their general concerns and specific proposals than are other groups. Everything else being equal, it is likely that they are also important coalition partners in EU policy networks. In sum, studying access helps to identify the features of those organizations that assume important positions in EU policy networks, in part acting as gate-keepers to the EU institutions, as well as important characteristics of the EU political process.

The institutional context at the EU level

The institutional context defines the *incentives* and *opportunities* of interest organizations to get in touch with EU decision-makers (Meynaud and Sidjanski 1971: 468; Marks and McAdam 1996; Pollack 1997; Lowery 2007). The second part of this book centres on the *vertical* dimension of this opportunity structure and illustrates that the European multilevel system offers interest organizations multiple points of access whose importance varies across different phases of the policy-making cycle. As Meynaud and Sidjanski have argued: 'la configuration et l'importance respective des accès dépendent du pouvoir officiel de décision depuis le stade de l'élaboration initiale jusqu'à celui de l'adoption finale' (1971: 468).[2] This chapter focuses on the *horizontal* opportunity structure at the EU level where the institutional task contingencies determine the 'target structure' (Almond 1958) of the interest groups and affect the choices of the EU institutions whether and whom to consult.

Notably, three elements of the EU institutional setting shape the access of the interest groups: its segmentation into three pillars, the allocation of powers to its institutions and their internal differentiation. The EU is marked by its pronounced institutional segmentation (see Peters 1992; Eising and Kohler-Koch 1994). In the first pillar of the EU, the European Community, interest groups enjoy relatively good access to the European institutions. This is less so in the other two pillars, which cover common foreign and security policy (CFSP) and police and judicial cooperation in criminal matters (formerly justice and home affairs). These two pillars operate more intergovernmentally, and, as such, involve much less input from the Commission, the European Parliament and the European Courts. This allows member governments to prevent interest groups from gaining access to the EU policy process. For example, during the development of the EU refugee and asylum policy in the early 1990s, Amnesty International complained that it was virtually shut out of EU decision-making (van der Klaauw 1994: 279). For most groups, then, the EC pillar provides the greatest potential for access to the EU institutions, not least because it comprises the vast majority of the Union's regulatory and distributive policies. Therefore, the subsequent analysis concentrates on the European Community.

Enjoying a monopoly over policy initiation and monitoring compliance with Community law in the member states, the European Commission is considered to be the most important contact partner for interest groups in the EC pillar (e.g. Coen 2002: 263–4; Mazey and Richardson 2002: 135–6). The Commission has also acquired important powers under the so-called delegated legislation which comprises the large majority of EU legal acts.[3] Many interest organizations emphasize the difficulty of obtaining substantial modifications of a Commission proposal once it has been presented to the European Parliament and the Council of the European Union (Meynaud and Sidjanski 1971: 550). Therefore, it is important for interest organizations to take action before the Commission has formed its opinion and finalized the details. Even though the Commission exercises its powers collectively, it is rarely approached as a collegiate body. Being organized into several Directorates-General (DGs) each of which is responsible for specific policy areas, interest groups tend to maintain relations with one or more of these DGs. Therefore:

H 4 Interest organizations maintain more contacts with the Commission than with the other EU institutions.

Over time, the European Parliament has acquired substantial legislative powers and 'is now a force to be reckoned with across a wide range of policy domains' (Wallace 2005: 65). The heads of its Standing Committees and the *rapporteurs* who are responsible for a policy dossier are the most important addressees for interest group demands. Despite the increase of its powers, the Parliament is often held to be less important to interest groups than the Council or the Commission because its influence still varies according to the issue and the decision-making procedure at hand. According to Mazey and Richardson (1993: 12) the normal pattern for producer groups is to see the EP 'very much as a secondary arena'. In general, the EP is considered to represent supranational interests in EU policy-making. But, being nominated by national parties and elected by national voters, its members are said to be more amenable to national pressures than the Commission and also more open to diffuse or public interests, including those representing the environment, consumers or large groups such as the unemployed and pensioners. Some analysts regard the links forged between interest groups and MEPs as 'coalitions of the weak' (Kohler-Koch 1997: 6–7).

Interest groups do not always find it easy to access the relevant MEPs because these commute between Strasbourg, Brussels and their electoral districts and because the parliamentary majorities are more unstable than in the parliamentary democracies of the member states. The EP is organized in party groupings of which the largest and most important are the European People's Party and the European Socialists. In many issues, the rules of the EU legislative process prescribe an absolute majority in the parliament and make necessary or facilitate an informal grand coalition of the two large parliamentary parties (see Hix 1998). However, given the lack of party-political discipline that emerges, in general, in parliamentary systems where the parliamentary majority supports the government that is in charge, in the EP, the importance of territorial, institutional, party-political and issue-specific decision criteria varies to a great extent.

Owing to its decisive position, the Council of the EU would seem to be a highly relevant point of access for interest groups and consists of a series of specialized councils in different issue areas. The meetings of the national ministers in the specialized councils are prepared by the Committee of Permanent Representatives (Coreper I and II) and the numerous Council Working Groups that are composed, for the most part, of national experts. Given its relatively few meetings and its composition of national delegates, the Council is rarely lobbied in Brussels. Rather, domestic interest groups address their concerns to national government departments (see Chapter 6). Although the Council's policy positions evolve along national lines, in part as a consequence of pressure by domestic interests, the European Council is more removed from interest group pressure. Not only does it comprise the heads of state or government (as well as the President of the Commission), thus representing cross-sectoral interests to a greater degree, but it also meets formally only once every six months, lessening its impact on the minutiae of day-to-day politics in the EU. Therefore, the analysis concentrates on the EU Council. The fifth hypothesis is:

H 5 Interest organizations maintain more contacts with the EP than with the Council of the EU.

Given the differentiation within the institutions, it can be expected that the interest organizations have more frequent interactions at the working level of EU institutions than with political leaders, partly because European integration consists largely of technical details (Mazey and Richardson 2002: 136). The desk officers in the DGs of the Commission, the Council working groups and also the parliamentary committees are responsible for drafting policy proposals or sorting out their details. It is estimated that some 70 per cent of Council texts are agreed in its working groups, another 15 per cent in Coreper or other senior committees, which leaves only some 10–15 per cent to clear for the ministers (Wallace 2005: 58). Accordingly, the bureaucratic staff depends heavily on external information and support. In contrast, the Commissioners and the ministers usually do not pay attention to every policy detail but focus on those aspects that are contested or deemed to be crucial. As far as interest groups are concerned, lobbying them aims either at establishing broad policy principles – such as the attempts of the European Roundtable of Industrialists to mobilize support for the Internal Market Program among the member state governments (see Cowles 1997) – at revising decisions that were taken before in the policy process – such as former German Chancellor Schröder's intervention in favour of the Volkswagen AG – or at raising the stakes in favour of one specific policy alternative rather than others. Hence, less frequent access to these leaders does not imply that these contacts are less important than those at the working level.

H 6 Interest organizations maintain more contacts with position holders at the working level of the European institutions than with their political leadership.

As the EU judiciary, the European Court of Justice (ECJ) monitors compliance with and interprets EU law. European law takes precedence over national law and grants rights to individual citizens that the national courts must uphold. As a consequence, the preliminary ruling procedure, which offers a channel for national courts to refer questions of European law to the ECJ, allows interest groups to challenge the compatibility of domestic and EU law. Inter alia, this was pointed out by Jill Lovecy in her study of the liberalization of professional services in the

EU. Lovecy concluded that their recourse to the ECJ allowed individual members of the professions to challenge, in some cases successfully, restrictive national practices. Ultimately, litigation led to policy change 'by the back door' because it involved issues which both national governments and the EU had earlier refused to discuss or amend (Lovecy 1999). However, in practice, to take a case to the European Court usually demands that a body of EU law already exists. And even where this is the case, the outcome of such action is uncertain, the financial costs heavy and the duration of the case generally lengthy, which means that this avenue is clearly not available to all citizens and interest groups, and will only be worthwhile when the stakes are felt to be especially high.

Finally, the Economic and Social Committee (ESC), set up to channel the opinions of organized interests within the European policy process, has only consultative rights in EU legislation. The ESC is a tripartite body composed of individual members representing employers, workers and other interests. It is generally considered to be of marginal importance for the representation of interests within the EU. Direct contacts between EU institutions and interest organizations are now much more important than this institutionalized forum for interest intermediation. In this context, at least, much the same may be said of the Committee of the Regions (CoR). So neither of these institutions is included in the empirical analysis.

The form and exchange goods of interest organizations

Besides institutional opportunities, the organizational form of business interests is likely to have an effect on the access to policy-makers because, to some extent, it is tied to the resources that are at the disposal of these actors (see Chapter 2). In that respect, it is helpful to distinguish among large and small firms, firms and business interest associations and among national associations and EU level associations.

As discussed in Chapter 2, not all firms are well equipped to take political action at the EU level. To a large extent, a firm's dependence on associations and its capacity to act at EU level is determined by its size. Small firms tend to rely on associations to represent their interests because they do not have the resources to sustain substantial public affairs capacities (see also Coen 1997, 1998) and, lacking individual investment power, they must unite to gain political clout. In contrast, large firms control substantial resources that allow them to act unilaterally and turn them into relevant interlocutors for state actors.

It is interesting to note that, despite these capacities, many large European firms relied for quite a while on national routes, highlighting the importance of domestic contexts. In his early study of the political activities related to transnational collaboration of business in the common market, Werner Feld (1970: 77) found that many incumbents were then preoccupied with regaining their national markets and lobbying routes, although the European authorities, especially the Commission, have not been completely neglected. By the late 1960s, only a limited number of firms, such as the Italian car manufacturer Fiat or the oil company

Shell, had established offices in Brussels. Maria Green Cowles (1997, 1998) discusses in detail the reasons of many companies to remain aloof from the EC institutions. Several firms were national champions in public ownership or received preferential treatment at the domestic level (see also Hayward 1995a, 1995b). They enjoyed excellent access to their national governments, which looked after their interests in the European arena and could veto European policies that ran against national business interests. Moreover, initially, the Commission had a preference for consulting community-wide interest organizations so that it would not need to arbitrate among different national points of view (Meynaud and Sidjanski 1971: 394–5).

Notably, firms responded to two major regulatory carrots and sticks in the 1970s and 1980s: on the one hand, they mobilized against the efforts to introduce regulations for works councils in multinational firms by the end of the 1970s (Vredeling directive). And, on the other hand, they supported the Internal Market Program when they were facing the European economic crisis and the growing international competition in the late 1970s and early 1980s (Sandholtz and Zysman 1989). The failure of national programmes to address these problems provided incentives for big business to organize at the European level (Cowles 1998: 112).

Given the economic and political 'Eurosclerosis', the Commission also reviewed its stance on the political involvement of firms. Its Industry Commissioner Etienne Davignon worked directly with a number of firms to find solutions for the problems plaguing industrial sectors such as the steel industry. Wayne Sandholtz (1992) and Edgar Grande (1994) discuss in detail the collaboration of major information technology firms and the Commission in the making of ESPRIT, the European Strategic Programme for Research and Development in Information Technology. Meanwhile, there are several important examples of the emergence of Commission bodies that brought together Chief Executive Officers (CEOs) from large firms: for example, the Competitiveness Advisory Group, the Bangemann Group in Telecommunications and Information Technology and the Transatlantic Business Dialogue on international regulatory issues (see Cowles 2001; Coen 2002).

As a consequence of the increasingly felt political weight of the European institutions and the loss of their governments' veto powers in the Council owing to EC treaty reforms, many firms pressed for changes of the membership rules and proceedings in EU associations such that UNICE, the European industry federation, allowed for the membership of large firms in its committees and made its cumbersome decision-making procedures more efficient. In 1990, the UNICE Advisory and Support Group was formed which included some 25 companies that provided both money and personnel to the associations. In 1991, CEFIC, the European association of the chemical industry, allowed for the full membership of companies and developed a bicameral structure that created a new organizational equilibrium between national associations and individual chemical firms (Grant 1993b: 33). Nowadays, several Eurogroups which organize large firms exclude national associations (Cowles 1997; Coen 2002). The public affairs activities of firms have also become more professional, including greater attempts to coordinate the lobbying efforts of international subsidiaries and the establishment of public affairs offices in Brussels. These activities are not just responses to European integration, they reflect the general professionalization of public affairs activities. According to Wyn Grant, the government relations divisions of many British firms were only set up in the mid-1970s (1991: 100), following the example that had been set by American firms.

In light of these developments, some analysts claim that the European Commission has come to work more closely with large firms than with associations (Cowles 2001; Coen 2002) labelling this a form of 'elite pluralism'. To the EU institutions it is important that different forms of organization control quite different resources. Associations are not in direct control of the economic resources of their members, whereas large firms command tremendous investment power. Furthermore, the economic and technical knowledge of firms is usually closer to the market than that of associations. Sonia Mazey and Jeremy Richardson (2001: 77) provide the example of a Commission official who set up a 'Market Practicioners' Group' in order to contact people 'whose bread and butter it was to work in the markets, who might come across the problems we identified in their day-to-day practices'. As they are also important players in their home markets, large firms can even serve the EU institutions as avenues to exert influence on national governments. In that vein, Maria Green Cowles (1997) highlights the role of the European Round Table of Industrialists in persuading national governments of the benefits of the Internal Market Program. And Stefan Collignon and Daniela Schwarzer (2005) discuss the support of the Association for the Monetary Union of Europe and the efforts of its members – banks, insurance companies and industrial firms – to persuade national policy-makers of the advantages of the European Monetary Union. In sum, while according to Meynaud and Sidjanski (1971) European associations dominated EC lobbying until the 1970s, there are good reasons to believe that a form of elite pluralism has emerged in which large firms have better access to the EU institutions than other interest organizations.

H 7 Large firms have better access to the EU institutions than business associations.

Just as small and large firms differ, not all business associations will have equal access to the EU institutions. Here, I don't consider the size of these organizations but their location in the EU multilevel setting because this position shapes their political strategies and activities. It is unlikely that domestic groups will be equally active at the EU and the national levels of government. These organizations are embedded in domestic structures and social relations and depend on routine exchanges with domestic partners. Only if EU regulation has an important impact on them and their members, if the division of labour among them and those EU associations which are supposed to represent them in EU politics is unsatisfactory, or if the terms of EU policy implementation at the national level must be worked out, will they extend their activities to the EU level. Hence, national associations concentrate on domestic institutions whereas EU associations focus on EU institutions.

Table 7.4 Expected and empirical ranking of interest organization contacts with EU institutions and national governments

EU institution	Expected and empirical rankings of interest organizations
	1. Firm > EU association > National association
European Parliament	2. EU association > National association > Firm
	3. EU association = National association > Firm
European Commission	2. Firm > EU association > National association
	3. EU association > Firm > National association
Council of Ministers	2. National association > EU association > Firm
	3. National association > Firm > EU association

Note: 1. Eising, expected ranking; 2. Bouwen, expected ranking 2002b: 17; 3, Bouwen, empirical ranking 2002b: 24.

H 8 EU business associations maintain more contacts with the EU institutions than national business associations.

I do not assume that the relative access of firms, national associations and EU interest groups varies across the Council, the Parliament and the Commission. In contrast, Pieter Bouwen has suggested that these institutions are in need of different exchange goods (Bouwen 2002a, 2002b: 13–16). Promoting European policies, the Commission very much depends on the economic and technological knowledge that firms possess. Given that it must ensure sufficient support for its policy proposals, it is also interested in the information that EU associations can provide about the 'European encompassing interest'. To the Commission, the least important exchange good is national associations' knowledge about 'the domestic encompassing interest'. Given that it is supposed to represent supranational interests but that its members are responsible to national voters, the EP seems to be most interested in the information provided by EU associations about the encompassing European interest, followed by the knowledge of national associations about their domain. Finally, the intergovernmental EU Council is most concerned about the 'domestic encompassing interest' that national associations can provide. As national governments usually seek to reach consensus in the Council and with the parliament when the co-decision procedure applies, the Council also needs some information about the 'European encompassing interest'. Table 7.4 summarizes the expected rank order of the contacts that the interest organizations maintain with EU institutions.

However, Bouwen (2002b: 24) does not find empirical support for his hypothesized rank orders: according to his data, EU associations maintain more contacts with the Commission than firms, and these have more frequent access than national associations. The first conclusion would be that the European Commission depends more on the European encompassing interest than on economic and technological knowledge. Second, Eurogroups do not have more contact with the EP than national associations. However, both maintain more contact with MEPs than large firms. It follows that the European Parliament demands as much information about the European as about the national encompassing interest. The firms' expert knowledge about markets is less relevant to the MEPs. Third, national associations have the best access to the Council of the EU, closely followed by firms and then EU associations. Thus, Council members are most interested in the domestic consequences of EU policies, and then they depend on market knowledge provided by firms. The subsequent section checks whether these empirical findings or whether H 4 and 5 are supported when using supply-side rather than demand-side data.

Empirical analysis of the access patterns

Access patterns

I test the presented hypotheses by comparing the mean access of the interest organizations to the EU institutions. As in the case of domestic institutions, access has been measured on a six-fold scale that includes the following classes: no contacts, annual contacts, half-yearly contacts, quarter-yearly contacts, monthly contacts, weekly contacts. I again use t-tests and analyses of variance to study these data. While these are designed to analyse interval data, as quite robust procedures, they are frequently considered to be applicable to the study of ordinal data such as is used in this analysis. T-tests (pairwise comparisons) compare the mean access of each form of interest organization – EU association, national association and large firm – to *different* EU institutions (H 4–H 6). Analyses of variance (ANOVA) identify whether the mean access to a *specific* institution varies across these types (H 7–H 8). They are supplemented by pairwise post hoc comparisons (not reported) that identify the significant differences.

Figure 7.1 illustrates the average access of business associations and firms, demonstrating that consultation practices vary both across and within EU institutions. The formal comparisons of these data largely confirm the expected access patterns to the EU institutions (H 4–H 6). On average, all three forms of organization maintain more contacts with the Commission (at working level) than with MEPs and position holders in the Council of the EU, confirming H 4: the Commission is clearly the most important addressee of interest group demands at EU level. Compared to the findings reached in earlier studies (Meynaud and Sidjanski 1971), the EP nowadays draws far greater attention to itself. Business associations and firms maintain least contact with the Council. Nonetheless, H 5 does not find full support: business associations have more frequent contacts with the EP than with the Council, which was expected, but this is not true for large firms. These present their arguments as often to the EP committees as to the Council machinery. Apparently, they find it easier to obtain access to the rather intractable Council machinery than their supposed interest intermediaries, the business associations. Finally, for each form of interest organization, contacts with officials at the working level outnumber those with the political leaderships of the Commission and the Council, supporting H 6. The interest organizations devote the bulk of their time and effort to influencing the details of EU legislation, whereas their exchanges with the leadership complement these activities.

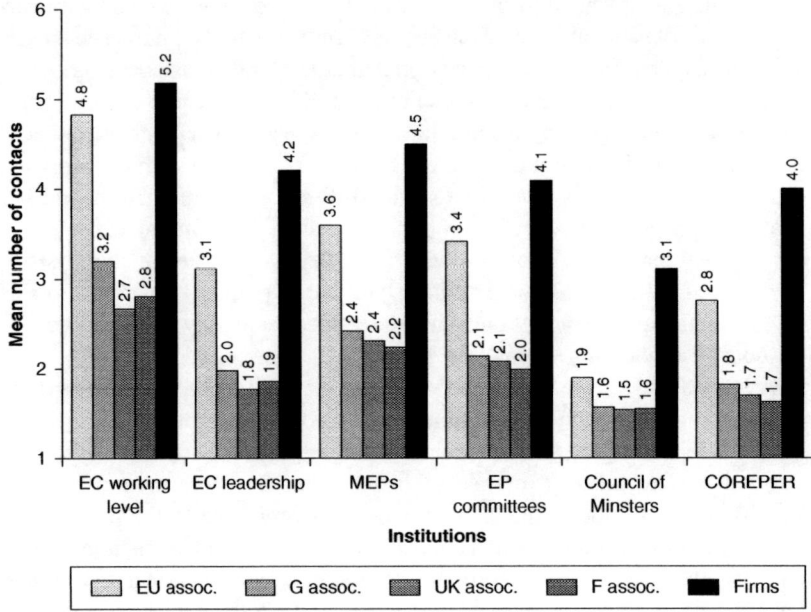

Figure 7.1 European Union contacts between state and business (means)

Note: 1 no contacts, 2 annual, 3 half-yearly, 4 quarter-yearly, 5 monthly, 6 weekly.
ANOVAs for access to EU institutions by firms and associations: European Commission working level: F 56.109 df between 4, df in 794, p = .000; European Commission leadership: F 52.172 dfb 4, df in 756, p = .000; MEPs F 29.229, dfb 4, df in 777, p = .000; EP committees F 36.357 dfb 4 df in 754; Council of Ministers F 17.829 dfb 4, df in 718, p = .000; COREPER F 36.969 dfb 4 df in 737, p .000. Post-hoc comparisons (not reported) indicate significant differences for all institutions between EU associations and firms, on the one hand, and national associations, on the other. There is just one significant difference among national associations: German groups are more frequently in touch with the working level of the Commission than British associations. Finally, large firms have better access than EU associations to the Commission leadership, the Council of the EU and the MEPs.

t-Tests indicate that the average access of one and the same form of organization to different EU institutions varies (pairwise comparisons for EU Council-EP, EP-European Commission, European Commission-EU Council not reported). The exception is the t-test for the access of firms to the EP and to the Council: T 1.034 (df 32), p .309.

Also the hypotheses about the importance of organizational form and location in the institutional setting find only partial support. As implied by H 7 and H 8, large firms and EU associations are more frequently in touch with the EU institutions than national associations. These tend to maintain only occasional contacts with the EU institutions. The EU institutions are dependent on the technical information and economic clout of firms and on the 'European encompassing interests' of Eurogroups and their members rather than on any 'domestic encompassing interest'. As a consequence, the majority of large firms and many EU associations have become regular interlocuters of the EU institutions. Communicating frequently with these institutions, EU associations serve as information brokers and act as interest intermediaries for their members. Evidently, their tremendous resources allow large firms to opt out of their domestic contexts when representing their interests, whereas most national associations remain firmly tied to their domestic arenas.

However, with respect to the expectation that elite pluralism is characteristic of the EU, it is important to register that, contrary to H 7, the access of large firms and EU associations does not differ as much as expected. The firms have better access to the EU Council, but they do not have more contacts with Commission officials and parliamentary committees. The differences between firms and EU associations are less pronounced than general characterizations of the EU as a political system marked by elite pluralism would suggest. Bouwen's analysis of the *aggregated* institutional contacts also backs this finding: according to this study, supranational bureaucrats and MEPs are more frequently in touch with EU associations than with large firms (see Table 7.4).

However, it should be noted that, according to the EUROLOB data, large firms have indeed better access to the Commission's leadership and to MEPs than EU associations, indicating important variations within the EU institutions. The economic clout and technical expertise of firms count for more among political leaders than among policy experts. These are also very open to the information provided by EU associations, which act and speak for EU-wide constituencies. It follows that the extent to which firms and associations can affect the policy-making process in the EU is, inter alia, conditional upon the degree to which EU bureaucrats and politicians shape this process. The bias in favour of large firms seems to be greater if the political leaders are in full control of the bureaucracy, whereas comparative studies of domestic state–society relations tend to suggest that bureaucratic segmentation in various sub-systems is likely to 'create privileged relationships from which the uninitiated are excluded' (Atkinson and Coleman 1992).

In conclusion, the decision-making rationality varies both across the EU institutions and within each institution: the political clout of firms counts more in the higher echelons of the Commission, among MEPs, and within the EU Council than among the policy experts in the Commission and in the Parliament. The latter are also open to the information provided by EU associations that act and speak for EU-wide constituencies and represent a 'European encompassing interest'. Access to the higher strata of the EU institutions is more selective and, for the most part, restricted to the corporate actors. However, in comparison with patterns in the member states, it is important to note that EU institutions are less inclined to grant firms privileged access than is the case in France, Germany and the United Kingdom (compare Figure 6.2). Even though these findings depend partly on the greater specialization of Eurogroups on interest representation than is common among national associations (Chapters 4 and 5), they suggest that associative interest intermediation is more important in EU politics than the notion of elite pluralism implies. It seems that a bias in favour of large firms is more pronounced in the member states than at the EU level – no matter if these nations are corporatist, statist or pluralistic.

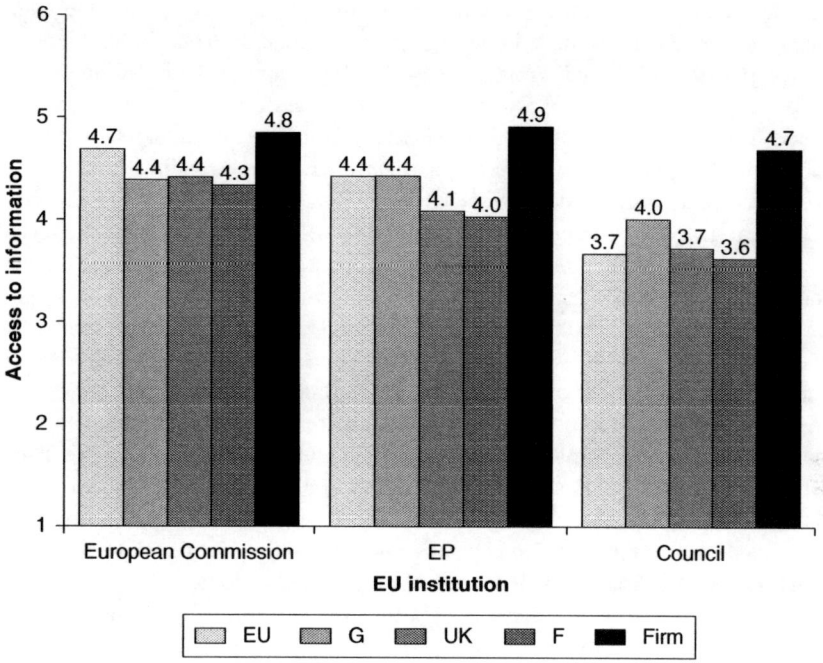

Figure 7.2 Access to information from EU institutions (means)

Note: (1) very difficult–(6) not difficult at all.
ANOVAs for access to information from EU institutions: European Commission: F 2.18 df between 4 df in 625, p = .069; European Parliament: F 3.64 dfb 4 df in 574, p = .006; Council of the EU: F 4.11 dfb 4 df in 531, p = .003.

Relations between EU institutions and interest organizations

A closer inspection of these contact patterns serves both to provide a more detailed account of the relations between EU institutions and interest organizations and to validate the findings of the access study. In what follows, I scrutinize whether the interest group access to information, their activities during the policy-making cycle and their initiation of the contacts support the outcome of the access analysis or shed new light on it. Figure 7.2 illustrates that, in general, those interest organizations with access find it not very difficult to obtain *information* from the Commission or the Parliament. On a scale ranging from 1 (very difficult) to 6 (not difficult at all), on average, the EU associations score 4.7 and 4.4, respectively. Without any noteworthy difference among French, German and British groups, the national associations achieve between 4.0 and 4.4, and the firms have scores between 4.8 and 4.9. By comparison, obtaining information from the Council is more difficult. EU and national associations score only between 3.6 and 4.0. With an average score of 4.7, firms find it easier than business associations to obtain information from the Council (except the German groups). Large firms also have better access to information from the Parliament than the British and French groups. These findings support the outcome of the access study, which indicated a somewhat better access for firms to the EU institutions. They also demonstrate that the EU institutions are as open to those national associations that manage to establish themselves as interest intermediaries in the EU multilevel system (see Chapter 5) as to EU business associations.

Comparing the access to *information* at the EU level with that at the national level (see Figure 6.3)[4] yields the following results: EU associations find it as easy to obtain information from the EU bureaucracy as national associations can obtain information from national officials. A similar picture emerges for the contact pattern with MPs. The national groups – apart from the French associations – find it as easy to attain information from national MPs as the Eurogroups can from MEPs.

All in all, the EU institutions do not provide their regular interlocuters with significantly more or less information than the domestic institutions in France, Germany and the UK. Those actors that maintain close ties with political institutions at both levels, namely large enterprises, find no significant difference in the ease with which they can acquire policy information at each level. In contrast, the national associations are still more rooted in domestic contexts so that British and German groups find it easier to attain information from national institutions than from EU bodies. However, given their comparatively poor access to information from domestic institutions, French associations are not of the opinion that they obtain less information at the EU level than in France.

Figure 7.3 illustrates whether interest organizations represent their interests never, sometimes, or often vis-à-vis the EU institutions during the *policy-making cycle*, ranging from the agenda-setting stage (left-hand pillar) to the implementation of EU policies (right-hand pillar). As the timing of interest representation is measured in only three categories, I use Chi^2 tests to analyse whether EU associations, national groups and large firms differ in their level of activity in these stages. The results demonstrate that the attention and efforts of the interest groups vary *across* the policy-making cycle. Moreover, the level of activities displayed by EU associations, firms and national groups *in each stage* of the policy-making cycle differs significantly, even though it is in order to note that the corresponding statistical associations are weak or at best modest.

Given that the primary task of EU institutions is the conception of common policies rather than their execution, interest organizations are more active when EU institutions design policy proposals and decide upon them than during the implementation stage. But, as was the case at the domestic level, only a minority of them is already present when the EU policy agenda is being set. Given the 'broad market for policy ideas' and 'the unpredictability of the European policy agenda' this is hardly surprising (Mazey and Richardson 1993: 22, 11). The EU political process is 'more difficult for everyone – including groups – to manage' than the national processes. '[N]ew ideas and proposals can emerge from nowhere with little or no warning, simply because the Commission has seen fit to

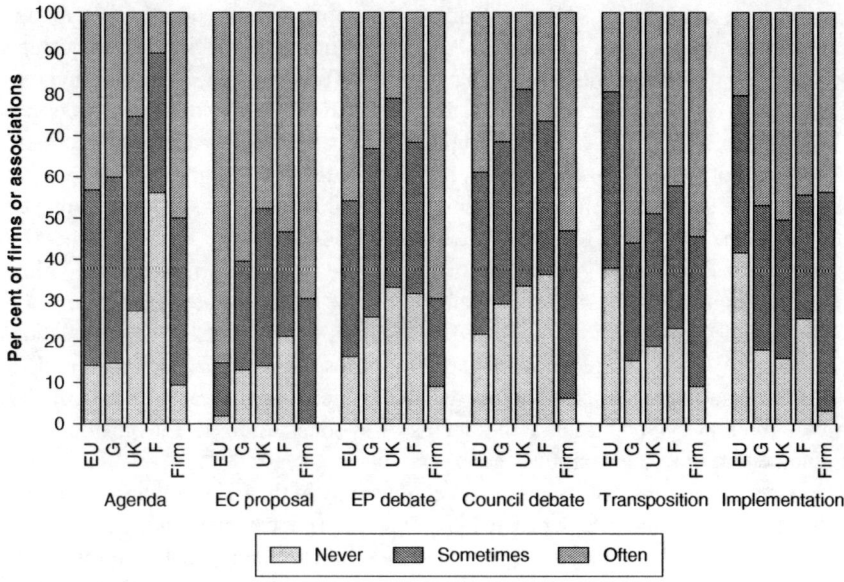

Figure 7.3 Timing of interest representation at EU level (per cent of associations and firms)

Note: Chi^2-tests for the timing of interest representation at the EU level by type of organization: Agenda Setting: Chi^2 95.005 (df 8), p .000; Commission proposal: Chi^2 69.152 (df 8), p .000; European Parliament debate: Chi^2 47.148 (df 8), p .000; EU Council debate: Chi^2 32.217 (df 8), p .000; Transposition: Chi^2 66.938 (df 8), p .000; Implementation: Chi^2 62.565, p .000. The Cramer-V measures indicating the strength of these statistical associations range between 0.147 (Council debate) and 0.250 (agenda setting).

consult a particular group or a particular expert' (Mazey and Richardson 1993: 22). Large firms and EU associations are more active than national associations when the political agenda is being set. Among the national groups, German associations are involved earlier in the game than the other groups. Replicating the domestic pattern, French groups are basically absent from the early stage of the policy-making process.

During the next stage, most interest organizations intensify their efforts. They seek to present their interests frequently to the European Commission when it devises its proposals for EU directives and regulations, underscoring the importance of its monopoly on policy initiation. Interest group activities decrease once the Commission has delivered its proposals to the Parliament and the Council. Many associations still regard the Parliament as an institution that is only of secondary importance even if the gap to the other institutions has narrowed over time. By contrast, the EP draws as much attention from large firms as the Commission. It seems that only particularly resourceful actors and those groups that consider its members to be likely allies include the EP regularly in their lobbying strategies. When the Council discusses the policy proposal, national groups direct their attention to its national members and the national bureaucracies rather than to the EU decision-making body: 70 per cent of the German associations, 58 per cent of the British groups, 68 per cent of the French organizations and 88 per cent of the large firms raise their voice frequently when national governments develop their positions on upcoming EU legislation (cf. Figure 6.4). A far smaller number of groups extend these activities to the Council. Only 31 per cent of the German groups, 19 per cent of the British organizations, 26 per cent of the French associations, but 53 per cent of the large firms claim to be frequently active at the EU level when the Council working groups meet, Coreper debates or the Council of Ministers takes its decision.

In the final stages of the policy-making cycle, when EU policies are being transposed into national law or implemented in the member states, domestic associations and firms are more interested in discussing the details of EU legislation and the nitty-gritty of the implementation process with EU institutions than EU associations. These confine themselves to influencing the early stages of the policy-making cycle and leave the details of the decentralized transposition and implementation to their national members.

In sum, large firms display a high level of activity at the EU level throughout the entire policy-making cycle, whereas EU associations concentrate heavily on the formulation of EU policies, focusing particularly on their relations with the European Commission. National associations spread their activities across the policy-making cycle, but maintain fewer contacts with EU institutions than EU associations and firms, such that the early stages of the policy-making process are even more dominated by firms and EU associations than was suggested by the access analysis.

According to Figure 7.4, most firms and associations *initiate the contacts* themselves rather than rely on other interest organizations or wait for invitations to participate in committee meetings, hearings or expert groups. Among the EU institutions, the Commission invites many organizations occasionally but only a minority of the groups frequently to its policy consultations. The EP recruits firms and business associations less often in its meetings and hearings than the Commission, and this applies even more to the EU Council. Nonetheless, it must be stressed that both the Commission and the Parliament bring EU associations more frequently into the policy-making process than the national institutions include national groups (cf. Figure 6.5). The Commission incorporates 36 per cent of the EU associations frequently into its deliberations, whereas the German government includes only 24 per cent of the German associations. The figures for the UK and France are 30 per cent and 17 per cent, respectively. Both at the EU level and in the member states, the executives draw regularly on the policy information of 27 per cent of the firms. In sum, the EU institutions structure the political participation of interest organizations to a greater extent than national institutions. The great variety of interest organizations that is present in EU politics, their dependence on multiple sources of information, the need to formulate sound policies that seem appropriate and acceptable to a great variety of actors and the requirement to legitimize their policy proposals have led them to establish a great variety of consultative fora and cooperative state–business relations (Eising and Kohler-Koch 1994, 1999b; Mazey and Richardson 1993, 2001).

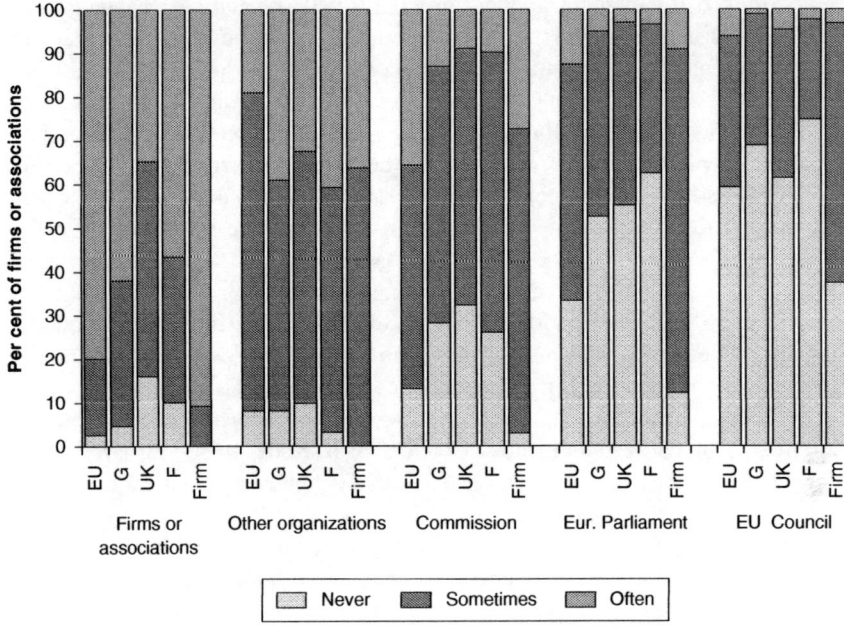

Figure 7.4 Contact initiatives at EU level (per cent of associations and firms)

Notes: Chi²-tests for the contact initiatives at EU level: Firms or associations themselves: Chi^2 99.049 (df 8) p = .000; Other interest organizations: Chi^2 26.756 (df 8) p = .001; European Commission: Chi^2 67.948 (df 8) p = .000; European Parliament: Chi^2 51.641 (df 8) p = .000; Council of the EU: Chi^2 26.556 (df 8) p = .001.

These patterns correspond well with the EU institutional structure. However, different organizational forms also trigger important variations. First of all, firms and EU associations are more likely to start political initiatives than national associations. Second, the EU institutions prefer to include firms and EU level groups into EU policy-making rather than national associations. This preferential treatment is an important asset of the Eurogroups vis-à-vis their national members. Finally, EU associations rely less on other interest organizations to provide a liaison to the EU institutions than national associations and firms, corroborating that many of them have evolved into important intermediaries between their members and the EU institutions.

Conclusion

The resource dependency perspective, interest group assessments of lobbying instruments and policy studies stress that it is important for interest groups to get access to EU policy-makers. The political access patterns are shaped by the resource dependencies among EU institutions and interest organizations, the institutional context of the EU and the organizational forms, structures and strategies of business interests. The empirical analysis in this chapter centred on the importance of the organizational form that is tied to specific exchange goods.

In line with former studies, the results indicate that policy experts in the EU institutions consult a multitude of stakeholders in EU policy-making. The European Commission assumes a central position in the policy-making process and the importance of the European Parliament for interest organizations has increased over time. However, only resourceful interest organizations such as large firms and groups that consider MEPs as likely allies include the EP regularly in their lobbying strategies. The conclusion is that the EU does not necessarily display a form of elite pluralism in which firms have invariably better access than associations to the policy-making process, even though EU interest intermediation displays important imbalances. The policy information and the economic clout of large firms and the ability of Eurogroups to represent the Europe-wide interests of their members matter more to EU policy-makers than the representation of domestic encompassing interests by national associations. Moreover, political leaders in the EU prefer to have dealings with large firms rather than with business associations such that a tightening political control of bureaucracy tips the balance in favour of big business.

Some of these imbalances are due to the institutional context of the EU. In the EU multilevel system, domestic interest organizations have developed a division of labour with EU associations (see Chapters 5 and 6). EU organizations focus on the EU level and also on the agenda-setting and policy-formulation stages of the policy cycle. Being privileged negotiation partners of the EU institutions during these stages, the Eurogroups evolved into intermediaries between these institutions and their national members, processing information about EU policies to their members, building a common platform with them and coordinating the representation of interests across member states.

To some extent, these findings put into perspective the results obtained in earlier access studies. There are two major reasons for the differences that have emerged: first of all, the different data and methodologies account for the different findings. Pieter Bouwen (2002b: 20) considered only 'insider groups' with access to the EU institutions in his analysis. Undoubtedly, this study has shed much light on the overall balance of interest organizations consulted by the EU institutions in the financial sector. However, the exclusive focus on organizations of a single economic sector that *have* access does not allow for the inference that, on average, national associations, EU interest organizations and firms have similar or dissimilar access to the EU institutions. In particular, excluding those organizations from the analysis that do not maintain contacts with EU institutions exaggerates the access of national associations because only a minority of them represents their interests regularly at the EU level (see Chapters 5 and 6). Only the 'multilevel players' among the domestic groups maintain as many contacts with EU institutions as EU associations and large firms.

Second, the studies conceptualized the access to the Council in different ways because Council members and officials have a dual affiliation: they are at the same time members of the EU legislative and their national governments. The EUROLOB survey conceived of the Council as a *collective* EU institution. When also taking the contacts of interest groups with their national governments into account (see Chapters 5 and 6), the ranking of the interest organizations' contacts with the Council changes: on average, firms still maintain the most contacts with the national representatives, but they are now followed by national associations and only then by EU associations. This comes closer to the previous outcome even though the ranking of firms and national groups is still reversed in the two studies. In sum, this chapter puts into question the results of previous studies on the access patterns in EU politics. Let us now move on to study the impact of factors other than organizational form on the access of interest groups to the EU institutions.

8 The politics of access in the European Union II
Towards a theory of interest group access

Analysing the impact of organizational form on access to EU policy-makers has yielded important insights into EU politics, but restricting the study of political access to this variable neglects the range of other factors that bear on the access patterns. Comparative studies suggest that policy information is not the only exchange good that is available to interest organizations (Schmitter and Streeck 1981; Cawson 1985; van Waarden 1991; see Chapter 2). In particular, these may render EU policy-making and implementation more manageable, provide political support to EU policy-makers and enhance the legitimacy of EU political programmes.

Therefore, I move now beyond the study of the organizational form, seeking to determine whether and to what degree institutional contexts, resource dependencies between state and business and interest group structures and strategies shape access to EU policy-makers (see also Shonfield 1965; J. Wilson 1973; Schmitter and Lehmbruch 1979; Schmitter and Streeck 1981; Atkinson and Coleman 1989). Earlier studies had a tendency to focus on just one of these dimensions. Vivien Schmidt (1999) highlights the importance of institutional contexts, pointing especially to the mode of interest intermediation that is prevalent in a political system. By contrast, Gerda Falkner (2000) concentrates on sectoral characteristics. She maintains that EU interest intermediation needs to be studied sector by sector. Finally, as shown in Chapter 7, Pieter Bouwen (2002a, 2002b) stresses the organizational features of interest groups, particularly emphasizing their control of policy information.

Each of these studies has great merits in pointing out major elements of the political exchanges in the EU. But none of them controls for the other potentially important dimensions, so they have not painted a coherent picture of what determines the access of interest groups to the EU institutions. Addressing this shortcoming, I seek to integrate their main dimensions in a consistent explanation of interest group access to the EU institutions, thus aiming at the consolidation and, when necessary, modification of our established understanding.

First, I discuss the impact of institutional contexts, resource dependencies and organizational factors when explaining interest group access. Second, I test these propositions by means of ordered logit regressions that control for the effects that each dimension has on the access patterns. The principal conclusion is that all dimensions must be taken into account. Focusing on just one of them leaves out important facets of the access patterns. In this analysis, I single out the general determinants of interest group access in the EU. These are the division of labour among European and national associations; the organizational resources of interests groups; and their political mobilization when they find the EU institutions to be important for representation of their interests. The effects of all other factors differ among the EU institutions because of the segmented institutional context and varying consultation criteria of the EU institutions. The findings also indicate that national contexts are less important for obtaining access to EU policy-makers than has been suspected.

Towards a theory of interest group access in the EU

Institutional context

I discuss two elements of the institutional context: the EU multilevel system and domestic modes of interest intermediation. The EU multilevel system offers multiple opportunities for interest organizations to represent their interests. Building on the discussion in previous chapters, I argue that EU associations and domestic groups will not be evenly represented at each level of government because they are nested in the context in which they emerged and depend on routine exchanges with their partners and members (see J. Wilson 1973). In short, their location in the EU multilevel setting shapes their political activities. EU business associations organize member firms and associations that are located within the EU member states and represent the so-called 'European encompassing interest' (Bouwen 2002a, 2002b). In contrast, national associations organize members and represent the so-called 'domestic encompassing interest' (Bouwen 2002a, 2002b) primarily at the domestic level. Because they must manage scarce resources, they tend to rely on EU associations for the representation of their interests at the EU level (Bennett 1997a, 1997b). Hence, EU associations have more contacts with EU institutions than do national associations.

H 1.1 EU associations have more frequent access than do national associations.

Not only the multilevel structure of the EU but also domestic institutional contexts should leave an imprint on the access patterns of national interest organizations to the EU institutions. Chapter 3 established that the national modes of interest intermediation and national varieties of capitalism vary less than has frequently been suggested. Nonetheless, France is still marked by some elements of statism, Germany has corporatist traits and the United Kingdom falls under the heading of pluralism. While in France, associations do not play a major role when policies are formulated, they may come back in when policies are implemented (Schmidt 1999, 2006). The UK government generally strives for consensus with interest groups but has a strong capacity to exclude them from political processes (Dyson 1980; Cowles 2001). Thus, being sometimes subject to stop-go consultation, British interest groups enjoy relatively good access to their government (Cowles 2001). In German federalism, associations have many access opportunities. As state institutions also have a distinct preference for associational self-regulation, many business interest organizations have routine access to the government and are regarded as legitimate spokespeople for their domains (Streeck 1999). Translating involvement of business interests in domestic politics to the EU level means:

H 1.2   Corporatism supports better access to the EU institutions than does pluralism, which leads to better access than does statism.

However, the relation among domestic modes of interest representation and political activities in the EU is not yet well understood so that there are two major contenders to H 1.2. First, some authors argue that *embeddedness* in domestic policy networks is decisive for the adaptation of national actors to the EU. On the one hand, those associations that enjoy excellent access to domestic institutions might continue to rely on their established national channels of communication and influence. On the other hand, those associations that are excluded from domestic policy networks might seek compensation at EU level (Beyers 2002). Accordingly, the correlation between national and EU level contacts should be negative.

Second, Vivien Schmidt (1999) and Maria Green Cowles (2001) suggest that the *degree of fit* between the EU and the national modes of interest intermediation matters most (see Chapter 6). According to this logic, those associations that are well acquainted with the EU mode adapt more easily to EU-level interest representation than do groups that have been socialized in a different setting. Both authors find that pluralism prevails in the EU. Accordingly, associations socialized in a pluralistic context should find it easier to extend their practices to the EU level than associations with a corporatist or a statist background.

Resource dependencies

The contacts between EU institutions and business interests are rooted in resource dependencies. In a fine-grained analysis of the exchange patterns between state and business in the EU, I seek to move beyond the focus on the organizational form in order to identify the role of various exchange goods. On the one hand, business bears the costs or obtains the benefits of EU regulation provided by the EU institutions. However, EU regulation needs to be apparent to the interest organizations if it is to trigger efforts to access the EU institutions. The EU environment is not a given reality; to some extent it is 'created through a process of attention and interpretation' (Pfeffer and Salancik 2003: 13). Therefore, I rely on the importance that associations ascribe to the EU institutions as an indicator of their perception of EU regulation. If the associations or their members are exposed to a higher degree of EU regulation, they are likely to attach greater relevance to the EU institutions for the representation of their interests and undertake greater efforts to access them.[1]

H 2.1   The more relevant associations find the EU institutions for the representation of their interests, the more they seek and have contacts with them.

EU regulation generates a huge demand for policy information. As discussed in Chapter 7, EU institutions are in need of information that enables them to devise policy proposals that solve the problems at hand, can be administered in the member states, and can win a sufficient majority among EU legislators (Meynaud and Sidjanski 1971: 552; Mazey and Richardson 2002: 148). Obviously, they have recourse to several sources of information. The policy information of business interests is deemed essential in the areas of market integration and regulation, standard-setting and external commercial policy. Here, business interests command specific and private information about the likely economic and technical effects of EU programmes, their repercussions on domestic law and the political responses of their members.

H 2.2 The more policy information associations can deliver, the better is their access.

EU institutions depend on interest groups not only for their information but for a variety of further exchange goods. In that respect, the consent of interest groups to EU policies and their ability to enhance the legitimacy of these policies seem crucial. EU institutions need the consent of business interest organizations if these are able to forestall an agreement at EU level or impede its implementation. Here, I consider the impact of the structural economic power of business on its ability to veto EU policies.[2] Given the strong focus of the EU on market-making and market-correcting policies, the internationalization and economic weight of business would seem to be as important as policy information. Internationalization increases the veto power of business because producers operating in international markets can more credibly threaten to shift investments than can producers that are nested in domestic markets.

H 2.3 A higher degree of internationalization increases the number of contacts.

Economic weight, which indicates the number of employees that the members of an association have, is a proxy for the relevance of these firms in the economy. The greater the economic weight of firms, the greater are 'the public consequences of [their] discretionary decisions in the market' (Lindblom 1977: 171) and the more will political actors be interested in the functioning of the economic domains that business associations represent. Needless to say, economic clout, investment decisions and employment effects cannot be invoked for each and every policy issue and their importance varies across time (Vogel 1987; see also Chapter 2).

H 2.4 Greater economic weight secures better access to EU policy-makers.

In recent years, EU institutions have also come to stress the contribution of civil society – in which the Commission counts business interest groups – to the legitimacy of European governance. Membership density indicates to what extent an association mobilizes its potential members. The more potential members an association organizes, the more it can claim to be representative of its domain. This should improve its access because it increases the democratic legitimacy of EU policies (European Commission 2002).

H 2.5 A higher membership density improves access to EU institutions.

The organizational structures of business interest associations

Organizational factors can have an independent effect on the relations of business interest associations with state institutions. I conceive business interest associations as boundedly rational organizations that define, aggregate, defend and promote the political interests of a distinct group of producers or employers (Schmitter and Streeck 1981: 33; see Chapters 2 and 3). They exchange resources with their members and with their political and economic environments to ensure their maintenance and to enhance their autonomy (J. Wilson 1973). Their organizational structures contain the core answers to the questions of how to deal with the demands of their members and of state institutions. They embody not only a 'more or less permanent acceptance of the participants on the division of authority and organizational tasks' (Truman 1993 [1951]: 113), but they also process 'the complex variety of motives and goals' existing in the membership and 'transform them into a more or less coherent set of political objectives' (Schmitter and Streeck 1981: 122). These structures shape their members' behaviour in ways that may be 'resistant to change' and 'may persist long after their usefulness as a means of guiding group activities is disappeared' (Truman 1993 [1951]: 113). Several interest groups studies that draw on organizational theory (J. Wilson 1973; Knoke 1990; Walker 1991; Truman 1993 [1951]; Grote and Lang 2003) have highlighted the importance of two key elements in organizational structures: the domain of the organization and organizational resources.

The organizational domain has a strong impact on the collective activity of associations. Separating the 'members and interests that are admitted into the association, from others that are excluded' (Schmitter and Streeck 1981: 122), it delimits the sectoral scope of the association. The size of the sector domain has two opposing effects on access to political institutions. A broader sector domain tends to enhance the relevance of an association to policy-makers but decreases its capacity for collective action. *Ceteris paribus*, a sub-sector domain is associated with a small number of policy issues and members, which allows the association to pursue its members' interests vigorously without much need for internal compromise. However, although its capacity for collective action may be high, an association with a narrow domain may turn out to be irrelevant to policy-makers. In contrast, a broader sector or cross-sector domain increases the number of members and policy issues the association must cope with such that the increased heterogeneity of member interests may render the definition of collective goals more difficult. Nonetheless, EU institutions have stated that they prefer to negotiate with broad-based associations because this facilitates political reforms and relieves them of the task of dealing with a vast array of narrow claims (European Commission 2002).

H 3.1 A broader sector domain improves access to EU institutions.

Furthermore, different actors may be eligible to join an association. To some extent, the types of members indicate the position that interest organizations assume in the associational system. Associations with a direct membership of entrepreneurs, business organizations and firms form the bottom layer. They tend to have narrow domains and aggregate interests at a relatively low level. By contrast, federations organize other associations and are located at the higher echelons of the associational population, which should improve their access to EU policy-makers. In addition, several business associations allow for the membership of both firms and associations. Firms thereby avoid the filtering of their interests in lower-order associations. In turn, mixed-membership groups obtain additional resources from the firms. Therefore, they should have better access than federations.

H 3.2 Mixed-membership groups have better access than federations, and these have better access than direct membership groups.

To ensure their survival and maintenance, associations need a more or less stable supply of resources from their members and their environment (J. Wilson 1973: 30). As voluntary organizations, associations draw on the time, money and effort of their members. Financial resources are a major prerequisite for their activities. A larger income allows them to develop an elaborate division of labour, with a permanent staff (Knoke 1990: 76). Bureaucratization and specialization enable them to pursue their objectives more effectively. They also make for the development of long-term goals, which can be conducive to the build-up of continuous relations with state authorities.

H 3.3 A larger budget improves access to the EU institutions.

To extract resources from their members, associations offer them incentives (Olson 1965; Wilson 1973; Schmitter and Streeck 1981; Knoke 1990). Business associations usually provide some collective goods (i.e. they seek to affect public policy-making or govern market exchanges) and some selective goods (i.e. services) to their members. However, Chapters 3 and 4 as well as empirical studies of EU interest groups (Aspinwall and Greenwood 1998; Greenwood and Aspinwall 1998) suggest that service provision is far less important than interest representation in EU interest intermediation. Hence, specializing in interest representation should equip groups with greater capacities to access political institutions.

H 3.4 Specialization in interest representation improves access to EU institutions.

The strategic choices: insider, outsider and nationalistic lobbying

Even though their activities are in part determined by their organizational domain and by their resources, associations have some latitude left in the choice of their strategy of interest representation. Business interest organizations rely on three strategies to pursue their political goals in the EU: insider, outsider and nationalistic strategies (see Chapter 7). Many business associations regard close relations with EU officials and parliamentarians as important assets and seek to get accepted as legitimate spokespeople for their domains (J. Wilson 1973: 314–16). This 'insider strategy' matches the need of the EU institutions for policy information and support. Associations with an insider strategy regard administrative responsibilities, personal contacts and position papers as important for representing their interests and selecting their contact partners at EU level.

H 4.1 An insider strategy increases the number of interactions with the EU institutions.

Other associations resort to the media and to the public to represent their interests. While generally staying out of the protest business, occasionally, adding well-timed public pressure to the demands they raise in direct negotiations with state institutions can enhance their access and influence. However, frequent campaigns against EU institutions and policies seem incompatible with an insider strategy. It is therefore not likely that business associations resort to an outsider strategy if they attach great value to close relationships with state institutions (J. Wilson 1973: 285). Often such campaigns, for example about the usefulness of genetically modified food, tend to be value loaded. In that case, the positions taken by the actors are not really negotiable if they do not want to lose their credibility. Moreover, the campaign success depends on the acknowledgement of public audiences that business has a just cause. Thus, a public strategy must appeal to a broad constituency, implying a relatively low degree of control over the outcome.

Arguably, the effects of a campaign depend on whether it is run by an EU association or by national groups. Because the European public is structured along national borders, national associations tend to mobilize distinct national publics. Their efforts are directed at national institutions even if they result from EU policies (Imig and Tarrow 2001a, 2001b; Balme, Chabanet and Wright 2002). In contrast, EU associations seek to mobilize a wider 'European public' or at least audiences from several member states, which should have a more favourable effect on their access to the EU institutions.

H 4.2 An outsider strategy reduces the number of contacts with the EU institutions. But EU associations pursuing an outsider strategy have better access than do national associations with such a strategy.

Finally, some business associations thrive on the heterogeneity of the EU member states and on their cleavages. To them, the nationality of EU officials and politicians as well as their language is of utmost importance in selecting contact partners. To a lesser extent, they select their contact partners on the basis of party affiliation and on the basis of personal acquaintance. This nationalistic strategy limits the number of contact partners in the EU because it relies on coalition building with like-minded national actors and is rooted in deeply engrained national differences among EU politicians and bureaucrats that are not conducive to EU problem-solving.

H 4.3 A nationalistic strategy reduces access to the EU institutions.

Table 8.1 summarizes these hypotheses and presents the operational definitions of the variables.

Table 8.1 Summary of hypotheses and definitions of variables

H	Variable[1]	Effect	Operational definition
Institutional opportunity structure[2]			
1.1	Task level: EU association	+	0 (French associations), 1 EU associations
1.2	Corporatism	+	0 (French associations), 1 German associations
	Pluralism	+	0 (French associations), 1 British associations
Resource dependencies			
2.1	Relevance of EU institution	+	Relevance of EU institution (Commission, EP or EU Council) for interest representation from 1 (not important at all) to 6 (very important)
2.2	Policy information[3]	+	Scale of providing political, legal, technical or economic policy information: 1 never, 2 sometimes, 3 often
2.3	Internationalization	+	Foreign turnover in per cent of total turnover
2.4	Economic weight	+	Employees of member firms in 1,000
2.5	Membership density	+	Percentage of potential members organized by the association
Organization			
3.1	Sector domain	+	1 Sub-sector 2 Sector 3 Cross-sector
3.2	Federation	+	0 (Other members) 1 Members: associations
	Mixed membership	+	0 (Other members) 1 Members: firms and associations
3.3	Budget	+	Revenue of the association in 10,000 €
3.4	Interest representation	+	Percentage of revenues spent on interest representation
Strategic choice[4]			
4.1	Insider strategy	+	Factor scores for the importance of personal contacts, position papers, administrative responsibilities
4.2	Outsider strategy	−	Factor scores for the importance of media, public mobilization, presence in committees
	EU outsider strategy	+	EU associations: factor scores for the importance of media, public mobilization, presence in committees
4.3	Nationalistic strategy	−	Factor scores for the importance of nationality, language and party affiliation

Notes
1 All variables are based on the EUROLOB questionnaire. Hence, the data are based on the information and the assessments of the respondents.
2 Corporatism is measured by a dummy variable for German associations, and pluralism is measured by a dummy variable for UK associations. French associations are the reference category. As a result of this operationalization, French associations are also the reference category for the effect of the task level which compares EU associations to national associations. To assess the difference between EU and national associations, I also take into account the size of the three regression coefficients.
3 The scale for 'policy information' is based on three variables that indicate how often (never, sometimes or often) associations provide legal, economic or political information to political institutions (Cronbach's alpha 0.68).
4 The construction of the three strategy factors is described in Chapter 7.

Table 8.2 Access of business associations to EU institutions

Institutions	Contacts of associations (in per cent)					
	No	Annual	Half-yearly	Quarterly	Monthly	Weekly
European Commission political leadership	46.3	21.4	15.0	9.4	5.4	2.6
European Commission working level	25.8	9.9	14.3	19.5	16.1	14.5
Council of Ministers	68.6	13.3	8.4	5.8	3.8	0.3
Coreper	61.0	10.6	10.4	9.9	6.0	2.1
Members of the European Parliament	38.0	17.4	13.4	12.9	12.8	5.6
European Parliament committees	45.4	15.6	13.0	13.0	9.4	3.6

Note: N = 800. Deviations from 100 per cent in row sums are due to rounding errors.

Empirical analysis

Ordered regression models

I analyse the impact of the three dimensions by means of ordered logit regressions because access to the EU institutions has been measured in six categories on an ordinal scale: no, annual, half-yearly, quarterly, monthly and weekly contacts. Accordingly, a regression technique for ordinal outcomes that calculates the probability of falling into either of these categories is more suitable than a technique for interval level data. For this analysis, missing values were estimated by multiple imputation because a significant number of cases would have been lost using listwise deletion (King et al. 2001; Honaker et al. 2003).

Table 8.2 describes the access of the business associations to the EU institutions. As discussed in Chapter 7, the groups maintain more contacts with the Commission than with the Parliament, and slightly more contacts with the EP than with the EU Council. They are more frequently in touch with the working levels of the Commission and the Council than with their political leadership. However, their access to the members and to the committees of the European Parliament is fairly similar. Hence, the vertical structures of the Commission and the Council account for major differences in the access patterns whereas the horizontal division of labour among committee and plenary work in the Parliament does not lead to tremendous variation.

Panel (b) of Table 8.3 presents the summary statistics of the maximum likelihood estimations.[3] The overall fit of the models can be gauged from the G^2 likelihood ratio tests, which are all statistically significant ($p < 0.001$). According to these measures, we can rule out that all coefficients apart from the intercept are zero. According to McKelvey and Zavoina's R^2, the models explain between 46 per cent (Council of Ministers) and 59 per cent (Commission working level) of the variance if the ordinal data were transformed into an underlying interval scale. They predict between 46 per cent (Commission working level) and 70 per cent (Council of Ministers) of the cases correctly. The adjusted Count R^2 indicates that the model for the EU bureaucracy improves the number of correct predictions compared to a guess based on the modal category 'no contacts' by 27 per cent. However, the models for the Council and Coreper do not do very well on that measure because the great majority of the associations do not maintain contacts with them. Thus, a prediction based on the modal category 'no contacts' already does a quite good job.

Panel (a) in Table 8.3 presents the regression results. Raw coefficients are ordered logit coefficients. They indicate the change in the logged odds of the dependent variable for a unit increase of the independent variable, controlling for all other factors that are included in the analysis.[4] Beyond their direction and significance, the raw coefficients are hard to interpret because, in these multiplicative models, the impact of a change in the value of an independent variable on the contact probabilities depends upon the values of all other independent variables.

To facilitate their substantive interpretation, I discuss the outcomes for sector federations, with all other variables kept at their means or moved from their minima to their maxima. Figure 8.1 displays their contact probabilities with the political leaders and desk officers in the Commission and the Council of Ministers and with the members of the European Parliament, separately for EU groups and national associations with all other independent variables kept at their means.[5] Table 8.4 shows the impact of moving an independent variable from its minimum to its maximum on the probability of having weekly contacts with these EU institutions, thus demonstrating its substantial effect. Contrasting EU associations with German groups, Figure 8.2 illustrates the effects of financial resources, institutional relevance and policy information on the contact probabilities with the EU bureaucracy when moved from their minima to their maxima. To obtain greater insights into the logic of these political exchanges, I check also whether and with which interest organizations the EU institutions have initiated these contacts (see Tables A 8.4, A 8.5).

Empirical results: access and explanations

The empirical results confirm that institutional context, resource dependencies, organizational structures and strategic choices must be taken into account when analysing the access of business interest organizations to the EU institutions. It is insufficient to focus on just one of these dimensions. Because the EU institutional context is highly segmented, EU interest intermediation is highly variegated. Only a few factors have a consistent impact on access patterns, namely the position of associations in the EU multilevel setting, the organizational resources they control and their perception of institutional regulation. The effects of all other factors are contingent upon the characteristics of the EU institutions.

The institutional context

Their location in the EU multilevel system has a significant impact on the contacts of interest organizations with EU institutions. EU associations tend to have

Table 8.3 Ordered logit regressions (N = 800)

	(1) EC political leaders	(2) EC working level	(3) Council of Ministers	(4) Coreper	(5) Members of EP	(6) EP committees
Panel a) Regression models						
Institutional context						
EU association	1.369**	2.027**	.475	1.487**	1.005**	1.272**
Corporatism	.131	.614**	.151	.405	−.047	−.129
Pluralism	.237	.408	.796**	.708*	.482*	.485
Resource dependencies						
Institutional relevance	.649**	.807**	.591**	.749**	.780**	.744**
Expertise	.888**	.584**	.625**	.481**	.719**	.764**
Internationalization	.010**	.019**	.008*	.009*	.005	.002
Economic weight	.001**	.001**	.000*	.001**	.001**	.000*
Membership density	−.006	−.003	−.003	.006	−.006	−.007*
Organizational structure						
Sector domain	.049	−.001	.337*	−.053	.071	.013
Federation	.349	.344*	.312	.502**	.157	.176
Mixed members	.162	.096	.270	.136	.090	.092
Budget	.003**	.003**	.002**	.002**	.003**	.003**
Interest representation	.007*	.006*	.008*	−.003	.006**	.013**
Strategy						
Insider strategy	.084	.418**	.172	.139	.236*	.316**
National strategy	.070	−.117	.113	.139	−.055	−.138
Outsider strategy	−.123	−.284**	.086	−.095	−.080	−.043
EU outsider strategy	.246	.306	.350	.184	.363**	.351
Panel b) Maximum Likelihood Estimation						
Log Likelihood	−923.52	−1062.60	−667.84	−807.78	−102.09	−925.78
G^2	465.95	672.65	322.26	39.97	566.63	582.42
McKelvey Zavoina R^2	.49	.59	.46	.49	.54	0.57
Correct predictions (%)	52	46	70	63	47	55
Adjusted predictions (%)	11	27	3	6	15	17

Notes: Ordered logit coefficients, * significant at 5%; ** significant at 1% (two-tailed tests).

better access than national groups, which supports H 1.1. According to Figure 8.1, this difference is most pronounced at the working level of the Commission and less obvious at the level of its political leaders and in the EP. The probability of EU associations maintaining weekly contacts with EU bureaucrats amounts

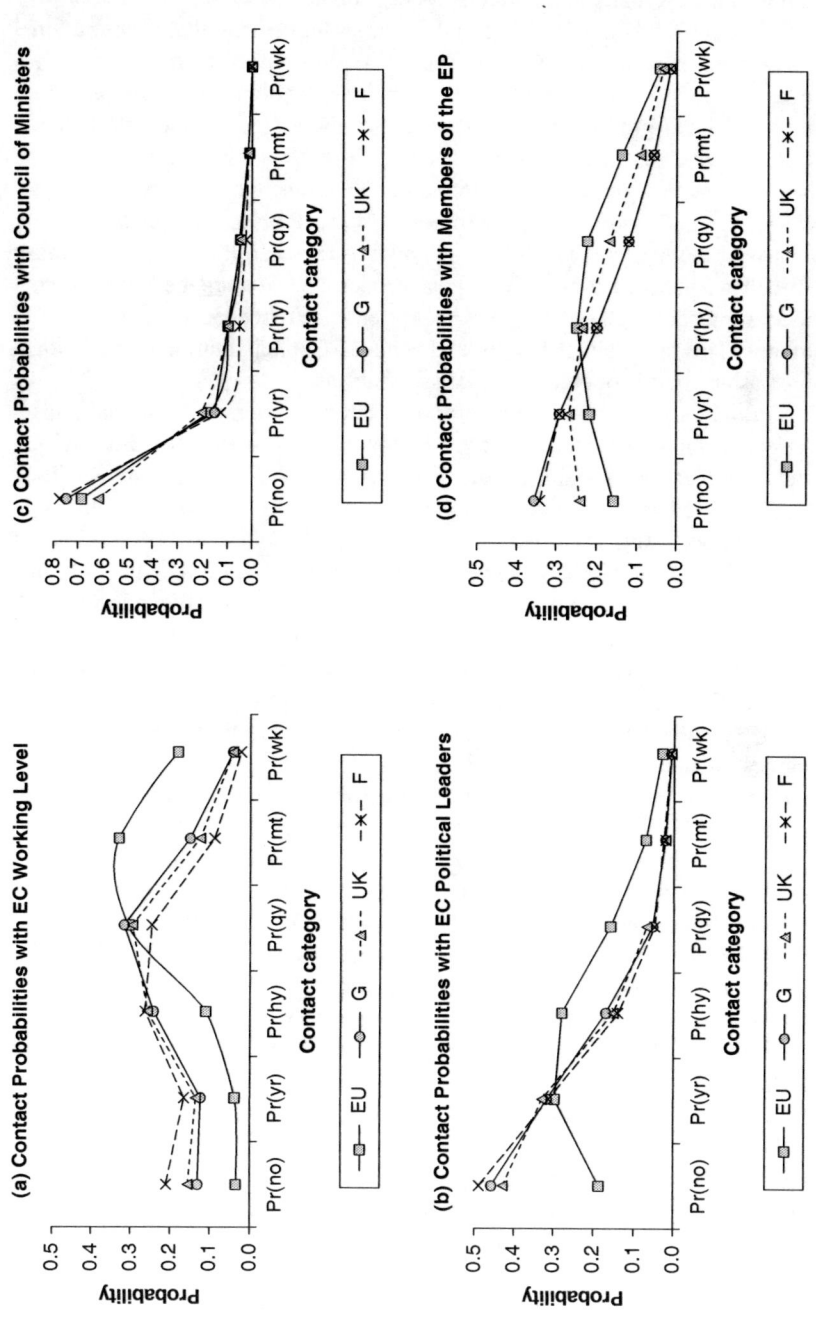

Figure 8.1 Contact probabilities with selected EU institutions

Note: Contact probabilities of national and EU sector federations, with all other variables set to their means.

to 0.18. While suggesting that only about one-fifth of EU groups tends to be in touch with the Commission very often, this figure is six times higher than that of French groups and three-and-a-half times higher than that of German groups. The probability of EU groups maintaining weekly contacts with MEPs is rather low. It amounts to 0.03, which is still two to three times higher than that of the national groups (see the base probabilities in Table 8.4). In contrast to previous studies (Bouwen 2002b: 17, 24) claiming that national associations are as frequently in touch as EU level groups with the Parliament, these figures illustrate that EU associations have become major interlocuters of both the Commission and the Parliament, whereas, on average, national associations are only occasionally in touch with these institutions. Only a minority of the domestic groups is regularly in touch with the MEPs (see Chapters 5 and 6). However, the EU groups find it as difficult as national associations to approach the Council because Council members represent national interests to a greater extent than do the other EU institutions. They also lack the additional venue to Council members and national administrations that is open to national associations.

The multilevel structure of the institutional setting has a more profound impact than domestic modes of interest intermediation. In fact, there is no clear-cut relation between these modes and the contact patterns at EU level. Figure 8.1 illustrates rather small and complex differences between the national groups: UK pluralism supports slightly better access than French statism to the EU Council and to the EP but not to the Commission. Corporatist practices enable German associations to establish more contacts with the Commission bureaucracy than the French associations but not with the other institutions. These findings are inconsistent with the expectation (H 1.2) that there is a clear rank order between corporatist, pluralist and statist groups when it comes to representing interests at EU level. Nor do these findings support the proposition that the degree of fit determines the adaptation of domestic interest groups.

Therefore, the rival hypothesis about the impact of the embeddedness of domestic actors in national policy networks needs to be scrutinized. A closer inspection (Table A8.3) yields moderate to strong correlations between the domestic and the EU-level contacts of national interest groups, which corroborates the outcomes of the cluster analysis in Chapter 5. Accordingly, it can be ruled out that weak embeddedness in national politics provides the grounds for close relations with the EU institutions. On the contrary, domestic embeddedness tends to reinforce access at the EU level. This correlation is strongest among the German groups, which translate the corporatist division of labour between peak associations and other interest groups to the EU level. In pluralist and statist regimes, in contrast, the domestic division of labour is under greater pressure. Thus, the modes of interest intermediation do not result in consistent access patterns at EU level. However, they condition the EU impact on the division of labour and the mode of competition in the domestic interest group systems.

Finally, when analysing the *predicted* access patterns by country, the French and particularly the UK organizations incorporate the European Parliament to a greater extent into their lobbying strategies than do the German associations.

Table 8.4 Impact of independent variables on the probability of having weekly contacts with EU institutions

	Eur. Com. working level				Eur. Com. political leaders				Council of Ministers				Members of the EP			
	EU	G	UK	F	EU	G	UK	F	EU	G	UK	F	EU	G	UK	F
Resource dependencies																
Institut. relevance	.384	.132	.110	.076	.054	.016	.018	.014	.007	.005	.009	.004	.224	.090	.143	.094
Policy information	.226	.074	.062	.042	.059	.018	.020	.015	.002	.001	.002	.001	.057	.021	.034	.022
Internationalization	.295	.112	.094	.066	.024	.007	.008	.006	.001	.001	.001	.000	.015	.005	.009	.005
Economic weight	.142	.050	.042	.029	.049	.015	.07	.013	.001	.001	.001	.001	.045	.016	.027	.017
Membership dens.	-.053	-.017	-.014	-.010	-.016	-.005	-.005	-.004	-.000	-.000	-.000	-.000	-.019	-.007	-.011	-.007
Organizational structure																
Budget	.455	.212	.182	.131	.090	.028	.031	.025	.003	.002	.004	.002	.111	.042	.069	.044
Interest represent.	.090	.029	.024	.016	.018	.005	.006	.005	.001	.001	.001	.000	.018	.006	.011	.007
Strategy																
Insider	.340	.117	.098	.068	.012	.004	.004	.003	.001	.001	.001	.001	.041	.015	.024	.015
Nationalism	-.102	-.033	-.027	-.019	.010	.003	.003	.003	.001	.000	.001	.000	-.010	-.003	-.006	-.004
Outsider[a]	-.036	-.081	-.067	-.046	.010	-.005	-.006	-.004	.002	.000	.001	.000	.036	-.005	-.008	-.005
Base probability	.182	.050	.041	.028	.025	.007	.008	.006	.001	.001	.001	.001	.031	.011	.018	.011

Note: The figures denote the change in the probability for *sector-federations* to have weekly contacts when the independent variable is moved from its minimum to its maximum, with all other variables kept at their means. (a) Outsider includes EU outsider for EU associations and sets it to zero for national associations.

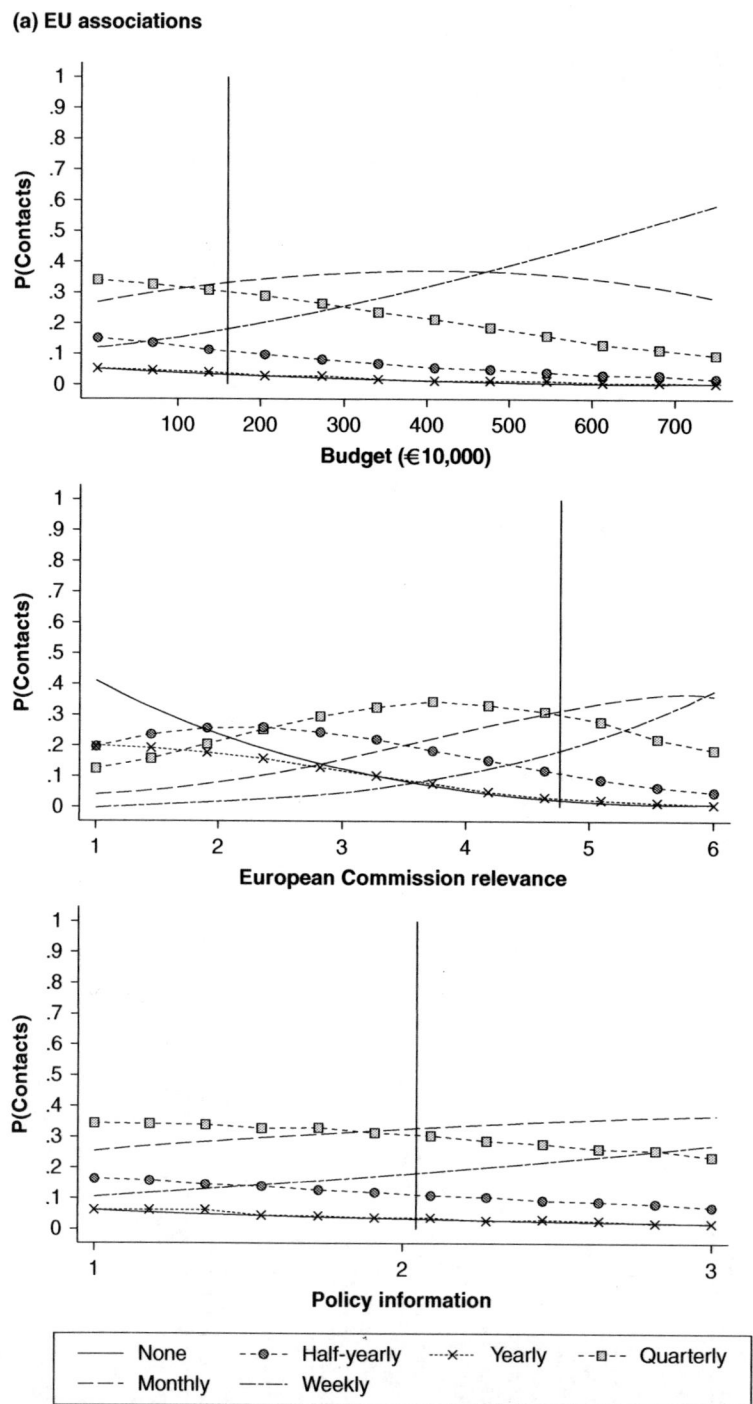

Figure 8.2 (continued opposite)

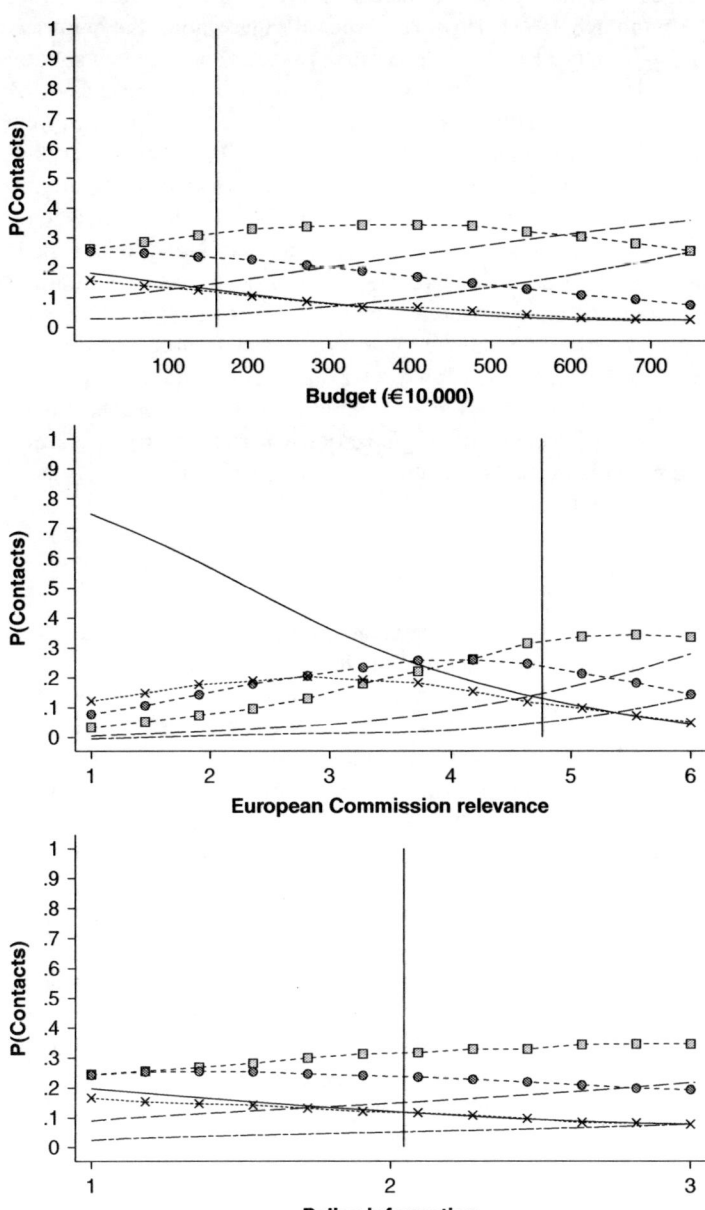

Figure 8.2 Contact probabilities with European Commission working level, contingent upon budget, political relevance and policy information

Notes: The figures illustrate the changing contact probabilities of sector federations when the independent variable is moved from its minimum to its maximum, with all other variables kept at their means. Vertical x-lines denote the means of the three variables.

These concentrate their efforts on the EU bureaucracy, apparently transferring their domestic focus on administrative interest intermediation to the EU level (Dyson 1980; Lehmbruch 1991). However, when disaggregating the empirical contact patterns by country (Table A8.1), German associations maintain slightly more contacts than UK or French groups with the Commission and have as many contacts as UK associations with the EU Council and the EP. According to the regression results, UK associations would be expected to have better access to these institutions, apart from the EU bureaucracy. Here, exchange goods, organizational resources and strategies of interest groups come into play, outweighing the effects of modes of interest intermediation. German associations tend to have broader domains and more resources than UK organizations, specialize more in interest representation and are more likely to pursue insider strategies. They control more policy information and find the EU institutions to be more important for the representation of their interests (Table A8.2). Altogether, these factors outweigh the domestic modes of interest intermediation, which therefore seem to be less relevant to the explanation than organizational structures, resources and strategies. Research on large firms corroborates the inconsistent impact of these modes on EU lobbying (Bernhagen and Mitchell 2007).

Resource dependencies

Resource dependencies are crucial to the explanation of access patterns. The relevance that associations ascribe to the EU institutions because of their political activities has a profound impact on the contact frequencies, as was expected in H 2.1. In fact, national associations are not likely to seek access if an EU institution seems irrelevant to the representation of their interests. For example, in that case, the likelihood of German associations *not* maintaining contacts with the Commission amounts to a striking 75 per cent (Figure 8.2 (b)). If they find the EU bureaucrats highly relevant to their cause, the German groups are most likely to have quarterly access to them.

The perception of the EU institutions also shapes the activities of the EU level groups. The probability of their maintaining weekly contacts with EU bureaucrats increases by 38 percentage points if they attach great rather than little importance to the EU officials for the representation of their interests (Figure 8.2 (a)). Even though the likelihood that associations maintain as many contacts with MEPs is well below these levels, the Parliament also appears to be quite open to major stakeholders in EU policies. Perceiving the Parliament as a very important institution enhances the probability of having weekly contacts with it more than any other factor (see Table 8.4). In fact, being a stakeholder in EU regulation is a necessary condition for getting invited to EU policy consultations by the Council, the Parliament or the Commission (see Table A8.5).

Furthermore, the exchange goods that interest organizations control are of major importance. As expected, the ability to provide policy information improves their access, corroborating that this capacity is important in EU politics (H 2.2). The probability of EU groups having weekly contacts with EU bureaucrats increases by 0.23 and that of German groups is raised by 0.07 if they command a maximum rather than a minimum of policy information (Table 8.4). However, compared with the importance that interest groups ascribe to EU regulation, their capacity to provide policy information has a more moderate effect on access patterns (see Figure 8.2). More generally, when controlling for other factors, policy information does not seem to be as important for obtaining access as has been suggested in earlier studies (Bouwen 2002a, 2002b). Note, however, that the Council, the Parliament and the Commission have a clear preference for incorporating interest groups into their policy consultations that control policy information (see Table A8.5).

In support of H 2.4, greater economic weight increases contact frequency. EU institutions cannot ignore the employment effects of European policies and they include groups that have economic clout more frequently in their political consultations. However, economic weight appears to be less relevant to the explanation of the contact patterns than the importance that groups ascribe to the EU institutions and their ability to provide policy information. The probability of EU groups having weekly contacts with the EU bureaucracy increases by 0.14 and that of national groups is raised by only 0.03 to 0.05 if the firms they represent have 1.5 million employees rather than none.

The remaining two exchange goods vary in their effects across the EU institutions. As expected (H 2.3), internationalization enables interest organizations to establish more contacts with the EU Council and the Commission. The likelihood of EU groups maintaining weekly contacts with EU bureaucrats increases by almost 30 percentage points if the firms they represent are highly internationalized (Table 8.4). However, internationalization does not support significantly better access to the Parliament. Depending on the support of their constituencies, the MEPs pay as much attention to domestic business as to multinational enterprises. In conclusion, the Parliament should prove to be more responsive to protectionist demands than the Council or the Commission.

Finally, greater membership density does not have a significant impact on the number of contacts with the Commission and the Council. In stark contrast to H 2.5, it even reduces the odds of having contacts with the EP. There are two reasons why there appears to be no real pull from the EU institutions to consult business associations that seem more representative of their domains. First, except for the social partners, the EU institutions have not yet developed clear standards as to what determines the representative character of an association. Hence, they might not be aware of the membership density of associations. Second, other exchange goods seem to be of greater importance to EU institutions when it comes to consulting business associations: they tend to consult groups that represent European rather than national interests, are stakeholders in EU regulation and can provide policy information or have economic clout.

Interest group organization

Among the organizational factors, the financial resources of interest organizations are of major importance. The probability of EU associations that are in command of considerable financial resources (i.e. a budget of 7.5 million Euros) having weekly contacts with the Commission is 46 percentage points higher than that of have-nots (Table 8.4 and Figure 8.2), which supports H 3.3. The corresponding increases for national associations range from 13 (French groups) to 21 percentage points (German groups). Of all factors, then, the financial endowment of groups has the greatest potential to leave an imprint on contacts with the Commission, and when it comes to accessing the Council and the Parliament it ranks second only to the importance that associations ascribe to these institutions. However, associations that want to 'buy' more contacts with the EU institutions need to invest heavily in their lobbying activities: increasing the associational budget from the overall mean of 1.59 million Euros by 250,000 raises the probability of EU associations having weekly contacts with the Commission by just one percentage points and that of national groups by 0.2 to 0.5 percentage points (cf. Table 8.4 and Figure 8.2).

Specializing in interest representation also pays off, improving the ability of groups to address the relevant contact partners and to deliver the requested exchange goods (H 3.4). But the extent to which groups concentrate on the representation of interests is less consequential than the material resources at their disposal. The probability of EU groups having weekly contacts with the Commission bureaucracy is raised by nine percentage points when fully concentrating on interest representation rather than on the coordination of markets or the provision of services.

Sector domain and the position of associations in the associational systems have ambiguous effects, reflecting both institutional variations and the contradictory logics built into these factors: associations with broader sector domains tend to have slightly better access to the Council than groups with narrower domains (Table 8.3). National ministers prefer to listen to broad-based interest groups that are affected by a large number of EU policy issues and represent a broad membership. However, in contrast to H 3.1, these organizations are not more frequently in touch with the other EU institutions. The policy experts in the Commission and the Parliament depend as much on the input of more specialized associations, which also suffer less from collective action problems.

Being located at the higher echelons of the associational population, federations are more frequently in touch with the Commission and with Coreper than are groups with a direct membership. But this does not hold for groups with a mixed membership, which invalidates H 3.2. The European Parliament, which might be expected to support broad-based political representation throughout the Union, rewards neither greater domain size nor a peak association function. In sum, the Council machinery has a preference for dealing with associations that are located at the peak of their domain or have a broad-based domain, whereas the Commission privileges peak associations. None of these associational properties is of relevance to the MEPs.

The strategic choices of interest organizations

Finally, the strategies that interest organizations pursue matter, even though a few caveats are in order. First, nationalistic strategies have no significant effects, thus invalidating H 4.3. Second, the impact of insider and outsider strategies is contingent upon the institutional context, which is contrary to H 4.1 and 4.2: they affect neither the number of contacts with the Council and its administration nor those with the Commission leaders. Nonetheless, these strategies have a significant bearing on access to policy experts in the Commission and in the Parliament.

As expected, an insider strategy improves access to both parliamentarians and bureaucrats. It has a profound impact on the number of contacts that interest groups maintain with the EU bureaucracy. Relying greatly on an insider strategy rather than not relying on insider tactics increases the probability of EU groups maintaining weekly contacts with EU bureaucrats by 0.34 and that of national groups by 0.07 (French associations) to 0.12 (German groups) (see Table 8.4). Hence, the insider strategy proves to be a highly efficient means of communicating policy information to the bureaucratic staff when policy proposals are being drafted. It is of less relevance when organizations seek to approach the Parliament on a regular basis, but even here it is still more effective than an outsider strategy.

The impact of the outsider strategy varies, which highlights important institutional differences. Under public scrutiny, the members of the European Parliament are attentive to media coverage and public debates. That is why national associations that pursue an outsider strategy do not have fewer contacts with the MEPs and why EU associations employing outsider tactics across national borders have even more contacts with them. Note that EU associations tend to combine outsider strategies with greater presence in parliamentary consultations whereas national groups use outsider strategies mainly in order to draw public or governmental attention to EU policies. As a corollary, the EU Council is also more inclined to draw groups into EU policy-making that pursue an outsider strategy (Table A8.5). Hence, these groups rely on the mobilization of domestic publics and politicians as well as on the activities of EU-level groups but do not necessarily seek redress through the European Parliament.

Finally, the bureaucratic rationality of the Commission staff clearly diverges from the Parliament's response to EU media coverage. Pursuing an outsider strategy tends to reduce access to the bureaucratic staff. On the one hand, groups pursuing outsider tactics use it to compensate for a lack of access to the EU bureaucracy; on the other hand, these tactics also interfere with the logic of the insider strategy. Hence, it seems possible to combine insider and outsider strategies vis-à-vis the Parliament but not vis-à-vis the Commission. This might place interest groups in a dilemma because it seems difficult to limit the effects of outsider strategies to specific institutions in a political system.

Conclusion

EU political exchanges are shaped by institutional context and resource dependencies as well as by organizational structures and strategic choices. It would be remiss to exclude either of these dimensions from the study of interest group access in the EU. Studies focusing on just one of these dimensions tend to overrate its importance. Nonetheless, the analysis confirms that it is difficult to identify general patterns of interest intermediation in the EU because the impact of many factors is conditioned by the segmented EU institutional context.

Several findings about the general determinants of EU interest intermediation consolidate the results of previous studies. To some extent, they modify our conventional wisdom and also establish the relative importance of these factors. First, EU regulation is a major incentive for associations to intensify their lobbying efforts and to get in touch more frequently with the EU institutions. It is indeed necessary for national associations to locate the EU institutions important for the representation of their interests if they are to establish contacts with them. The Commission and the Parliament prove to be quite open to those interest groups that are affected by EU regulation and that consider them to be important.

Second, in the EU multilevel setting, EU and national associations act primarily at their main level of operation and have developed a division of labour that extends to different phases of the policy cycle: EU associations concentrate their activities on its early stages, whereas national groups tend to follow the process from the formulation of EU policies until their implementation in the member states. All in all, EU associations have evolved into routine interlocutors of the EU institutions when EU policies are being drafted. To say the least, they have turned into important negotiation arenas, and in some cases even into actors in their own right. By contrast, only a minority of national associations acts routinely at the EU level. Because these actors are usually also well embedded in domestic policy networks, they are vital to the representation of business interests in the EU multilevel system (see Chapters 4 and 5).

Third, resources are crucial to the representation of interests in EU politics. Well-endowed associations have much better access than poor associations, underscoring that EU lobbying needs substantial material backing. The ability to provide policy information also improves the standing of interest groups even though it appears to be less important for obtaining access than has been suggested in previous studies. The analysis indicated that state–group relations are clearly not confined to the exchange of policy information. Economic clout and internationalization have also proven to be of some importance because the EU institutions must take the economic effects of EU policies into account. In sum, those organizations that find the EU institutions important to the representation of their interests, command sufficient financial resources, can bring in policy information and have economic clout tend to have better access than other groups, which gives them a greater chance to have a say in EU policies. The significance of these political exchange goods and material resources in EU politics raises genuine doubts that the current efforts of the EU institutions to strengthen civil society participation and working towards more equitable consultation patterns (see European Commission 2002) will significantly reduce the bias that exists in favour of resourceful actors. In fact, the Parliament, the Council and the Commission alike tend to invite those interest organizations to policy consultations that are subject to EU regulation and can provide helpful policy information (Table A8.4). Beyond these general criteria, the Council and the Parliament take notice of the organizations' ability to mobilize the public while the Commission prefers to deal with organizations that pursue insider strategies. Council and Commission pay also close attention to the economic clout of their negotiation partners. To reduce bias, not only would the EU institutions need to pay a substantially higher premium on the interest groups' contribution to policy legitimacy and public support for the EU, but civil society organizations would also need to be able to follow EU policy issues across the policy cycle and table detailed policy information that is backed by large constituencies.

In that respect, it is important to note that, among the EU institutions, the European Parliament is most attentive to outsider strategies enhancing the public debate. The political rationality of the MEPs, who are subject to national election pressures, differs from the bureaucratic rationality of the Commission, which encourages an insider strategy and punishes an outsider strategy in its attempt to devise innovative and workable policy proposals. It appears that the Parliament is a more promising venue for civil society concerns and protectionist demands than the Council or the Commission, even though it is important to bear in mind that it still has limited legislative powers (see also Kohler-Koch 1997).

Finally, the relationship between national modes of interest intermediation and EU access patterns is less pronounced than was posited in earlier studies (Schmidt 1999; Cowles 2001). The differences among statist, pluralistic and corporatist groups were both smaller and more complex than expected. There are several explanations for the resulting ambiguity. First, factors other than these national modes may be more important in EU politics. In part, organizational structures, strategies and exchange goods outweigh their impact. Second, the domestic modes may be less different than is often claimed. It is likely that, after 50 years, European integration has levelled out some differences. Moreover, these modes are rarely found in their pure form, rather more often being blurred. Finally, the modal studies have not paid much attention to institutional differentiation, which is of great importance in this study.

Appendix

Table A8.1 Access to EU institutions by country (per cent of associations)

	Contacts						
	No	Annual	Half-yearly	Quarter yearly	Monthly	Weekly	N
Panel a) Access to European Commission political leadership							
EU associations	14.2	26.5	17.9	23.5	9.9	8.2	162
G associations	49.2	22.4	16.2	6.5	4.4	8.0	321
UK associations	60.3	18.6	11.8	3.9	3.9	1.5	204
F associations	58.4	15.9	13.3	7.1	4.4	0.9	113
Panel b) Access to European Commission working level							
EU associations	3.1	4.9	6.8	19.1	23.5	42.6	162
G associations	25.9	10.9	17.1	19.3	16.8	10.0	321
UK associations	39.2	9.3	17.2	19.1	10.3	4.9	204
F associations	33.6	15.0	11.5	21.2	14.2	4.4	113
Panel c) Access to the Council of Ministers							
EU associations	50.6	25.3	11.1	5.6	7.4	.0	162
G associations	72.0	11.2	8.1	5.6	2.5	.6	321
UK associations	75.5	8.8	5.9	5.9	3.9	.0	204
F associations	72.6	9.7	9.7	6.2	1.8	.0	113
Panel d) Access to Coreper							
EU associations	32.7	14.8	18.5	17.3	11.1	5.6	162
G associations	67.0	9.4	7.5	9.0	5.6	1.6	321
UK associations	70.6	8.8	8.3	5.9	4.9	1.5	204
F associations	67.3	11.5	10.6	8.9	1.8	.0	113
Panel e) Access to the members of the European Parliament							
EU associations	16.1	14.2	14.2	19.1	22.2	14.2	162
G associations	42.1	17.8	13.7	12.2	10.3	4.1	321
UK associations	48.0	13.7	12.8	10.8	10.8	3.9	204
F associations	39.8	27.4	12.4	9.7	9.7	.9	113
Panel f) Access to the EP committees							
EU associations	16.7	16.1	13.6	25.3	19.1	9.3	162
G associations	49.2	19.6	12.5	8.7	6.9	3.1	321
UK associations	57.8	8.3	12.8	11.8	7.4	2.0	204
F associations	53.1	16.8	14.2	9.7	6.2	.0	113

Table A8.2 Descriptive statistics by country

Variable	Mean	Std. Dev.	Min	Max
Panel a) EU associations (N = 162)				
Sectoral domain	1.75	0.67	1	3
Membership density (%)	79.47	16.07	13	100
Budget (10,000€)	128.08	196.90	0	750
Resources for Interest representation (%)	57.58	26.44	5	100
Expertise (Scale)	2.01	.53	1	3
Insider strategy (Factor scores)	.34	.61	−2.33	1.20
Nationalistic strategy (Factor scores)	−.39	.95	−1.61	2.87
Outsider strategy (Factor scores)	.35	.88	−2.65	2.07
Economic weight (1,000 employees)	448.91	489.12	0	1,500
Internationalization (%)	40.07	23.45	0	88
EC regulation	5.55	.92	1	6
EP regulation	4.77	.29	1	6
Council regulation	4.35	1.43	1	7.12
Panel b) German associations (N = 321)				
Sectoral domain	1.76	0.62	1	3
Membership density (%)	70.20	24.20	13	99.98
Budget (10,000€)	177.05	222.07	0	750
Res. for Interest representation (%)	49.95	25.15	0	100
Expertise (Scale)	2.28	.58	.307	3
Insider strategy (Factor scores)	−.09	1.11	−4.06	2.32
Nationalistic strategy (Factor scores)	.06	.98	−1.42	3.08
Outsider strategy (Factor scores)	−.20	1.01	−2.73	2.15
Economic weight (1,000 employees)	191.86	322.05	0	1,500
Internationalization (%)	25.35	20.11	0	88
EC regulation	4.61	1.26	1.18	6.10
EP regulation	3.94	1.49	.52	6.88
Council regulation	3.68	1.47	.15	6.60
Panel c) UK associations (N = 204)				
Sectoral domain	1.67	0.74	1	3
Membership density (%)	61.31	26.78	0	100
Budget (10,000€)	151.22	214.70	0	750
Res. for Interest representation (%)	42.53	26.19	0	100
Expertise (Scale)	1.72	.51	1	3.17
Insider strategy (Factor scores)	−.54	1.08	−4.15	1.18
Nationalistic strategy (Factor scores)	.08	.94	−2.83	2.82
Outsider strategy (Factor scores)	−.24	1.01	−2.61	2.09
Economic weight (1,000 employees)	240.30	370.21	0	1,500
Internationalization (%)	24.85	22.89	0	88
EC regulation	4.39	1.35	1	6.01
EP regulation	3.69	1.43	.13	6
Council regulation	3.45	1.45	.057	6.45
Panel d) French associations (N = 113)				
Sectoral domain	1.81	0.69	1	3
Membership density (%)	68.96	23.82	13	88
Budget (10,000€)	167.46	205.72	0	750

(Continued)

Table A8.2 (Continued)

Variable	Mean	Std. Dev.	Min	Max
Res. for Interest representation (%)	46.20	25.72	0	100
Expertise (Scale)	2.02	.49	1	3
Insider strategy (Factor scores)	.08	.78	−3.01	1.13
Nationalistic strategy (Factor scores)	.25	.98	−1.85	2.80
Outsider strategy (Factor scores)	.16	.93	−2.41	3.10
Economic weight (1,000 employees)	187.91	304.92	0	1,500
Internationalization (%)	26.44	21.49	0	88
EC regulation	4.74	1.14	1	6
EP regulation	3.83	1.26	.78	6.88
Council regulation	4.12	1.38	.15	6.05

Note: In the multiple imputation, variables measuring percentages have been bound to values between 0 and 100. The lowest value of other variables has been bound to 0 when negative values were meaningless on these variables.

Table A8.3 Rank correlations among national and EU-level contacts

	German associations	British associations	French associations	EU associations
Nat. government pol. leadership – EC political leadership	.630	.389	.454	.233
Nat. government working level – EC working level	.580	.503	.531	.128
Nat. government pol. leadership – Council of Ministers	.465	.427	.525	.429
Nat. government working level – Coreper	.383	.363	.387	.293
Nat. parliament members – EP members	.676	.657	.504	.239
Nat. parliament committees – EP committees	.670	.568	.414	.247

Note: All rank correlations (Spearman's r) are significant at $p = .05$.

Table A8.4 Frequency of contact initiatives between EU institutions and business associations (per cent, N = 800)

Initiative taken by	Frequency of initiative		
	Never	Sometimes	Often
Business association	9.3	33.6	57.1
European Commission	28.5	54.4	17.1
EU Council	65.4	30.8	3.9
European Parliament	53.0	40.8	6.3

Table A8.5 Contact initiatives with interest organizations by EU institutions: ordered logit regressions (N = 800)

	Institutional initiative by		
	European Commission	European Parliament	Council of the EU
Institutional context			
EU association	.847**	1.007**	.212
Corporatism	.143	.460	.006
Pluralism	.300	.747**	.813**
Resource dependencies			
Institutional relevance	.237**	.406**	.294**
Policy information	.389*	.366*	.459**
Internationalization	.008*	.004	.002
Economic weight	.001**	.000	.001*
Membership density	.005	.003	−.001
Organizational Structure			
Sector domain	−.258*	−.214	−.241
Federation	.078	.126	.195
Mixed membership	−.055	.210	.284
Budget	.001	.001**	−.000
Interest representation	−.008**	−.000	−.003
Organizational strategy			
Insider	.483**	.093	.077
National	.033	.161	.129
Public	.105	.408**	.291**
Eupublic	−.019	−.018	−.094
Maximum likelihood estimations			
Log Likelihood	−680.03	−582.362	−557.706
G2	225.90	236.22	110.91
McKelvey Zavoina R^2	.30	.33	.19
Correct predictions (%)	60	68	68
Adjusted predictions (%)	13	31	8

Notes: Ordered logit coefficients, * significant at 5%; ** significant at 1% (two-tailed tests).

9 Conclusion

This book analyses the adaptation of business interest representation to EU politics by drawing on institutional theory, organizational theory and the concept of resource dependence. In a cross-level, cross-national and quantitative comparison, I have sought to consolidate, modify (when necessary) and enhance our established understandings of EU interest intermediation. The aim was to identify and explain the structured relations, the enduring division of labour, the rules of the game, and the predominant strategies and modes of political behaviour that have emerged within the EU institutional context.

Three general conclusions emerge from this analysis. First, with regard to domestic institutional contexts, political-economy theories overdraw the differences between national modes of interest intermediation and varieties of capitalism. They are in need of being fine-tuned. Second, the evolution of a multilevel polity in Europe has given rise to a multitiered system of interest groups. Placing a premium on the resources of interest organizations, multilevel policy-making makes for a notable division of labour among EU level and national groups as well as for biased interest representation. It causes moderate changes in domestic interest group systems and extensions of domestic practices to the changed institutional context. Third, EU level interest intermediation displays only very few general characteristics. The segmented EU institutional context gives rise to important inter- and intra-institutional variations.

The book presents the participation of business interest associations and large firms in EU policy-making as rational organizational choices. However, organizational rationality is but a starting point for the analysis of participation (see Olsen 1983: 154). Given limits to the rationality of interest organizations it is crucial to identify the parameters of organizational calculations and the variables that enter into their strategic choices. Drawing on institutional theory and on the organizational theory of resource dependence, this study scrutinizes the European institutional setting, the national varieties of capitalism and modes of interest intermediation and the organizational characteristics of business interests as influences on the political behaviour of firms and associations in the EU. The empirical analysis suggests that the literature on varieties of capitalism and modes of interest intermediation overdraws the extent of cross-national differences among business interest organizations and of the systems they operate in.

Only when fine-tuning the analysis, cross-national differences between the interest group systems become apparent. Thus, the French interest group system resembles the structure of the German system, but French associations differ from German groups in functional terms. In particular, higher order associations in Germany play a greater role in the representation of interests and in integrating the system. In contrast, British groups resemble German groups in functional terms, that is, in their concentration on political interest representation rather than market coordination or service provision, but the British interest group system differs in structural terms as it is much more fragmented and less integrated. Despite manifold similarities, the interaction between state and business continues to vary in some respects across national borders. French statism shows in the relatively poor access that French groups have to information from government and parliament and in their late arrival on the political scene during the policy-making process. British pluralism and the fragmentation of the British interest group system are evident in the greater inability of British groups to initiate contacts with state institutions. German corporatism is noticeable in the function of higher-order associations as main channels for the representation of business interests.

However, the extent of cross-national similarities does not correspond well with the prevailing assumptions about statism, corporatism and pluralism. The book develops four explanations. Partly, business interest associations in France, Germany and the UK cope with similar task contingencies. In addition, the interest group systems seem to have converged over time during the decades of European integration and have become subject to pressures from economic globalization. Moreover, a good part of this finding is owed to the methodological problems inherent in typological studies. These types hardly ever exist in their pure form, so the differences among these countries are less pronounced than is often posited. Last but not least, the political-economy theories pay only scant attention to the internal differentiation of the state apparatus which is of great importance in this study. It may therefore be more useful to rephrase the notion of domestic embeddedness in more specific institutional terms. Hence, German associations have translated a focus on administrative interest intermediation onto the EU level and British associations that are used to considering the domestic parliament in their lobbying strategies now also include the European Parliament into them.

The transformation of the European system of nation states into the EU multilevel polity has led to the co-evolution of a multitiered system of interest groups. While the landscape of interest groups at the EU level was initially confined to European business associations, in recent decades it has considerably broadened to also encompass large firms, national associations and consultants that complement the collective efforts of EU associations. The extension of EU activities to social regulation following the Single European Act has strengthened the presence of non-occupational interests, thus reducing the bias in the EU interest group system that existed in favour of business interests. According to several observers, major societal cleavages and value conflicts now find their way into EU politics so that they become far more politicized than they have been in the past.

This widening of EU policy networks may put established policy communities and traditional patterns of alliance formation among business interests under duress. While various case studies have underlined that the formation of ad hoc coalitions becomes more important in campaigning for specific issues, the empirical analysis demonstrated that, in general, business interest organizations have a strong preference for dealing with 'likes' and with like-minded actors. They find that the cooperation with supposedly countervailing environmental, social or labour interests is of much less use to them. After all, the patterns of alliance formation and associative cooperation may display a greater stability than is implied in the case studies on the formation of issue networks. This suggests that 'baptist-and-bootlegger-coalitions' are rare phenomena that revolve around rather stable cores.

Business interests in all three countries have adapted to European integration by joining EU associations and by incorporating them into their lobbying strategies. Earlier interest group studies suggest that these large firms and business interest associations pursue insider rather than outsider strategies (J. Wilson 1973; Walker 1991), that is, they seek direct access to policy-makers rather than rallying in the street or starting press campaigns. But the strategic repertoire of these actors encompasses more than these two options. Due to the international composition of the EU, several organizations pursue a nationalist strategy, mostly addressing their fellow countrymen in the EU institutions and making appeals to national interests.

Despite the emergence of multilevel polity, a multilevel strategy, pursuing direct access to politicians and bureaucrats at each level of the European polity has not become the dominant way of representing interests in the EU. This option is open only to large firms and to business interest associations that are very resourceful, that possess substantial negotiation capacities and that are not confined to operating in their domestic contexts by their membership. In the EU multilevel system, associations tend to focus on one primary level of operation and most domestic interest organizations are embedded in the division of labour that has emerged among EU associations and domestic interest groups.

EU organizations focus on the EU level and also on the agenda-setting and policy formulation stages of the policy cycle. Being privileged negotiation partners of the EU institutions during these stages and being aided by the legalistic implementation of EU law in the member states that forms an important incentive for their members to agree on a common position, they evolved into intermediaries between these institutions and their national members. The Eurogroups have become experts in processing information about EU policies to their members, in building a common platform among them and in coordinating the representation of interests across member states. To say the least, they have turned into important negotiation arenas, and in some cases even into actors in their own right.

Accordingly, European integration does not replace the established division of labour and power structure in national interest group systems. For the most part, it has stimulated extensions and modifications of established practices, reaffirming the positions of those organizations that had already developed capacities to articulate, aggregate, organize and represent the interests of their members. This tendency is more pronounced in corporatist settings that channel political representation through peak associations than it is in pluralist or statist settings. Those national organizations that have evolved into multilevel players are now the nodal points that link the domestic with the European arenas. They do no longer rely solely on their national governments or on EU associations to look after their interests in EU politics. They are able to communicate directly with the EU institutions and enter into coalitions with interest organizations that are present in the European arena. By contrast, those domestic associations that continue to rely exclusively on national communication channels, the so-called national players, tend to lose political ground because they come to depend on the EU associations, multilevel players and the national government for the promotion of their interest at the EU level.

The state institutions in the European multilevel setting are not just arenas for the pursuit of group interests or merely referees that ratify the outcome of the group struggle. Rather, they set the terms of trade with interest groups, by providing them with exclusive or privileged access, by delegating policy-making competencies to them and by regulating policy consultation. As a consequence, access to EU policy-making is very much shaped by the characteristics, roles and activities of the European Commission, the European Parliament and the Council of the EU.

An important consequence of the institutional segmentation of the EU is that access patterns to EU institutions display only very few *general characteristics*. First, as has been indicated, the multilevel setting makes for a division of labour among EU associations and national associations. Second, the resources at the disposal of interest groups matter greatly in EU politics. Well endowed associations have much better access than have-nots because they can provide specialized and highly relevant policy information. However, unlike the dominant view in earlier studies, EU state–business relations are not just about the exchange of policy-information. The economic clout of business interest organizations is as important as their expert advice because the EU institutions need to take into account the economic effects of EU policies and because these economic actors carry some weight in the member states. In fact, all EU institutions have a strong preference for incorporating those groups in the policy-making process that can contribute policy information and whose members have investment power. In particular, access to the political leaders of the Commission and the Council is limited to the privileged few, namely to those organizations with considerable financial means, information and economic clout. It appears that multilevel policy-making has an in-built tendency to work to the disadvantage of weaker interests even though not each and every policy decision needs to reflect this asymmetry.

Third, many earlier studies highlighted the openness of the EU institutions to interest organizations. This book confirms that the policy experts in the EU institutions consult a multitude of stakeholders in EU regulation and it indicates that the quality of this information exchange compares to that in national state–business relations in the UK or Germany. However, it is also apparent that the openness of the EU institutions outweighs neither the division of labour among EU and national associations nor the relevance of organizational resources. Hence, unless poorly endowed actors receive very strong support from the EU institutions, it is doubtful that the institutionalization of the political participation of civil society in the Lisbon treaty and the regulation of the consultation patterns will offset the structural bias in the access patterns. The fact that business interests value their informal contacts with EU decision-makers more than their committee work underscores this point. In the perception of the interest groups, the institutionalized consultations and negotiations allow for less influence on EU policies and for a less fruitful exchange of information than the more selective informal relations.

Given their institutional segmentation, decision-making practices vary across the EU institutions. Such differences show prominently in their responses to the strategies and economic internationalization of interest organizations. Generally, EU institutions encourage an insider strategy. In fact, the use of an outsider strategy, that is, the mobilization of the media and the public, goes hand in hand with less frequent consultations by the Commission. The Parliament and the Council are more perceptive to public pressures. To some extent, these differences place the associations in a dilemma: it is difficult to target public campaigns at the Council and the Parliament but not at the Commission. It is therefore mostly those groups that feel they are shut out from policy-formulation by the Commission, that have recourse to an outsider strategy and that seek to re-enter the game via the Parliament and the Council. Regarding economic internationalization, the Commission and the Council grant business interest organizations with international economic activities better access. They are wary of their ability to shift investments to other locations and also seek to benefit from the international experiences of these actors with different regulators. By contrast, Members of the European Parliament credit these actors neither for their investment power nor for their international expertise. They pay as much attention to the worries of those firms and associations that concentrate on domestic markets because these are also important parts of their constituencies. MEPs should therefore be more open to demands for protectionism than the Commission or the Council.

Given these results of the study as well as its limitation to the analysis of business interests from the three large EU member states, three major research desiderata emerge from it. First, the quantitative empirical study of interest representation in the European Union can usefully be extended to other types of interest organization and a greater number of EU member states in order to allow for more general statements about European interest intermediation. This would allow us to evaluate more thoroughly the extent of bias that seems to be present in the multilevel system in favour of business interests. Statistical multilevel analysis could serve to assess the impact of various domestic and sectoral factors that could not be addressed in this study.

Second, the importance of multilevel policy-networks and negotiation systems in EU policy-making calls for a move away from the predominant focus on EU level groups to the comparative study of these structures in different issue areas. Such analyses should explicitly address those theoretical and empirical gaps that can best be tackled in configurative analyses. This would not only include the study of inter- and intra-organizational coordination mechanisms and dynamics in these networks but also the more detailed, yet controlled analysis of the roles and functions of EU level associations, national associations and their members in such settings.

Finally, to some extent, the research focus of EU interest group studies needs to be broadened to also incorporate the study of social movements, political cleavages and political parties that are all part of the European political space in which interest groups are situated. This might help place political scientists in a position to come to terms with major aspects of the cleavage structure and the democratic quality of the European polity.

Appendix: Questionnaire
Intermediation of Interests in the European Union

Questionnaire for Associations and Companies

Universität Mannheim
Prof. Dr. Beate Kohler-Koch

Guidelines for filling in this questionnaire

In most cases, you simply need to tick the box (q) which corresponds most closely to your opinion. Any row of boxes forms a continuum between two extremes.

Example: most certainly   not at all
                    ❑   ❑   ❑   ❑   ❑   ❑
                    1   2   3   4   5   6

Please answer the questions in the given order and jump ahead only when asked to do so in the text as follows: → *Please continue with question No. ...*

If you wish to make comments on any of the questions, or wish to give a more detailed answer, please feel free to do so using the last page of this queationnaire (indicating to which question your statement relates).

Having completed the questionaire, please return it to:

> **Prof. Dr. Beate Kohler-Koch**
> **--Reference: Intermediation of Interests--**
> **Lehrstuhl für Politische Wissenschaft II**
> **Seminargebäude A5**
> **Universität Mannheim**
> **D-68161 Mannheim**

In case of further questions do not hesitate to contact :

Prof. Dr. Beate Kohler-Koch: Tel.: +49-(0)621-292/5287   Fax: +49-(0)621-292/5289
Rainer Eising: Tel.: +49-(0)621-292/5263   Fax: +49-(0)621-292/5289

email: bkohler@sowi.uni-mannheim.de
       reising@sowi.uni-mannheim.de

Thank you very much for your time and effort, it is sincerely appreciated.

Intermediation of Interests in the European Union

Our research project analyses the relations between interest organisations and political institutions in the European Union (EU). Its aim is to identify the advantages and deficiencies of the existing system of interest intermediation as well as to develop strategies to improve it.

On the basis of this questionnaire, we would like to ask you about **your opinion** on this topic.

Definition of terms:

For the purpose of this survey, we summarise all associations which have the task of representing their members' interests vis-à-vis the EU institutions under the term "EU association".

Under the term "trade association", we subsume professional, producers' and employers' associations.

I. **First, we want to examine the relations between associations and companies, on the one hand, and European and national institutions, on the other hand. This allows us to determine the importance of the various political institutions for the representation of your interests.**

---

1. Contacts with the EU institutions

a) Do you maintain contacts with the EU institutions?

  yes ❏   no ❏

If <u>not</u>, please continue with → *question 3*.

If yes, please indicate how often you have contacts with EU-institutions. *(Please tick a box in every row.)*

	none	yearly	½ a year	¼ a year	monthly	weekly
European Commission						
- Top level (Commissioners and cabinets)	❏	❏	❏	❏	❏	❏
- Desk officer (director-general, department manager)	❏	❏	❏	❏	❏	❏
EU regulatory and standardisation authorities (e.g. CEN, CENELEC)	❏	❏	❏	❏	❏	❏
Council						
- Level of Ministers	❏	❏	❏	❏	❏	❏
- COREPER, working groups	❏	❏	❏	❏	❏	❏
- General Secretariat of the Council	❏	❏	❏	❏	❏	❏
European Parliament (EP)						
- Committees and rapporteurs	❏	❏	❏	❏	❏	❏
- Individual members of the EP and their assistants	❏	❏	❏	❏	❏	❏
- Secretariat of the EP	❏	❏	❏	❏	❏	❏

2. Please characterise your relations to the EU institutions in more detail. *(Please tick a box in every row.)*

a) In order to represent the firm's or association's interests, how important are contacts with the EU institutions?

	no contacts	not important at all					very important
European Commission							
- Top level (Commissioners and Cabinets)	❑	❑	❑	❑	❑	❑	❑
- Desk officer (director-general, department manager)	❑	❑	❑	❑	❑	❑	❑
EU regulatory and standardisation authorities (e.g. CEN, CENELEC)	❑	❑	❑	❑	❑	❑	❑
Council							
- Level of Ministers	❑	❑	❑	❑	❑	❑	❑
- COREPER, working groups	❑	❑	❑	❑	❑	❑	❑
- General Secretariat of the Council	❑	❑	❑	❑	❑	❑	❑
European Parliament (EP)							
- Committees and rapporteurs	❑	❑	❑	❑	❑	❑	❑
- Individual members of the EP and their assistants	❑	❑	❑	❑	❑	❑	❑
- Secretariat of the EP	❑	❑	❑	❑	❑	❑	❑

b) Would you characterise your relationship to EU institutions as cooperative or as conflictual?

	no contacts	cooperative					conflictual
- European Commission	❑	❑	❑	❑	❑	❑	❑
- EU regulatory and standardisation authorities	❑	❑	❑	❑	❑	❑	❑
- Council	❑	❑	❑	❑	❑	❑	❑
- European Parliament	❑	❑	❑	❑	❑	❑	❑

c) Is it difficult for you to obtain information from the EU institutions?

	not difficult at all						very difficult
- European Commission	❑	❑	❑	❑	❑	❑	❑
- EU regulatory and standardisation authorities	❑	❑	❑	❑	❑	❑	❑
- Council	❑	❑	❑	❑	❑	❑	❑
- European Parliament	❑	❑	❑	❑	❑	❑	❑

3. Contacts with national institutions concerning EU law making (*Please tick a box in every row.*)

a) Do you maintain contacts with national institutions concerning EU law making?

yes ❏   no ❏

If not, please continue with → *question 5.*

b) If yes: How often do you maintain such contacts?

	none	yearly	½ a year	¼ a year	monthly	weekly
National government						
- Top level (prime minister, ministers national secretaries)	❏	❏	❏	❏	❏	❏
- Working level (Department managers)	❏	❏	❏	❏	❏	❏
National regulatory and standardisation authorities	❏	❏	❏	❏	❏	❏
Houses of Parliament						
- Parliamentary parties	❏	❏	❏	❏	❏	❏
- Individual members of parliament	❏	❏	❏	❏	❏	❏
- Parliamentary committees	❏	❏	❏	❏	❏	❏
Others (please specify):						
_____	❏	❏	❏	❏	❏	❏

4. Please characterise your contacts with the national institutions concerning EU-law making in more detail. (*Please tick a box in every row.*)

a) How important are your contacts with the national institutions with regard to EU law making?

	no contacts	not important at all					very important
National government							
- Top level (prime minister, ministers national secretaries)	❏	❏	❏	❏	❏	❏	❏
- Working level (department managers, referents)	❏	❏	❏	❏	❏	❏	❏
National regulatory and standardisation authorities	❏	❏	❏	❏	❏	❏	❏
Houses of Parliament							
- Parliamentary parties	❏	❏	❏	❏	❏	❏	❏
- Individual members of parliament	❏	❏	❏	❏	❏	❏	❏
- Parliamentary committees	❏	❏	❏	❏	❏	❏	❏

4.

b) Would you characterise your relationship to the national institutions as cooperative or as conflictual?

	no contacts	cooperative					conflictual
- National government	☐	☐	☐	☐	☐	☐	☐
- National regulatory and standardisation authorities	☐	☐	☐	☐	☐	☐	☐
- Houses of Parliament	☐	☐	☐	☐	☐	☐	☐

c) Is it difficult for you to obtain information from the national institutions?

	not difficult at all						very difficult
- National government	☐	☐	☐	☐	☐	☐	☐
- National regulatory and standardisation authorities	☐	☐	☐	☐	☐	☐	☐
- Houses of Parliament	☐	☐	☐	☐	☐	☐	☐

---

5. Please note the <u>three</u> political institutions which are most important for the representation of your interests and with whom you maintain contacts. (You can note national and EU institutions.) *(Please use capital letters.)*

1. _____

2. _____

3. _____

---

6. Do you take recourse to legal action in order to represent your interests? *(Please tick a box in every row.)*

a) How often do you take recourse to litigation in order to represent your interests?

never   very often
☐ ☐ ☐ ☐ ☐ ☐

b) How important is legal action for the representation of your interests?

not important at all   very important
☐ ☐ ☐ ☐ ☐ ☐

c) Did your recourse to legal action lose or gain in importance due to the EU law and the European Court of Justice?

The recourse to legal action ...
- lost in importance   ☐
- remained on the same level   ☐
- gained in importance   ☐

So far, we have examined the general importance of several political institutions. Now we want to assess if their relevance has varied over time or in different policy areas and issues.

7. **Since the mid 1980s, the powers of the different EU institutions have changed and the competences of the European Union have been extended. How did this affect the representation of the firm's or association's interests? Did the importance of the following institutions decrease or increase?** *(Please tick a box in every row.)*

	decreased	remained on the same level	increased
- European Commission	☐	☐	☐
- EU regulatory and standardisation authorities	☐	☐	☐
- Council	☐	☐	☐
- European Parliament	☐	☐	☐
- national government	☐	☐	☐
- national regulatory and standardisation authorities	☐	☐	☐
- Houses of Parliament	☐	☐	☐

8. **Political observers often emphasise that the right timing of representing interests is very important. When do you represent your interests vis-à-vis ...** *(Please tick a box in every row.)*
a) EU-institutions?

	never	sometimes	often
- when the political agenda is set	☐	☐	☐
- when the Commission formulates its proposal	☐	☐	☐
- during the debate in the European Parliament	☐	☐	☐
- during the debate in the Council	☐	☐	☐
- when EU law making is transposed into national law	☐	☐	☐
- during implementation by the national administration	☐	☐	☐

b) national institutions?

	never	sometimes	often
- when the political agenda is set	☐	☐	☐
- when the national position with regard to the Commission proposal is formulated	☐	☐	☐
- when EU legislation is transposed into national law	☐	☐	☐
- during implementation by the national administration	☐	☐	☐

9. **What relevance do the following criteria have when you select your contact partners?** *(Please tick a box in every row.)*

a) EU-institutions

	not important at all					very important
- nationality	☐	☐	☐	☐	☐	☐
- language	☐	☐	☐	☐	☐	☐
- personal relationship	☐	☐	☐	☐	☐	☐
- administrative responsibility	☐	☐	☐	☐	☐	☐
- party membership	☐	☐	☐	☐	☐	☐

b) National institutions

	not important at all					very important
- regional origin	☐	☐	☐	☐	☐	☐
- personal relationship	☐	☐	☐	☐	☐	☐
- administrative responsibility	☐	☐	☐	☐	☐	☐
- party membership	☐	☐	☐	☐	☐	☐

10. There are many ways of representing your firm's or association's interests in the EU. How useful do you find the following ways? *(Please tick a box in every row.)*

	not useful at all					very useful
- position papers	☐	☐	☐	☐	☐	☐
- personal contacts	☐	☐	☐	☐	☐	☐
- regular contacts and background information	☐	☐	☐	☐	☐	☐
- targeted contacts and information	☐	☐	☐	☐	☐	☐
- presence in committees and hearings	☐	☐	☐	☐	☐	☐
- presentation of scientific expertise	☐	☐	☐	☐	☐	☐
- mobilisation of the public and the media	☐	☐	☐	☐	☐	☐
- others (please specify): _____	☐	☐	☐	☐	☐	☐

11. Who mostly initiates the contacts with the political actors? *(Please tick a box in every row.)*

a) on the EU-level

	never	sometimes	often
- your organisation	☐	☐	☐
- other associations or companies	☐	☐	☐
- European Commission	☐	☐	☐
- EU regulatory and standardisation authorities	☐	☐	☐
- Council	☐	☐	☐
- European Parliament	☐	☐	☐

b) on the national level

	never	sometimes	often
- your organisation	☐	☐	☐
- other associations or companies	☐	☐	☐
- national government	☐	☐	☐
- national regulatory and standardisation authorities	☐	☐	☐
- Houses of Parliament	☐	☐	☐

12. How important are the following interest organisations on the EU level? *(Please tick a box in every row.)*

	not important at all					very important
- national trade associations	❏	❏	❏	❏	❏	❏
- EU trade associations	❏	❏	❏	❏	❏	❏
- international trade associations	❏	❏	❏	❏	❏	❏
- companies	❏	❏	❏	❏	❏	❏
- consultants	❏	❏	❏	❏	❏	❏
- scientific organisations	❏	❏	❏	❏	❏	❏
- trade unions	❏	❏	❏	❏	❏	❏
- national environmental, social and consumer associations	❏	❏	❏	❏	❏	❏
- EU environmental, social and consumer associations	❏	❏	❏	❏	❏	❏

13. Comparing the EU level to the national level, are these interest organisations on the EU level more or less important than on the national level? *(Please tick a box in every row.)*

	less important	same important	more important
- national trade associations	❏	❏	❏
- EU trade associations	❏	❏	❏
- international trade associations	❏	❏	❏
- companies	❏	❏	❏
- consultants	❏	❏	❏
- scientific organisations	❏	❏	❏
- trade unions	❏	❏	❏
- national environmental, social and consumer associations	❏	❏	❏
- EU environmental, social and consumer associations	❏	❏	❏

14. Cooperation with other organisations *(Please tick a box in every row.)*

a) Do you cooperate with other organisations to represent your interests?
   never ❏   sometimes ❏   often ❏

If <u>never</u>, please continue with → *question 15*.

14.

b) If you do cooperate with other organisations: How useful do you find this cooperation?

Cooperation with other organisations:	no cooperation	not useful at all					very useful
- British trade associations	❏	❏	❏	❏	❏	❏	❏
- foreign trade associations	❏	❏	❏	❏	❏	❏	❏
- EU trade associations	❏	❏	❏	❏	❏	❏	❏
- international trade associations	❏	❏	❏	❏	❏	❏	❏
- companies	❏	❏	❏	❏	❏	❏	❏
- consultants	❏	❏	❏	❏	❏	❏	❏
- scientific organisations	❏	❏	❏	❏	❏	❏	❏
- trade unions	❏	❏	❏	❏	❏	❏	❏
- national environmental, social and consumer associations	❏	❏	❏	❏	❏	❏	❏
- EU environmental, social and consumer associations	❏	❏	❏	❏	❏	❏	❏
Cooperation within associations							
- your association (for representatives of asscociations only)	❏	❏	❏	❏	❏	❏	❏
- your sectoral associations (for firm representatives only)	❏	❏	❏	❏	❏	❏	❏
- British umbrella associations	❏	❏	❏	❏	❏	❏	❏
- EU sectoral associations (e.g. CEFIC)	❏	❏	❏	❏	❏	❏	❏
- EU umbrella associations (e.g. CEEP, UNICE)	❏	❏	❏	❏	❏	❏	❏
- international federations of association		❏	❏	❏	❏	❏	❏

c) Of how many EU associations is your association, or company, a member?

0 ❏   1 ❏   2–5 ❏   6–10 ❏   more than 10 ❏

15. If you need expert knowledge, who provides it? *(Please tick a box in every row.)*

	never	sometimes	often
- external consultancies	❏	❏	❏
- scientific institutes	❏	❏	❏
- governmental institutions	❏	❏	❏
- your organisation's expertise (for associations: also expertise provided by your members)	❏	❏	❏
- other associations	❏	❏	❏
- other companies	❏	❏	❏

16. Which kind of information do political institutions ask from you? *(Please tick a box in every row.)*

	never	sometimes	often
- legal expert knowledge	❏	❏	❏
- technical expert knowledge	❏	❏	❏
- economic expert knowledge	❏	❏	❏
- assessment of political effects	❏	❏	❏
other (please specify): _____	❏	❏	❏

II. In the second part of this questionnaire we want to concentrate on the role of the European parliament (EP).

17. Some political observers emphasise that the influence of the European Parliament varies due to the characteristics of political problems. How do you assess its influence in EU decision processes? *(Please tick a box in every row.)*

Influence of the European Parliament	no influence at all					very high
a) in detailed technical questions	❏	❏	❏	❏	❏	❏
b) in questions of general public interest	❏	❏	❏	❏	❏	❏

18. Like all parliaments in democratic systems, the European Parliament has different functions. How important are the following activities of the European Parliament for its influence in EU decision making processes? *(Please tick a box in every row.)*

	not important at all					very important
- legislative function	❏	❏	❏	❏	❏	❏
- agenda setting	❏	❏	❏	❏	❏	❏
- consultations with the Council	❏	❏	❏	❏	❏	❏
- consultation with the European Commission	❏	❏	❏	❏	❏	❏
- parliamentary control of the Council	❏	❏	❏	❏	❏	❏
- parliamentary control of the European Commission	❏	❏	❏	❏	❏	❏
- representation of the European public	❏	❏	❏	❏	❏	❏

19. A member of the European Parliament should be in contact with as many interest groups as possible. Which interest organisations should get more attention and which should receive less attention?

	less attention					more attention
- trade associations	❑	❑	❑	❑	❑	❑
- companies	❑	❑	❑	❑	❑	❑
- consultants	❑	❑	❑	❑	❑	❑
- trade unions	❑	❑	❑	❑	❑	❑
- political parties	❑	❑	❑	❑	❑	❑

III. The third and final part of the questionnaire is only relevant for associations. <u>Company</u> <u>representative</u>s please continue with → *the indications on the last page* of this questionnaire. In this part, we want to gather some information about your association and about the structure of your economic sector.

20. Please indicate if you work for a national, an EU or an international association and how many branches the association represents. *(Please tick one box in each part.)*

a) According to the association's statute, you work for

- a national association	❑
- an EU association	❑
- an international association	❑

b) The association represents

- part of an economic sector (e.g. industrial chemicals)	❑
- the whole sector (e.g. chemicals)	❑
- more than one sector (e.g. chemicals and pharmaceuticals)	❑

21. Organisational characteristics of the association

a) How many employees does your association have?
  1–5 ❑   6–25 ❑   26–50 ❑   51–100 ❑   more than 100 ❑

When was your association founded?   Year: _____

c) How many members does your association have?
  1–50 ❑   51–100 ❑   101–250 ❑   251–500 ❑   more than 500 ❑

d) How many of the potential members (according to your statute) are represented by your association?
  1–25 % ❑   26–50 % ❑   51–75 % ❑   76–100 % ❑

21.
e) What is the budget of your association in ECU (1 ECU ≅ 0.66 GBP)?

Up to 100,000 ❏   up to 500,000 ❏   up to 1 Mill. ❏   up to 5 Mill. ❏   more than 5 Mill. ❏

f) How is your association financed? *(Please quote in percent of the total budget. Total: 100%)*
- membership subscriptions   _____ %
- payments for services   _____ %
- EU subsidies   _____ %
- other public subsidies   _____ %
- other finance: _____   _____ %

g) Does the association, according to its staute, admit to regular membership ...?

	yes	no
- individuals	❏	❏
- companies	❏	❏
- associations	❏	❏
- other organisations	❏	❏

If you do not represent a company or a companies' association please continue with→ *question 23*.

h) Does the association, according to its statute, specify rules of exclusion according to ...

firm size?
- small firms excluded	❏
- large firms excluded	❏
- no regulation at all	❏

type of ownership?
- public firms excluded	❏
- private firms excluded	❏
- no regulation at all	❏

i) Does your association have a liaison office or branch in Brussels?

  ❏ no   ❏ yes, since (year): _____

---

22. Which economic characteristics do your member companies and your sector display?
(Please tick a box in every row.)

a) How many employees do your member companies have in total?
Up to 100,000 ❏   up to 500,000 ❏   up to 1,000,000 ❏   more than 1,000,000 ❏

b) What percentage share does your members' foreign turnover have in their total turnover?
0 ❏   1–25 % ❏   26–50 % ❏   51–75 % ❏   76–100 % ❏

c) What percentage share do the three biggest companies have in the total turnover of your member companies?
0 ❏   1–25 % ❏   26–50 % ❏   51–75 % ❏   76–100 % ❏

23. Activities of your association. *(Please tick a box in every row.)*

a) Please estimate the proportion of resources spent on the following activities: *(In percent; total: 100 %.)*

- representation of interests _____ %
- provision of services _____ %
- market coordination (e.g. standard setting) _____ %
- other: _____ _____ %

b) With regard to the representation of interests, do you practise the following activities?

	yes	no
- monitoring of political developments	☐	☐
- informing the members about political developments	☐	☐
- representation of the members in political committees and hearings	☐	☐
- representation of interests vis-à-vis other interest organisations	☐	☐
- representation of interests vis-à-vis trade unions	☐	☐

c) Do you provide the following services?

	yes	no
- statistics and branch information	☐	☐
- market research	☐	☐
- individual legal and economic consulting	☐	☐
- access to consultancies	☐	☐
- advertising and public relations activities	☐	☐
- furthering education and qualification of members	☐	☐

d) With regard to market coordination, do you practise the following activities?

	yes	no
- definition of technical norms and standards	☐	☐
- fixing of quality and education standards	☐	☐
- coordination of research and development	☐	☐
- regulation of market entrance	☐	☐
- issuance of licences and certificates	☐	☐
- resolution of conflicts between members	☐	☐

Please don't forget to send us the filled out questionnaire by separate mail.

If you would like to receive a short version of our results, please fill out the form and send it to us by separate mail. We would highly appreciate if you could attach your latest annual report and also the statute of your association.

Your cooperation is sincerely appreciated.
We thank you very much for your time and effort!

Comments

Notes

1 Introduction

1 In May 2008, CONECCS was replaced by a new register of interest organizations in the European Union.
2 The sample is based on Henderson and Henderson (1995); European Commission (1996) Le Conseil National du Patronat Francais (1997); Oeckl (1997).
3 The addressees of the survey were reminded twice by mail to respond in case they hadn't; the second reminder included once again the survey.
4 Every tenth German, British or EU association that did not respond was addressed by phone and, due to the lower response rate, every fifth French association was asked why it did not respond.

2 Studying interest groups in the European Union: the theoretical terrain

1 In this respect, EU studies of interest groups are in good company with the American analyses of interest groups (see Baumgartner and Leech 1998.)
2 See the seminal study of Ernst Haas (1958). Later analyses in this tradition took a more sceptical view (Lindberg and Scheingold 1971).
3 For a critical perspective, see Kassim 1994.
4 Barbara Finke (2007) and Sabine Saurugger (2008) provide good reviews of this literature.
5 According to Beate Kohler-Koch (1992: 81), this was characteristic of EU interest group studies until the 1990s.
6 It goes without saying that firms may support the build-up of welfare states and political regulation if they expect positive effects on their commercial activities because labour unrest is reduced, product quality is enhanced, the qualifications of their staff are improved or the costs of their competitors are relatively more increased than their own costs.
7 For the general argument on the role of organizations in political processes, see Salisbury 1984; Mayntz 1986: 178.
8 For example, the so-called 'G-8' is a long-standing coalition of EU environmental groups. Its members pursue environmental policy goals and have agreed on an informal division of labour in EU environmental policy (see Webster 1998).
9 Some associations are advocacy coalitions that do not represent their members but act on behalf of third parties. These associations do not usually represent business

interests. For example, the European and national consumer associations hardly organize any consumers, but represent their interests in national and EU policy-making.
10 Oliver Williamson (1985: Ch. 2) discusses these issues in his transaction cost theory of economic behaviour.
11 The following discussion draws on Eising 2000 and on Eising and Cini 2002: 169–75.

3 State–business relations in the EU member states

1 Due to the small number of political systems, I could not apply a multilevel analysis.
2 The countries have been sorted on the basis of various corporatism scales presented in Pennings, Keman and Kleinnijenhuis (1999), on Siaroff's typology (1999) and on the basis of the contributions in Kohler-Koch and Eising (1999).
3 The importance of the institutional configuration of the economy for governing political-economic interactions has also been stressed, among others, by Katzenstein (1978a); Hollingsworth, Schmitter and Streeck (1994); Hollingsworth and Boyer (1997); and Kitschelt *et al.* (1999).
4 For the following, see Hall and Soskice 2001b.
5 Among the non-EU member states falling under this type are Switzerland, Norway and Japan.
6 In particular, they make for different degrees of fit with the European quasi-pluralist or network–mode of interest intermediation that will be explored in Chapter 5.
7 Employers' associations and producer associations affected by competition law must meet some reporting requirements (Greenwood 2004). The majority of trade associations are companies limited by guarantee, followed by those that are unincorporated and a relatively small number of associations that are limited by shares or take another legal form. In its 1999 benchmarking exercise, the Trade Association Forum (1999: 10) analysed 140 trade associations. Sixty-eight per cent were companies limited by guarantee; 27 per cent were unincorporated; four per cent were companies limited by shares; and one per cent had another legal form. The company format gives the association its own legal personality and limits the liability of its members (Greenwood 2004: 7).
8 Between 2001 and 2004, 71 per cent to 80 per cent of the consultations conformed to the twelve weeks period (website of the Cabinet office: www.cabinetoffice.gov.uk/regulation/ consultation/index.asp, accessed 15 December 2005). Ministers maintain discretion to deviate from the code, for example, if issues are highly specialized or address only few stakeholders. But they are supposed to give the reasons for such deviations and should follow the principles of the code as far as possible.
9 The TAF is now self-financing and located within the Confederation of British Industry (CBI).
10 This is also the reason why I refrain from applying Peter J. Katzenstein's characterization of the UK as a 'state-nation' (1978c), by which he denotes that the British institutions of government had been in place before the nation came into being.
11 'political representation, aiming at influencing the policy agenda by cultivating contacts with those persons in charge of its elaboration, is traditionally the domain of large public firms or quasi-public firms'.
12 Thus, more than half of the British trade associations that have been surveyed by the Trade Association Forum (TAF) in 1999 indicated that they compete with other associations for members (Boleat 2000: 16; see also Lane 1997: 24).
13 Givovanni Sartori distinguishes mostly the degree of fragmentation, that is, the number of relevant parties in the party system and the degree of polarization, or the ideological distance among the parties. I leave out the second dimension because interest organizations

Notes 205

seek to realize their interests and do not compete on the left–right axis for votes and political positions even if they may be closer to some parties than to others.
14 For example, the CBI organizes both firms and associations.
15 On average, British sub-sectoral associations organize 62.5%, British sectoral groups represent 68.7% and British cross-sectoral associations stand for 48.2% of their potential members (Analysis of variance (ANOVA): sum of squares (ss) between 7,905.73 (degrees of freedom [df] 2), sum of squares (ss) in 120,788.4 (df 176), F 5.760 p = .004). The figures for France are 73.7%, 70.1% and 63.0% (ANOVA between 1,209.99 (df 2) in 53,328.84 (df 100), F 1.134 p = .326), those for Germany amount to 66.7%, 72.5% and 71.0% (ANOVA between 2,177.97 (df 2) in 173,249.8 (df 298), F 1.873 p = .155).
16 The mean membership densities of German direct and mixed-membership organizations amount to 69.7% and 69.9%, and that of federations amounts to 72.9% (ANOVA 358.45 (df between 2) 176,393.44 (df in 295), F 0.275 p = .760). The results for British associations are 61.9%, 58.5% and 71.3% (ANOVA 1,236.65 (dfb 2) 130,925.5 (df in 182), F 0.860 p = .425), those for the French groups amount to 70.2%, 67.7% and 78.6%, respectively (ANOVA 768.2 (dfb 2) 57,675.19 (df in 103), F 0.686 p = .506).
17 Chi^2-tests for the type of members: D 5.738 (df 4) p = .220; UK 3.062 (df 4) p = .547; F 0.157 (df 2) p = .924. Chi^2-tests for the domain size: D 2.585 (df 4) p = .629; UK 3.654 (df 4) p = .455; F 0.693 (df 2) p = .707.
18 ANOVA for the relationship among the financial resources and the share of income derived from services: France 1,796.06 (df between 4) 32,386.77 (df in 97) F 1.34 p = .259; United Kingdom 12,285.67 (dfb 4) 90,231.32 (df in 177), F 6.02 p = .000; Germany 1,611.43 (dfb 4) 53,552.94 (df in 285), F 2.14 p = .076.
19 Small British associations have narrow functional profiles and provide only a few services to their members. In contrast, small French and German associations have broader profiles. The average number of services offered by associations with an income below 100,000 € in the UK is 2.6, in Germany it is 3.5 and in France it is 3.9. ANOVAs for the relation between the number of services and the associational income in each country: United Kingdom (111.11 (df between 4) 382.63 (df in 176) F 12.78 p = .000), France 7.91 (dfb 4) 138.60 (df in 95) F 1.36 p = .255, Germany 17.19 (dfb 4) 470.13 (df in 287) F 2.62 p = .035.
20 On average, German federations spend 67.7% of their resources on interest representation, mixed-membership groups allocate 48.3% to this task, and direct membership groups spend 47.7% of their resources on it (ANOVA 13,181.89 (df between 2) 169,640.20 (df in 287), F 11.15 p = .000). The corresponding figures for British associations are 54.3%, 35.6% and 43.2% (ANOVA 2,587.4 (dfb 2), 121,534.31 (df in 174), F 1.85 p = .160); and those for French associations amount to 83.0%, 40.4% and 43.7% (ANOVA 7,889.55 (dfb 2), 46,193.16 (df in 83), F 7.09 p = .001).

4 The evolution of the EU interest group system: to join or not to join?

1 The various directories of interest groups in the European Union list different types of organization and vary with regard to the total number of actors in each class, so that the entire population of interest organizations in the EU is not known. For example, see the 10,000 actors data set of the EU online-newsserver EurActiv, the European Public Affairs Directory and the CONECCS data of the European Commission. For a useful discussion, see Berkhout and Lowery 2008.
2 In May 2008, CONECCS was replaced by a new directory of EU level interest groups.

206 *Notes*

3 Jean Meynaud and Dusan Sidjanski (1971) describe in detail the formation, the organization and the operation of major Eurogroups in different issue areas in the 1950s and 1960s.
4 H.-W. Platzer (1984: 126) quotes officials of the Federation of German Industry, the BDI.
5 The large increase in the number of UNICE position papers from the 1960s to the 1970s is attributed to the initial moves from negative to positive integration (Platzer 1984: 133–6).
6 Pamela Camerra-Rowe (1994) analysed the different strategies that British and German companies and trade associations pursued in response to the Internal Market Program and the Single European Act (SEA). Wayne Sandholtz and John Zysman (1989) drew attention to the influence of large firms on these institutional developments. Sandholtz also analysed their role in the formulation of European information technology and telecommunications policies in the late 1980s (1992).
7 Recall that 33.6 per cent of the German groups, 16 per cent of the UK organizations and 27.3 per cent of the French associations have not hired professional consultants.
8 The cooperatives founded EURO COOP in 1957. The European Consumers' Organization BEUC was set up in 1962, but has its own secretariat only since 1973. In 1969, the committee of family organizations in the EU (COFACE) was installed.
9 See Truman 1951: 66–108. On the importance of some of these factors for the European interest group system, see Meynaud and Sidjanski 1971: 17–19.
10 European Information, Communications and Consumer Electronics Technology Industry Association.
11 EURELECTRIC: European Grouping of the Electricity Supply Industry. UNIPEDE: Union Internationale des Producteurs et Distributeurs d'Energie Electrique.
12 See the studies of social capital in a number of Western European countries, in Putnam 2001.
13 Given the lack of data on statist practices of interest intermediation, I refrain here from including this mode of interest intermediation in the analysis.
14 Table A 4.1 in the appendix to this chapter presents the correlation matrix of the variables included in the regression analysis.
15 ANOVA: F 15.67, 25,755.05 (df between 3) 411,013.0 (df in 750), $p = .000$.
16 Chi^2 tests for the financial means of EU associations, on the one hand, and German (21.651 df 6, $p = .000$), French (Chi^2 18.812, $p = .001$) or British groups (Chi^2 4.773, $p = .311$), on the other.
17 Note that the same finding holds for the national BIAs: for the most part, the incentives that the German, French and British associations provide are not significantly related to their membership densities, putting into question the importance of selective material incentives for business' organized collective action.

5 Multilevel governance and business interests in the European Union

1 This means that I do not restrict the analysis to peak associations as Andrew Moravcsik does.
2 The cluster analysis has been calculated by k-means clustering which assigns the interest organizations by means of an algorithm into k clusters so that the within-cluster sum of squared Euclidean distances is minimized. Using SPSS starting values, those interest organizations with the largest distances to each other were the starting points. Missing cases were excluded pairwise. There were ties in the data. Three criteria helped in identifying the number of clusters. First, each of the clusters needed to have a clear substantive interpretation. Second, the number of clusters has been determined with test statistics for solutions ranging from one to ten clusters (see appendix Table A5.2).

These include the explained variance of a k-cluster solution (ETA), its proportional reduction of error (PRE) and its explained variance adjusted for by the number of clusters (F-MAX). Finally, the chosen solution had to be stable.

3 The picture changes only slightly when taking the mean of national percentages in France, Germany and the UK. In that case 21.8% of the groups are multilevel players.

4 Among the German (Chi^2 24.020, df 3, p = .000) and the British associations (Chi^2 8.375, df 3, p = .036), these differences are significant, among the French associations, they are not (Chi^2 6.880, df 3, p = 0.760).

6 The Europeanization of interest groups and interest intermediation

1 This conceptualization differs from Risse, Cowles and Caporaso (2001), who mean by Europeanization the build-up of European institutions, as well as from Radaelli (2003) whose concept includes developments both at the EU level and at the national level. For useful overviews and applications of the concept, see Kohler-Koch 2000; Cowles, Caporaso and Risse 2001; Dyson and Goetz 2003; Eising 2003; Featherstone and Radaelli 2003; Lenschow 2005; Graziano and Vink 2006.

2 The EU has usually been regarded as variant of pluralism (Streeck and Schmitter 1991; Coen 1998; Schmidt 1999) or as a variety of network governance (Kohler-Koch and Eising 1999; Ansell 2000; Peterson 2003), showing inroads to corporatism mostly in social policy-making (Falkner 1998) and standardization and harmonization policies (Eichener and Voelzkow 1994c). Germany has frequently been labelled a case of corporatism (Streeck 1999), but also a form of organized pluralism (Sebaldt 1997), corporative pluralism (Maier 1977) and even statism (Baltz, König and Schneider 2005). The UK has been marked as either statist (Schmidt 1996) or pluralist (Siaroff 1999), but displaying corporatist traits in several issue areas (Crouch and Dore 1990). And France is either filed as statist (Hayward 1982; Schmidt 1996) or pluralist (F. Wilson 1987) with corporatism being the rule in the agricultural sector (Keeler 1988).

3 An inspection of the German literature indicates that the Federation of German Industry may never have been a monopoly player in foreign trade policy. The importance of large firms and even individual entrepreneurs is a long-standing feature of German state–economy relations (Feldman 1978: 241; Bührer and Grande 2000: 167). Prior studies emphasized the important role of both sectoral associations and large firms in German foreign economic policy (Kreile 1978: 195–5). Thus, the degree of fit among the EU and German patterns of foreign trade policy formation does not seem to be as poor as Cowles finds it.

4 Asked to assess the importance of the regions for their lobbying efforts in EU policy-making on a scale from 1 (not important at all) to 6 (very important), German associations scored an average of 3.3, whereas British groups scored 2.1 and French organizations scored 2.0.

5 For the German Bundestag, see Saalfeld (1996: 12), and for the British House of Representatives, compare Norton (1996: 107). For a comparative study of Denmark, the UK and Germany, see Auel and Benz 2004.

6 Cluster membership of British and German associations (Chi^2 5.059, df = 4, p = .281), cluster membership of German and French associations (Chi^2 23.980, df = 4, p = .000), cluster membership of British and French associations (Chi^2 13.607, df = 4, p = .009).

7 Three variables indicate the share of *financial resources* (in per cent) spent on interest representation (1), service provision (2) and market coordination (3), respectively. Ten variables indicate whether the associations perform certain *tasks or not*: monitoring of political activities (4); political information to members (5); political representation of members (6);

statistics and sector information (7); market research (8); legal and economic consulting (9); technical standards (10); education and quality standards (11); issuance of licenses (12); dispute resolution (13). Variables 4, 5 and 6 load highly positively (component >0.7) on *interest representation*. Variables 3, 10 and 11 load moderately (0.5 component <0.7) or highly positively on *market coordination*. Variable 2 loads highly positively and variable 1 loads highly negatively (component <-0.7) on *service provision*. Variable 12 loads moderately and variable 13 loads moderately on *licensing*. Finally, variable 7 loads moderately and variable 8 loads highly positively on *market information*.

8 Analysis of variance for the mean factor scores on the associational tasks by clusters: German associations (df between 3, df in 280) – interest representation F 28.459, ss between 58.51 ss in 191.87, p = .000; market standards F 2.254, between 6.72 in 278.08, p = .082; services F 1.130, between 3.15 in 260.11, p = .337; licensing F 2.246, between 6.28 in 260.83, p = .083; market information F .416, between .725 in 162.38, p = .741. British associations (df between 3, df in 166) – interest representation F 11.796, between 19.15 in 89.85, p = .000; market standards F .755, between 2.17 in 159.04, p = .521; services F 2.386, between 7.17 in 166.295, p = .071; licensing F .177, between .641 in 200.15, p = .912; market information F 3.233, between 12.98 in 222.15, p = .024. French associations (df between 3, df in 75) – interest representation F 1.959, between 7.11 in 90.75, p = .127; market standards F .901, between 2.35 in 65.17, p = .445; services F .695, between 2.04 in 73.31, p = .558.

9 The effects of the political systems are controlled because the domestic modes of interest intermediation may affect not only the negotiation capacities of associations but also their financial endowment. This two-way analysis of variance indicates significant differences of the mean budget sizes both by cluster and by country (Corrected model F 7.075, df 19, p .000; country F 3.829, df 3, p = .010; clusters F 12.432, df 4, p .000; Interaction country and clusters F 1.345, df 12, p .188; df between 704). But according to the post hoc comparisons, only German and EU associations differ significantly in their resource endowment. There are no significant differences among German, French and British associations. It follows that the international composition of the clusters is not the outcome of resource asymmetries across borders. The further breakdown in analyses for each country demonstrates that the average budget sizes differ significantly along the clusters in each member state. The results are: German (F 22.428, dfb 3 df in 290, p = .000), British (F 9.208, dfb3, df in 175, p = .000), French (F 5.876, dfb3 df in 94, p = .001), EU associations (F 2.142, dfb 4 df in 135, p = .079).

7 The politics of access in the European Union I: towards elite pluralism?

1 To some extent, Bouwen also considers professional consultancies, but less systematically than the other three forms of organization, so I do not consider them here.
2 'The configuration and the importance of access to decision-makers depends on the allocation of decision-making powers ranging from the early phase of policy formulation to the final adoption of these policies'.
3 According to Rinus van Schendelen (2002: 63–4), 82 per cent of the EU legal acts in the year 2000 were matters of delegated legislation in the comitology system of the EU. Only 18 per cent fell under the secondary legislation upon which the Council, and, depending on the decision-making procedure, the European Parliament decide.
4 Pairwise T-tests comparing the mean access to information of firms and associations from EU institutions to that from national institutions: European Commission-National

government: EU associations (T 1.46, df 93, p = .148), German associations (T –5.01, df 213, p = .000), British associations (T –3.31, df 117, p = .001), French associations (T 1.77, df 66, p = 0.082) and firms (T 0.81, df 31, p = .423). European Parliament-National Parliament: EU associations (T 0.15, df 78, p = .884), German associations (T –4.35, df 189, p = .000), British associations (T –4.57, df 107, p = .000), French associations (T –1.02, df 57, p = .311) and firms (T 1.07, df 30, p = .292).

8 The politics of access in the European Union II: towards a theory of interest group access

1 The counter argument runs as follows: these assessments are highly subjective. Associations consider only those institutions as important with whom they maintain contacts. However, this begs the question why they established these contacts in the first place. Conceiving of business associations as rational organizations that depend on resources they obtain from both members and state institutions, it is reasonable to expect that they seek contacts with those EU institutions which can provide crucial resources, namely organizational support, policy information and influence on EU regulation.
2 I discuss three exchange goods – political regulation, the degree of internationalization and economic weight – that are frequently considered to be sectoral characteristics (see Cawson 1985; Atkinson and Coleman 1989; Hollingsworth, Schmitter and Streeck, 1994; Falkner 2000). Here, I depart from these sectoral analyses in order to stress the logic of political exchanges that emanates from these factors.
3 I used SPost (Long and Freese 1997) to calculate these measures.
4 A logged odds ratio is the change in the logarithm of the ratio between the probability of being in a lower category than *m* (e.g. monthly contacts) and that of being in *m* (e.g. weekly contacts).
5 Table A8.1 in the appendix to this chapter presents the descriptive statistics of these variables.

References

Aberbach, J. D., Putnam, R. D., and Rockman, B. A. (1981) *Bureaucrats and politicians in Western democracies*, Cambridge MA: Harvard University Press.

Abromeit, H. and Schmidt, T. (1998) 'Grenzprobleme der Demokratie – konzeptionelle Überlegungen', in B. Kohler-Koch (ed.) *Regieren in entgrenzten Räumen*, Opladen: Westdeutscher Verlag, 293–320. Politische Vierteljahresschrift, Special issue 29/1998.

Adshead, M. (1996) 'Beyond clientelism: agricultural networks in Ireland and the EU', *West European Politics*, 19(3): 563–608.

Almond, G. A. (1958) 'A comparative study of interest groups and the political process', *American Political Science Review*, 52(2): 270–82.

Andersen, S. S. and Eliassen, K. A. (1991) 'European Community lobbying', *European Journal of Political Research*, 20: 173–87.

Ansell, C. (2000) 'The networked polity: regional development in Western Europe', *Governance. An International Journal of Policy, Administration and Institutions*, 13(3): 303–33.

Appleton, A. (2001) 'France: party–group relations in the shadow of the state', in C. S. Thomas (ed.) *Political parties and interest groups. Shaping democratic governance*, Boulder, CO: Lynn Rienner, 45–62.

Armstrong, K. and Bulmer, S. J. (1998) *The governance of the Single European Market*, Manchester: Manchester University Press.

Aspinwall, M. (1998) 'Collective attraction – the new political game in Brussels', in J. Greenwood and M. Aspinwall (eds) *Collective action in the European Union. Interests and the new politics of associability*, London: Routledge, 196–213.

—— (1999) 'Planes, trains, and automobiles: transport in the European Union', in B. Kohler-Koch and R. Eising (eds) *The transformation of governance in the European Union*, London: Routledge, 119–34.

Aspinwall, M. and Greenwood, J. (1998) 'Conceptualising collective action in the European Union', in J. Greenwood and M. Aspinwall (eds) *Collective action in the European Union. Interests and the new politics of associability*, London: Routledge, 1–30.

Atkinson, M. M. and Coleman, W. D. (1989) 'Strong states and weak states: sectoral policy networks in advanced capitalist economies', *British Journal of Political Studies*, 19(1): 47–67.

—— (1992) 'Policy networks, policy communities and the problems of governance', *Governance. An International Journal of Policy and Administration*, 5(2): 154–80.

Auel, K. and Benz, A. (2004) 'National parliaments in EU multi-level governance: dilemmas and strategies of adaption', *FernUniversität in Hagen. Polis-Heft* 60.

Averyt, W. F. (1975) 'Eurogroups, clientela, and the European Community', *International Organization*, 29(4): 949–72.
—— (1977) *Agropolitics in the European Community. Interest groups and the Common Agricultural Policy*, New York: Praeger.
Bacher, J. (2001) 'Teststatistiken zur Bestimmung der Clusterzahl für QUICK CLUSTER', *ZA-Information*, 48: 71–97.
Balme, R. and Chabanet, D. (2002) 'Action collective et gouvernance de l'Union européenne', in R. Balme, D. Chabanet, and V. Wright (eds) *L'action collective en Europe/Collective action in Europe*, Paris: Presses de Science Po, 21–120.
—— (2008) *European Governance and Democracy. Power and Protest in the EU*, Lanham, MD: Rowman & Littlefield.
Balme, R., Chabanet, D., and Wright, V. (eds) (2002) *L'action collective en Europe/ Collective action in Europe*, Paris: Presses de Sciences Po.
Baltz, K., König, T., and Schneider, G. (2005) 'Immer noch ein etatistischer Kontinent: Die Bildung nationaler Positionen zu EU-Verhandlungen', in R. Eising and B. Kohler-Koch (eds) *Interessenpolitik in Europa*, Baden-Baden: Nomos, 283–310.
Bartle, I. (1999) 'Transnational interests in the European Union: globalization and changing organization in telecommunications and electricity', *Journal of Common Market Studies*, 37(3): 363–84.
Bartolini, St. (1998) 'Exit options, boundary building, political structuring. Sketches of a theory of large-scale territorial and membership "retrenchment/differentiation" versus "expansion/integration" (with references to the European Union)', European University Institute Working Paper, 98.
—— (2005) *Restructuring Europe. Centre formation, system building, and political structuring between the nation state and the European Union*, Oxford: Oxford University Press.
Baumgartner, F. R. (1996) 'Public interest groups in France and the United States', *Governance. An International Journal of Policy and Administration*, 9(1): 1–22.
Baumgartner, F. R. and Leech, B. (1998) *Basic interests. The importance of groups in politics and political science*, Princeton, NJ: Princeton University Press.
Baumheier, U. (1992) 'Öffentliche Verwaltung und Pharmaindustrie. Muster der Zusammenarbeit bei der Sicherheitskontrolle von Arzneimitteln, der Kostendämpfung im Gesundheitswesen und der Industrieförderung in der Bundesrepublik Deutschland, Großbritannien und Frankreich', unpublished thesis (Dissertation), Universität Konstanz.
Bennett, R. J. (ed.) (1997a) *Trade associations in Britain and Germany. Responding to internationalisation and the EU*, York: Anglo-German Foundation for the Study of Industrial Society.
—— (1997b) 'Trade associations: new challenges, new logic?', in R. J. Bennett (ed.) *Trade associations in Britain and Germany. Responding to internationalisation and the EU*, York: Anglo-German Foundation for the Study of Industrial Society, 1–11.
—— (1997c) 'Trade associations: Britain and Germany compared', in R. J. Bennett (ed.) *Trade associations in Britain and Germany. Responding to internationalisation and the EU*, York: Anglo-German Foundation for the Study of Industrial Society, 12–22.
—— (1997d) 'The impact of European economic integration on business associations: the UK case', *West European Politics*, 20(3): 61–90.
Benz, A. (1998) 'Politikverflechtung ohne Politikverflechtungsfalle – Koordination und Strukturdynamik im europäischen Mehrebenensystem', *Politische Vierteljahresschrift*, 39(4): 558–89.
Benz, A. and Lehmbruch, G. (eds) (2002) *Föderalismus. Analysen in entwicklungsgeschichtlicher und vergleichender Perspektive*, Wiesbaden: Westdeutscher Verlag. PVS-Special issue 32/2001.

Berkhout, J. and Lowery, D. (2008) 'Counting organized interests in the European Union: a comparison of data sources', *Journal of European Public Policy*, 15(4): 489–513.

Bernhagen, P. and Mitchell, N. (2007) 'Transnational business actors and lobbying in the European Union', paper presented at the ESRC Workshop 'Organized Interests and Democratic Governance', Newcastle, 25–26 January.

Beyers, J. (2002) 'Gaining and seeking access: the European adaptation of domestic interest associations', *European Journal of Political Research*, 41(5): 585–612.

Beyers, J. and Kerremans, B. (2005) 'Bürokraten, Politiker und gesellschaftliche Interessen: Ist die Europäische Union entpolitisiert?', in R. Eising and B. Kohler-Koch (eds) *Interessenpolitik in Europa*, Baden-Baden: Nomos, 123–50.

Beyers, J., Eising, R., and Maloney, W. (2008) 'Much we study, little we know? The study of interest group politics in Europe and elsewhere', *West European Politics*, 31(6), forthcoming.

Beyme, K. von (1993) 'West Germany and the New Germany: centralization, expanding pluralism, and new changes', in C. S. Thomas (ed.) *First World Interest Groups. A Comparative Perspective*, Westport, CT: Greenwood, 165–81.

Bischoff, I. (2003) 'Determinants of the increase in the number of interest groups in Western Democracies: theoretical considerations and evidence from 21 OECD countries', *Public Choice*, 114(1–2): 197–218.

Blank, O. (2002) 'The impact of changing sectoral definition upon associability: the convergence of business interests in the information and communications technology sector in Europe', in J. Greenwood (ed.) *The effectiveness of EU business associations*, New York: Palgrave, 115–21.

Blank, St. (1978) 'Britain: the politics of foreign economic policy, the domestic economy, and the problem of pluralistic stagnation', in P. J. Katzenstein (ed.) *Between power and plenty: foreign economic policies of advanced industrial states*, Madison: The University of Wisconsin Press, 89–137.

Block, F. (1977) 'The ruling class does not rule: note on the Marxist theory of the state', *Socialist Review*, 33: 5–23.

Boleat, M. (2000) *Models of trade association cooperation*, London: Trade Association Forum.

Borragán, N. Pérez-Solórzano (2003) 'The organisation of business interests in Central and East European countries for EU representation', in J. Greenwood (ed.) *The Challenge of change in EU business associations*, Basingstoke: Macmillan, 213–25.

Börzel, T. A. (1997) 'What's so special about policy networks? An exploration of the concept and its usefulness in studying European governance', *European Integration online Papers* 1(16). Available: http://eiop.or.at/eiop/texte/1997-016a.htm (accessed February 2009).

Bouwen, P. (2002a) 'Corporate lobbying in the European Union: the logic of access', *Journal of European Public Policy*, 9(3): 365–90.

—— (2002b) 'A comparative study of business lobbying in the European Parliament, the European Commission and the Council of Ministers', *Discussion Paper* (02/7), *Max-Planck-Institute for the Study of Societies*.

Bührer, W. and Grande, E. (eds) (2000) *Unternehmerverbände und Staat in Deutschland*, Baden-Baden: Nomos.

Burkhardt-Reich, B. and Schumann, W. (1983) *Agrarverbände in der EG. Das agrarpolitische Entscheidungsgefüge in Brüssel und den EG-Mitgliedstaaten unter besonderer Berücksichtigung des Euro-Verbandes COPA und seiner nationalen Mitgliedsverbände*, Kehl: Engel.

Butt-Philipp, A. (2000) 'The role of non-state actors in the European Union integration theory: an everyday overview of the literature', paper presented at 'The Effectiveness of EU Business Associations' conference in Brussels, 18–22 September.

Camerra-Rowe, P. G. (1994) 'Lobbying in the new Europe: firms and politics in the Single European Market', unpublished thesis (PhD-Dissertation), Duke University.

Caporaso, J. A. (1974) *The structure and function of European integration*, Pacific Palisades, CA: Goodyear.

Cawson, A. (1985) 'Introduction. Varieties of corporatism: the importance of the meso-level of interest inermediation', in A. Cawson (ed.) *Organized interests and the state. Studies in meso-corporatism*, London: Sage, 1–21.

Clark, P. B. and Wilson, J. Q. (1961) 'Incentive systems: a theory of organizations', *Administrative Science Quarterly*, 6(3): 219–66.

Coen, D. (1997) 'The evolution of the large firm as a political actor in the European Union', *Journal of Public Policy*, 4(1): 91–108.

—— (1998) 'The European business interest and the nation state: large-firm lobbying in the European Union and member states', *Journal of Public Policy*, 18(1): 75–100.

—— (2002) 'Business interests and European integration', in R. Balme, D. Chabenet, and V. Wright (eds) *L'action collective en Europe/Collective action in Europe*, Paris: Presses de Science Po, 255–77.

—— (ed.) (2007) 'Empirical and theoretical studies in EU-lobbying', *Special Issue of the Journal of European Public Policy*, 14(3), 333–488.

Cohen, E. (1995) 'France: national champions in search of a mission', in J. E. S. Hayward (ed.) *Industrial enterprise and european integration. From national to international champions in Western Europe*, Oxford: Oxford University Press.

Coleman, W. D. (1997) 'Associational governance in a globalizing era: weathering the storm', in J. R. Hollingsworth and R. Boyer (eds) *Contemporary capitalism. The embeddedness of institutions*, Cambridge: Cambridge University Press, 127–53.

Collignon, St. and Schwarzer, D. (2005) 'Unternehmen und Banken auf dem Weg zur Währungsunion: Die "Association for the Monetary Union of Europe" als Motor eines transnationalen Konsenses', in R. Eising and B. Kohler-Koch (eds) *Interessenpolitik in Europa*, Baden-Baden: Nomos, 203–26.

Commission (Commission of the European Communities) (1992) *An open and structured dialogue between the Commission and special interest groups*, Brussels: SEC (92) 2272 final.

—— (1999) *The Commission and non-governmental organisations. Building a stronger partnership*, Brussels: Commission discussion paper presented by President Prodi and Vice-President Kinnock.

—— (2001) *European governance. A white paper*, Brussels: COM(2001) final, 25.7.2001.

—— (2002) *Consultation document. Towards a reinforced culture of consultation and dialogue – Proposal for general principles and minimum standards for consultation of interested parties by the Commission*, Brussels: COM(2002) 277 final, 5.6.2002.

Commission (Commission of the European Communities) General Secretariat (2002) *Consultation, the European Commission and civil society* (CONECCS), Brussels. Available: http://europa.eu.int/comm/civil_society/coneccs/index_en.htm (accessed May 2002).

Constantelos, J. (1996) 'Multi-level lobbying in the European Union: a paired sectoral comparison across the French–Italian border', *Regional and Federal Studies*, 6(1): 28–55.

Cowles, M. G. (1997) 'Organizing industrial coalitions: a challenge for the future?', in H. Wallace and A. R. Young (eds) *Participation and policy-making in the European Union*, Oxford: Clarendon Press, 116–40.

—— (1998) 'The changing architecture of big business', in J. Greenwood and M. Aspinwall (eds) *Collective action in the European Union. Interests and the new politics of associability*, London: Routledge, 108–25.

—— (2001) 'The transatlantic business dialogue and domestic business–government relations', in M. G. Cowles, J. A. Caporaso, and T. Risse (eds) *Transforming Europe. Europeanization and domestic change*, Ithaca, NY: Cornell University Press, 159–79.

Cowles, M. G., Caporaso, J., and Risse, T. (eds) (2001) *Transforming Europe. Europeanization and domestic change*, Ithaca, NY: Cornell University Press.

Cram, L. (1998) 'The EU institutions and collective action: constructing a European interest', in J. Greenwood and M. Aspinwall (eds) *Collective action in the European Union. Interests and the new politics of associability*, London: Routledge, 63–80.

Crombez, Ch. (2002) 'Information, lobbying, and the legislative process in the European Union', *European Union Politics*, 3(1): 7–32.

Crouch, C. and Dore, R. (1990) *Corporatism and accountability*, Oxford: Clarendon Press.

Cullen, P. P. (1999) 'Pan-European non governmental organizations: European Union sponsored mobilization and activism for social rights', paper presented at the 6th biennial conference of the European Community Studies Association, Pittsburgh, 2–5 June.

Culpepper, P. D. (2001) 'Employers, public policy, and the politics of decentralized cooperation in Germany and France', in P. A. Hall and D. Soskice (eds) *Varieties of capitalism. The institutional foundations of comparative advantage*, Oxford: Oxford University Press, 275–306.

Czada, R. M. (1991) 'Interest groups, self-interest, and the institutionalization of political action', in R. M. Czada and A. Windhoff-Héritier (eds) *Political choice. Institutions, rules, and limits of rationality*, Frankfurt a.M.: Campus, 257–300.

DiMaggio, P. and Powell, W. W. (1991) 'The iron cage revisited: institutional isomorphism and collective rationality in organizational fields', in P. DiMaggio and W. W. Powell (eds) *The New Institutionalism in organizational analysis*, Chicago, IL: The University of Chicago Press, 63–82.

Döring, H. (1992) 'Parlament und Regierung', in O. W. Gabriel (ed.) *Die EG-Staaten im Vergleich*, Bonn: Bundeszentrale für politische Bildung, 334–56.

Department of Trade and Industry (DTI) (1996) *A best practice guide for the model trade association*. London: DTI.

Dür, Andreas and De Bièvre, D. (2007) 'Inclusion without influence? NGOs in European trade policy', *Journal of Public Policy*, 27(1): 79–101.

Dyson, K. (1980) *The state tradition in Western Europe*, Oxford: Martin Robertson.

Dyson, K. and Goetz, K. H. (2003) *Germany, Europe and the politics of constraint*, Oxford: Oxford University Press.

Ebbinghaus, B. and Hassel, A. (1999) 'Striking deals: concertation in the reform of continental welfare states', unpublished thesis (Discussion Paper (99/3)), Max-Planck-Institute for the Study of Societies.

Ebbinghaus, B. and Visser, J. (1994) 'Barrieren und Wege "grenzenloser Solidarität": Gewerkschaften und Europäische Integration', in W. Streeck (ed.) *Staat und Verbände*, Opladen, 223–55. PVS Special issue 25/1994.

Eder, K., Hellmann, K. U., and Trenz, H.-J. (1998) 'Regieren in Europa jenseits öffentlicher Legitimation? Eine Untersuchung zur Rolle von politischer Öffentlichkeit in Europa', in B. Kohler-Koch (ed.) *Regieren in entgrenzten Räumen*, Opladen: Westdeutscher Verlag, 321–44. Politische Vierteljahresschrift, Special issue 29/1998.

Eichener, V. and Voelzkow, H. (eds) (1994a) *Europäische Integration und verbandliche Interessenvermittlung*, Marburg: Metropolis.

—— (1994b) 'Europäische Integration und verbandliche Interessenvermittlung: Ko-Evolution von politisch-administrativem System und Verbändelandschaft', in V. Eichener and H. Voelzkow (eds) *Europäische Integration und verbandliche Interessenvermittlung*, Marburg: Metropolis, 9–27.

—— (1994c) 'Europäische Regulierung im Arbeitsschutz: Überraschungen aus Brüssel und ein erster Versuch ihrer Erklärung', in V. Eichener and H. Voelzkow (eds) *Europäische Integration und verbandliche Interessenvermittlung*, Marburg: Metropolis, 385–419.

Eising, R. (1999) 'Reshuffling power: the liberalization of the EU electricity markets and its impact on the German governance regime', in B. Kohler-Koch and R. Eising (eds) *The transformation of governance in the European Union*, London: Routledge, 208–28.

—— (2000) *Liberalisierung und Europäisierung. Die regulative Reform der Elektrizitätsversorgung in Großbritannien, der Europäischen Gemeinschaft und der Bundesrepublik Deutschland*, Opladen: Leske + Budrich.

—— (2001) 'Assoziative Demokratie in der Europäischen Union?', in A. Zimmer and B. Wessels (eds) *Verbände und Demokratie in Deutschland*, Opladen: Leske + Budrich, 293–330.

—— (2002) 'Policy learning in embedded negotiations: explaining EU electricity liberalization', *International Organization*, 56(1): 85–120.

—— (2003) 'Integration und Europäisierung: Konzepte in der EU-Forschung', in M. Jachtenfuchs and B. Kohler-Koch (eds) *Europäische Integration*, Opladen: Leske + Budrich, 387–416.

Eising, R. and Cini, M. (2002) 'Disintegration or reconfiguration? Organized interests in Western Europe', in P. Heywood, E. Jones, and M. Rhodes (eds) *Developments in West European Politics 2*, New York: Palgrave, 168–83.

Eising, R. and Jabko, N. (2001) 'Moving targets: national interests and European Union electricity liberalization', *Comparative Political Studies*, 34(7): 242–67.

Eising, R. and Kohler-Koch, B. (1994) 'Inflation und Zerfaserung: Trends der Interessenvermittlung in der Europäischen Gemeinschaft', in W. Streeck (ed.) *Staat und Verbände*, Opladen: Westdeutscher Verlag, 175–206. PVS-Special issue 25/1994.

—— (1999a) 'Introduction: network governance in the European Union', in B. Kohler-Koch and R. Eising (eds) *The transformation of governance in the European Union*, London: Routledge, 3–13.

—— (1999b) 'Governance in the European Union: a comparative assessment', in B. Kohler-Koch and R. Eising (eds) *The transformation of governance in the European Union*, London: Routledge, 267–85.

—— (eds) (2005a) *Interessenpolitik in Europa*, Baden-Baden: Nomos.

—— (2005b) 'Interessenpolitik im europäischen Mehrebenensystem', in R. Eising and B. Kohler-Koch (eds) *Interessenpolitik in Europa*, Baden-Baden: Nomos, 11–75.

Eriksen, E. O., Jörges, C., and Neyer, J. (eds) (2003) *European governance. Deliberation and the quest for democratisation*, Oslo: ARENA Report No. 2.

ESC (Economic and Social Committee) (2004) *Final report of the ad hoc group on structured cooperation with European civil society organisations and networks*, Brussels: CESE 1498/2003, 17 February 2004.

European Commission (ed.) (1996) *Directory of interest groups/repertoire des groupes d'Interérêt/Verzeichnis der Interessenverbände*, Office for Official Publications of the EC: Luxembourg.

—— (2002) *Communication from the Commission. Towards a reinforced culture of consultation and dialogue – General principles and minimum standards for consultation of interested parties by the Commission*. COM (2002) 704 final, Brussels, 11 December.

216 References

Everitt, B. S. (1980) *Cluster analysis*, New York: Halsted Press.

Fairbrass, J. (2003) 'The Europeanisation of business interest representation: British and French firms compared', *Comparative European Politics*, 1(3): 313–34.

Falkner, G. (1998) *EU Social Policy in the 1990s. Towards a corporatist policy community*, London: Routledge.

—— (2000) 'Policy networks in a multi-level system: convergence towards moderate diversity?', *West European Politics*, 23(4): 94–121.

Falkner, G., Hartlapp, M., Leiber, S., and Treib, O. (2005) 'Die Kooperation der Sozialpartner im Arbeitsrecht: Ein europäischer Weg?', in R. Eising and B. Kohler-Koch (eds) *Interessenpolitik in Europa*, Baden-Baden: Nomos, 341–62.

Falkner, G., Treib, O., Hartlapp, M., and Leiber, S. (2005) *Complying with Europe. EU harmonization and soft law in the member states*, Cambridge: Cambridge University Press.

Featherstone, K. and Radaelli, C.M. (eds) (2003) *The politics of Europeanization*, Oxford: Oxford University Press.

Feld, W. J. (1970) *Transnational business collaboration among common market countries*, New York: Praeger.

Feldman, G. D. (1978) 'The large firm in the German industrial system: the M.A.N. 1900–1925', in D. Stegmann, B.J. Wendt, and P.-C. Witt (eds) *Industrielle Gesellschaft und politisches System*, Bonn: Verlag Neue Gesellschaft, 241–57.

Finke, B. (2007) 'Civil society participation in EU governance', *Living Review in European Governance* 2(2), www.livingreviews.org/lreg-2007-2 (accessed February 2009).

Geddes, A. (2000) 'Lobbying for migrant inclusion in the European Union: new opportunities for transnational advocacy?', *Journal of European Public Policy* 7, 4(4): 632–49.

Goetz, K. H. (2000) 'European integration and national executives: a cause in search of an effect?', *West European Politics*, 23(4): 211–31.

Goetz, K. H. and Hix, S. (eds) (2000) 'Europeanised politics? European integration and national political systems', *West European Politics* 23(4), Special Issue.

Grande, E. (1989) *Vom Monopol zum Wettbewerb? Die neokonservative Reform der Telekommunikation in Großbritannien und der Bundesrepublik Deutschland*, Wiesbaden: Deutscher Universitäts-Verlag.

—— (1994) *Vom Nationalstaat zur europäischen Politikverflechtung. Expansion und Transformation moderner Staatlichkeit – untersucht am Beispiel der Forschungs- und Technologiepolitik*, Universität Konstanz, Habilitationsschrift zur Erlangung einer venia legendi in Politischer Wissenschaft und Verwaltungswissenschaft.

—— (1996) 'The state and interest groups in a framework of multi-level decision-making: the case of the European Union', *Journal of European Public Policy*, 3(3): 318–38.

—— (2000) 'Multi-level governance: Institutionelle Besonderheiten und Funktionsbedingungen des europäischen Mehrebenensystems', in E. Grande and M. Jachtenfuchs (eds) *Wie problemlösungsfähig ist die Europäische Union?*, Baden-Baden: Nomos, 11–25.

Granovetter, M. (1992) 'Economic action and social structure: the problem of embeddedness', in M. Granovetter and R. Swedberg (eds) *The sociology of economic life*, Boulder, CO: Westview Press, 53–81.

Grant, W. (1991) 'DIY: the government relations functions of large companies', in G. Jordan (ed.) *The commercial lobbyists. Politics for profit in Britain*, Aberdeen: Aberdeen University Press, 99–110.

—— (1993a) *Business and politics in Britain*, London: Macmillan.

—— (1993b) 'Pressure groups and the European Community: an overview', in S. Mazey and J. Richardson (eds) *Lobbying in the European Community*, Oxford: Oxford University Press, 27–46.
—— (2000) *Pressure groups and British politics*, New York: St. Martin's Press.
Gray, V. and Lowery, D. (2001) 'The expression of density dependence in state communities of organized interests', *American Politics Research*, 29(4): 374–91.
Graziano, P. and Vink, M. (2007) *Europeanization. New research agendas*, Basingstoke: Palgrave Macmillan.
Greenwood, J. (2002a) *Inside the EU business associations*, London: Palgrave.
—— (2002b) 'EU interest groups and their members: when is membership a "collective action problem"?', in R. Balme, D. Chabenet, and V. Wright (eds) *L'action collective en Europe/Collective action in Europe*, Paris: Presses de Science Po, 227–53.
—— (2003) *Interest representation in the European Union*, New York: St. Martin's Press.
—— (2004) *The association of small and medium sized enterprises. United Kingdom.* Aberdeen. Available: www.rgu.ac.uk/files/UK%20SME%20associations%20final%20version.pdf (accessed November 2005).
Greenwood, J. and Aspinwall, M. (eds) (1998) *Collective action in the European Union. Interests and the new politics of associability*, London: Routledge.
Greenwood, J. and Ronit, K. (1994) 'Interest groups in the European Community: newly emerging dynamics and forms', *West European Politics*, 17(1): 31–52.
Greenwood, J. and Webster, R. (2000) 'Are EU business associations governable?', *European Integration online Papers*, 4(3). Available: http://eiop.or.at/eiop/texte/2000-003a.htm (accessed February 2009).
Greenwood, J., Grote, J., and Ronit, K. (eds) (1992) *Organized interests and the European Community*, London: Sage.
Grossmann, E. and Saurugger, S. (2004) 'Challenging French interest groups: the state, Europe and the international political system', *French Politics*, 2(2): 203–20.
Grote, J. R. and Lang, A. (2003) 'Europeanization and organizational change in national trade associations: an organizational ecology perspective', in K. Featherstone and C. M. Radaelli (eds) *The politics of Europeanization*, Oxford: Oxford University Press, 225–54.
Grove, J. W. (1962) *Government and industry in Britain*, London: Longmans.
Guéguen, D. (2003) 'David against Goliath: are big lobbying organizations more efficient than smaller ones?', in J. Greenwood (ed.) *The challenge of change in EU business associations*, New York: Palgrave Macmillan, 139–49.
Haas, E. B. (1958) *The uniting of Europe. Political, social and economic forces 1950–1957*, Notre Dame, IN: University of Notre Dame Press. Reprint of the second edition with a new introduction by Ernst Haas and a foreword by Desmond Dinan.
—— (1975) *The obsolescence of regional integration theory*, Berkeley, CA: Institute of International Studies. University of California, Berkeley.
Hall, P. A. (1986) *Governing the economy. The politics of state intervention in Britain and France*, Oxford: Oxford University Press.
Hall, P. A. and Soskice, D. (eds) (2001a) *Varieties of capitalism. The institutional foundations of comparative advantage*, Oxford: Oxford University Press.
—— (2001b) 'An introduction to varieties of capitalism', in P. A. Hall and D. Soskice (eds) *Varieties of capitalism. The institutional foundations of comparative advantage*, Oxford: Oxford University Press, 1–68.
Hall, P. A. and Taylor, R. C. R. (1996) 'Political science and the three new institutionalisms', *Political Studies*, 44: 936–57.

Hancké, B. (2001) 'Revisiting the French model: coordination and restructuring in French industry', in P. A. Hall and D. Soskice (eds) *Varieties of capitalism. The institutional foundations of comparative advantage*, Oxford: Oxford University Press, 307–34.

Harvey, B. (1993) 'Lobbying in Europe: the experience of voluntary organization', in S. Mazey and J. Richardson (eds) *Lobbying in the European Community*, Oxford, 188–200.

Hassel, A., Höpner, M., Kurdelbusch, A., Rehder, B., and Zugehör, R. (2000) 'Dimensionen der Internationalisierung: Ergebnisse der Unternehmensdatenbank', "Internationalisierung der 100 größten Unternehmen in Deutschland", *Max-Planck-Institute for the Study of Societies Working Paper* (00/1).

Haverland, M. (1999) *National autonomy, European integraton, and the politics of packaging waste*, Amsterdam: Thela Thesis.

Hayes-Renshaw, F. and Wallace, H. (1997) *The Council of Ministers*, Houndmills, Basingstoke: Macmillan.

Hayward, J. (1982) 'Mobilising private interests in the service of public ambitions: the salient element in the dual French policy style', in J. Richardson (ed.) *Policy styles in Western Europe*, London: George Allen & Unwin, 111–40.

—— (1995a) *Industrial enterprise and European integration. From national to international champions in Western Europe*, Oxford: Oxford University Press.

—— (1995b) 'Introduction: Europe's endangered industrial champions', in J. Hayward (ed.) *Industrial enterprise and European integration. From national to international champions in Western Europe*, Oxford: Oxford University Press, 1–20.

—— (1996) 'Organized interests and public policies', in J. Hayward and E. C. Page (eds) *Governing the new Europe*, Cambridge: Polity Press, 224–56.

Heinelt, H. (1998) 'Zivilgesellschaftliche Perspektiven einer demokratischen Transformation der Europäischen Union', *Zeitschrift für Internationale Beziehungen*, 5(1): 79–107.

Helm, D. (1989) 'The economic borders of the state', in D. Helm (ed.) *The economic borders of the state*, Oxford: Oxford University Press, 9–45.

Henderson, S. P. A. and Henderson, A. J. W. (eds) (1995) *Directory of British Associations and Associations in Ireland*, 12th ed., Beckenham.

Héritier, A. (1996) 'The accomodation of diversity in European policy-making and its outcomes: regulatory policy as a patchwork', *Journal of European Public Policy*, 3(2): 149–67.

Héritier, A., Kerver, D., Knill, C., and Lehmkuhl, D. (2001) *Differential Europe. The EU impact on national policy-making*, Boulder, CO: Rowman & Littlefield.

Hey, C. and Brendle, U. (1994) *Umweltverbände und EG. Strategien, politische Kulturen und Organisationsformen*, Opladen: Westdeutscher Verlag.

Hix, S. (1998) 'Elections, parties and institutional design: a comparative perspective on European Union democracy', *West European Politics*, 21(3): 19–52.

Hix, S. and Raunio, T. (2000) 'Backbenchers learn to fight back: European integration and parliamentary government', in K. H. Goetz and S. Hix (eds) *Europeanised politics? European integration and national political systems*', 142–68, *West European Politics. Special Issue* 23(4).

Hoffmann, S. (1966) 'Obstinate or obsolete? The fate of the nation-state and the case of Western Europe', *Daedalus*, 95(2): 862–915.

Hollingsworth, J. R. and Boyer, R. (eds) (1997) *Contemporary capitalism. The embeddedness of institutions*, Cambridge: Cambridge University Press.

Hollingsworth, J. R., Schmitter, P. C., and Streeck, W. (eds) (1994) *Governing capitalist economies. Performance and control of economic sectors*, Oxford: Oxford University Press.

Honaker, J., Joseph, A., King, G., Scheve, K., and Singh, N. (2003) *Amelia. A program for missing data*, Cambridge, MA: Harvard University Press. Available: http://GKing.Harvard.edu (accessed November 2003).

Hooghe, L. (2001) *The European Commission and the integration of Europe*, Oxford: Oxford University Press.

—— (2002) 'The mobilisation of territorial interests and multilevel governance', in R. Balme, D. Chabenet, and V. Wright (eds) *L'action collective en Europe/Collective action in Europe*, Paris: Presses de Science Po, 347–74.

Hooghe, L. and Marks, G. (2003) 'Unraveling the central state, but how? Types of multilevel governance', *American Political Science Review*, 97(2): 233–43.

Hueglin, T. O. (1999) 'Government, governance, governmentality: a comparative assessment', in B. Kohler-Koch and R. Eising (eds) *The transformation of governance in the European Union*, London: Routledge, 249–66.

Imig, D. and Tarrow, S. (2001a) *Contentious Europeans. Protest and politics in an emerging polity*, Lanham, MD: Rowman & Littlefield.

—— (2001b) 'Studying contention in an emerging polity', in D. Imig and S. Tarrow (eds) *Contentious Europeans. Protest and politics in an emerging polity*, Lanham, MD: Rowman & Littlefield, 3–26.

—— (2001c) 'Mapping the Europeanization of contestation: evidence from a quantitative data analysis', in D. Imig and S. Tarrow (eds) *Contentious Europeans. Protest and politics in an emerging polity*, Lanham, MD: Rowman & Littlefield, 27–49.

Jachtenfuchs, M. and Kohler-Koch, B. (1996) 'Einleitung: Regieren im dynamischen Mehrebenensystem', in M. Jachtenfuchs and B. Kohler-Koch (eds) *Europäische Integration*, Opladen: Leske + Budrich, 15–44.

—— (2003) 'Regieren und Institutionenbildung', in M. Jachtenfuchs and B. Kohler-Koch (eds) *Europäische Integration*, Opladen: Leske + Budrich, 11–46.

Jordan, G. (1998) 'What drives associability at the European level? The limits of the utilitarian explanation', in J. Greenwood and M. Aspinwall (eds) *Collective action in the European Union. Interests and the new politics of associability*, London: Routledge, 31–62.

Jordan, G. and Maloney, W. (2001) 'Britain: change and continuity within the new realities of British politics', in C. S. Thomas (ed.) *Political parties and interest groups. Shaping democratic governance*, Boulder, CO: Lynne Rienner, 27–44.

Jordan, G. and Richardson, J. (1982) 'The British policy style or the logic of negotiation?', in J. Richardson (ed.) *Policy styles in Western Europe*, London: George Allen & Unwin, 80–110.

Judge, D. (1990) *Parliament and industry*, Aldershot: Dartmouth.

Kassim, H. (1994) 'Policy networks, networks and European policy-making: a sceptical view', *West European Politics*, 17(4): 15–27.

Kassim, H., Peters, B. G., and Wright, V. (eds) (2000) *The national co-ordination of EU policy. The domestic level*, Oxford: Oxford University Press.

Katzenstein, P. J. (ed.) (1978a) *Between power and plenty. Foreign economic policies of advanced industrial states*, Madison: The University of Wisconsin Press.

—— (1978b) 'Introduction: domestic and international forces and strategies of foreign economic policy', in P. J. Katzenstein (ed.) *Between power and plenty. Foreign economic policies of advanced industrial states*, Madison: The University of Wisconsin Press, 3–22.

—— (1978c) 'Conclusion: domestic structures and strategies of foreign economic policy', in P. J. Katzenstein (ed.) *Between power and plenty. Foreign economic policies of advanced industrial states*, Madison: The University of Wisconsin Press, 295–336.

—— (1985) *Small states in world markets*, Ithaca, NY: Cornell University Press.
—— (1987) *Policy and politics in West Germany. The growth of a semisovereign state*, Philadelphia, PA: Temple University Press.
—— (ed.) (1997) *Tamed power. Germany in Europe*, Ithaca, NY: Cornell University Press.
Keeler, J. T. S. (1988) *The politics of neocorporatism in France. Farmers, the state, and agricultural policy-making in the Fifth Republic*, Oxford: Oxford University Press.
Keohane, R. O. (1984) *After hegemony. Cooperation and discord in the world political economy*, Princeton, NJ: Princeton University Press.
Keohane, R. O. and Hoffmann, S. (1991) 'Institutional change in Europe in the 1980s', in R. O. Keohane and S. Hoffmann (eds) *The new European Community. Decisionmaking and institutional change*, Boulder, CO: Westview Press, 1–39.
Key, V. O. (1956) *American state politics. An introduction*, New York: Knopf.
King, G., Honaker, J., Joseph, A., and Scheve, K. (2001) 'Analyzing incomplete political science data: an alternative algorithm for multiple imputation', *American Political Science Review*, 95(1): 49–68.
Kitschelt, H., Lange, P., Marks, G., and Stephens J. D. (eds) (1999) *Continuity and change in contemporary capitalism*, Cambridge: Cambridge University Press.
Klein, A., Koopmans, R., Trenz, H. -J., Klein, L., Lahusen, C., and Rucht, D. (eds) (2003) *Bürgerschaft, Öffentlichkeit und Demokratie in Europa*, Opladen: Leske + Budrich.
Knill, C. (2001) 'Private governance across multiple arenas: European interest associations as interface actors', *Journal of European Public Policy*, 8(2): 227–46.
Knill, C. and Lehmkuhl, D. (1999) 'How Europe matters: different mechanisms of Europeanization', *European Integration online Papers* 3(7).
Knill, C. and Lenschow, A. (1998) 'Coping with Europe: the impact of British and German administrations on the implementation of EU environmental policy', *Journal of European Public Policy*, 5(4): 595–614.
Knoke, D. (1990) *Organizing for collective action. The political economies of associations*, New York: Aldine de Gruyter.
Kohler-Koch, Beate (1992) 'Interessen und Integration: Die Rolle organisierter Interessen im westeuropäischen Integrationsprozeß', in M. Kreile (ed.) *Die Integration Europas*, Opladen: Westdeutscher Verlag, 81–119. Politische Vierteljahresschrift Special Issue 23/1992.
—— (1993) 'Germany: fragmented but strong lobbying', in M. P. C. M. van Schendelen (ed.) *National public and private EC lobbying*, Aldershot: Dartmouth, 23–48.
—— (1997) 'Organized interests in the EC and the European Parliament' *European Integration online Papers* 1(9). Available: http://eiop.or.at/eiop/texte/1997-009a.htm (accessed February 2009) .
—— (ed.) (1998) *Interaktive Politik in Europa. Regionen im Netzwerk der Integration*, Opladen: Leske + Budrich.
—— (1999) 'The evolution and transformation of European governance', in B. Kohler-Koch and R. Eising (eds) *The transformation of governance in the European Union*, London: Routledge, 14–35.
—— (2000) 'Europäisierung: Plädoyer für eine Horizonterweiterung', in M. Knodt and B. Kohler-Koch (eds) *Deutschland zwischen Europäisierung und Selbstbehauptung*, Frankfurt a.M.: Campus, 11–31.
Kohler-Koch, B. and Eising, R. (eds) (1999) *The transformation of governance in the European Union*, London: Routledge.
Kohler-Koch, B., Brümmer R., Myrzik, B., and Platzer, H.W. (1988) *Wirtschaftsverbände als transnationale Akteure. Der Beitrag deutscher Verbände zum Management internationaler Interdependenz im Kontext der EG-Süderweiterung*, Darmstadt: DFG-Abschlußbericht.

Kotzian, P. (2003) *Verhandlungen im europäischen Arzneimittelsektor. Initiierung – Institutionalisierung – Ergebnisse*, Baden-Baden: Nomos.
Kratochwil, F. V. (1989) *Rules, norms, and decisions. On the conditions of practical and legal reasoning in international relations and domestic affairs*, Cambridge: Cambridge University Press.
Kreile, M. (1978) 'West Germany: The dynamics of expansion – foreign economic policies of advanced industrial states', in P. J. Katzenstein (ed.) *Between power and plenty. Foreign economic policies of advanced industrials states*, Madison: The University of Wisconsin Press, 191–223.
Kriesi, H. -D. (2000) 'Reflections on the Swiss case', paper presented at the workshop on 'The impact of Europeanization and globalization on national patterns of interest intermediation', Florence: European University Institute, 1–3 June.
Lahusen, C. (2002) 'Commercial consultancies in the European Union: the shape and structure of professional interest intermediation', *Journal of European Public Policy*, 9(5): 695–714.
—— (2003) 'Moving into the European orbit: commercial consultants in the European Union', *European Union Politics*, 4(2): 191–218.
Lahusen, C. and Jauß, C. (2001) *Lobbying als Beruf – Interessengruppen in der Europäischen Union*, Baden-Baden: Nomos.
Lane, C. (1992) 'European business systems: Britain and Germany compared', in R. Whitley (ed.) *European business systems. Firms and markets in their national contexts*, London: Sage, 64–97.
—— (1997) 'Trade associations and inter-firm relations in Britain and Germany', in R. J. Bennett (ed.) *Trade associations in Britain and Germany. Responding to internationalisation and the EU*, York: Anglo-German Foundation for the Study of Industrial Society, 23–32.
Le Conseil National du Patronat Francais (1997) Annuaire Officiel 1997, CIRNOV SA, Paris. Kap. 2, I Groupement Professionnels, A Industrie, B Prestataire de Services, C Commerce, Kap. 3, Adhérents Membres Associés.
Lehmbruch, G. (1977) 'Liberal corporatism and party government', *Comparative Political Studies*, 10(1): 91–126.
—— (1991) 'The organization of society, administration strategies, and policy networks: elements of a development theory of interest systems', in R. M. Czada and A. Windhoff-Héritier (eds) *Political choice. Institutions, rules, and the limits of rationality*, Frankfurt a.M.: Campus, 121–58.
Lehmkuhl, D. (2000) *The importance of small differences. The impact of European integration on road haulage associations in Germany and the Netherlands*, Amsterdam: Thela Thesis.
Lenschow, A. (2005) 'Europeanisation of public policy', in J. R. Richardson (ed.) *European Union. Power and policy-making*, New York: Routledge.
Liefmann, R. (1897) *Die Unternehmerverbände (Konventionen, Kartelle). Ihr Wesen und ihre Bedeutung*, Freiburg i. Br.: J.C.B. Mohr (Paul Siebeck).
Lijphart, A. (1975) 'The comparable cases strategy in comparative research', *Comparative Political Studies*, 8(2): 158–77.
—— (1999) *Patterns of democracy. Government forms and performance in thirty-six countries*, New Haven, CT: Yale University Press.
Lindberg, L. N. (1963) *The political dynamics of European economic integration*, Stanford, CT: Stanford University Press.
Lindberg, L. N. and Scheingold, S. A. (eds) (1971) *Regional integration. Theory and research*, Cambridge, MA: Harvard University Press.

Lindblom, C. E. (1977) *Politics and markets. The world's political-economic systems*, New York: Basic Books.

Long, J. S. and Freese, J. (1997) *Regression models for categorical dependent variables using Stata*, College Station, TX: Stata Press.

Lovecy, J. (1999) 'Governance transformation in professional services sector: a case of market integration "by the back door"?', in B. Kohler-Koch and R. Eising (eds) *The transformation of governance in the European Union*, London: Routledge, 135–52.

Lowery, D. (2007) 'Why do organized interests lobby? A multi-goal, multi-context theory of lobbying', *Polity*, 39(1): 29–54.

Lowery, D., Gray, V., and Fellowes, M. (2005) 'Sisyphus meets the Borg: economic scale and inequalities in interest representation', *Journal of Theoretical Politics*, 17(1): 41–74.

Lütz, S. (2002) *Der Staat und die Globalisierung von Finanzmärkten. Regulative Politik in Deutschland, Großbritannien und den USA*, Frankfurt a.M.: Campus.

MacLaughlin, A., Jordan, G., and Maloney, W. A. (1993) 'Corporate lobbying in the European Community', *Journal of Common Market Studies*, 31(2): 191–212.

Mahoney, C. (2004) 'The power of institutions: state and interest-group activity in the European Union', *European Union Politics*, 5(4): 441–66.

—— (2008) *Brussels versus the Beltway. Advocacy in the United States and the European Union*, Washington, DC: Georgetown University Press.

Maier, C. S. (1977) 'Coal and economic power in the Weimar Republic: the effects of the coal crisis of 1920', in H. Mommsen, Petzina, D., and Weisbrod, B. (eds) *Industrielles System und politische Entwicklung in der Weimarer Republik 2*, Düsseldorf: Droste, 530ff.

Majone, G. (1989) 'Regulating Europe: problems and prospects', in T. Ellwein *et al.* (ed.) *Jahrbuch zur Staats- und Verwaltungswissenschaft, Bd. 3*, Baden-Baden: Nomos, 159–77.

—— (1996) *Regulating Europe*, London: Routledge.

Mansbridge, J. (1990) *Beyond self-interest*, Chicago, IL: The University of Chicago Press.

March, J. G. and Olsen, J. P. (1989) *Rediscovering institutions. The organizational basis of politics*, New York: The Free Press.

Marks, G. and Hooghe, L. (2001) *Multi-level governance and European integration*, Lanham, MD: Rowman & Littlefield.

Marks, G. and McAdam, D. (1996) 'Social movements and the changing structure of political opportunity in the European Union', *West European Politics*, 19(2): 249–78.

Marks, G. and Steenbergen, M. (2002) 'Understanding political contestation in the European Union', in M. Steenbergen and G. Marks (eds) *Dimensions of contestation in the European Union, Comparative Political Studies. Special Issue*, 35(8): 879–92.

Marsh, D. (1983) 'Interest group activity and structural power: Lindblom's 'Politics and markets'', *West European Politics*, 6(2): 3–17.

Martin, A. and Ross, G. (1999) 'In the line of fire: the Europeanization of labor representation', in A. Martin and G. Ross *et al.* (eds) *The brave new world of European labor. European trade unions at the millennium*, New York: Berghahn, 312–67.

Mayntz, R. (1986) 'Corporate actors in public policy: changing perspectives in political analysis', *Norsk Statsvitenskapelig Tidsskrift*, 3: 7–25.

—— (1992) 'Modernisierung und die Logik von interorganisatorischen Netzwerken', *Journal für Sozialforschung*, 32(1): 19–32.

—— (1999) 'Multi-level governance: German federalism and the European Union', in C. Lankowski (ed.) *Governing beyond the nation state. Global public policy, regionalism, or going local?* Washington, DC: American Institute for Contemporary German Studies, 101–14. The Johns Hopkins University AICGS Research Report 11.

—— (2002) 'Zur Theoriefähigkeit makro-sozialer Analysen', in R. Mayntz (ed.) *Akteure – Mechanismen – Modelle. Zur Theoriefähigkeit makro-sozialer Analysen*, Frankfurt a.M.: Campus, 7–43.
Mayntz, R. and Scharpf, F. W. (1975) *Policy making in the German federal bureaucracy*, Amsterdam: Elsevier.
—— (eds) (1995) *Gesellschaftliche Selbstregulierung und politische Steuerung*, Frankfurt a.M.: Campus.
Mazey, S. and Richardson, J. R. (1993) 'Introduction: transference of power, decision rules, and rules of the game', in S. Mazey and J. R. Richardson (eds) *Lobbying in the European Community*, Oxford: Oxford University Press, 2–26.
—— (2001) 'Institutionalising promiscuity: Commission-interest group relations in the EU', in A. Stone-Sweet, W. Sandholtz, and N. Fligstein (eds) *The institutionalization of Europe*, Oxford: Oxford University Press, 71–93.
—— (2002) 'Pluralisme ouvert ou restreint? Les groupes d'interêt dans l'Union européenne', in R. Balme, D. Chabenet, and V. Wright (eds) *L'action collective en Europe/Collective action in Europe*, Paris: Presses de Science Po, 123–61.
Mény, Y. (1999) 'Interessengruppen in Frankreich: von Pluralismus keine Spur', in M. Christadler and H. Uterwedde (eds) *Länderbericht Frankreich. Geschichte – Politik – Wirtschaft – Gesellschaft*, Bonn: Bundeszentrale für politische Bildung, 348–62.
Meynaud, J. and Sidjanski, D. (1971) '*Les groupes de pression dans la Communauté Européenne, 1958–1968. Structure et action des organisations professionnelles*', Brussels: Université Libre, Institut de Sociologie.
Michalowitz, I. (2004) *EU Lobbying. Principals, agents and targets: Strategic interest intermediation in EU policy-making*, Münster: LIT-Verlag.
Moe, T. M. (1980) *The organization of interests. Incentives and internal dynamics of political interests groups*, Chicago, IL: Chicago University Press.
Moravcsik, A. (1998) *The choice for Europe. Social purpose and state power from Messina to Maastricht*, Ithaca, NY: Cornell University Press.
Nicolaïdis, K. and Howse, R. (eds) (2001) *The federal vision. Legitimacy and levels of governance in the United States and the European Union*, Oxford: Oxford University Press.
Norton, P. (1996) 'The UK: political conflict, parliamentary scrutiny', in P. Norton (ed.) *National parliament and the European Union*, London: Frank Cass, 92–109.
Oeckl, A. (ed.) (1997) *Taschenbuch des öffentlichen Lebens. Deutschland, 46. Jahrgang*, Bonn: Festland Verlag, Kap.: Wirtschaft I–XIV.
Offe, C. (1995) 'Some skeptical considerations on the malleability of representative institutions', in J. Cohen and J. Rogers (eds) *Associations and democracy*, London: Verso, 114–32.
Offe, C. and Wiesenthal, H. (1985) 'Two logics of collective action', in C. Offe (ed.) *Disorganized capitalism. Contemporary transformations of work and politics*, Cambridge: Polity Press, 170–220. First printed in: M. Zeitlin (ed.) *Political power and social theory* (1980), Greenwich, CT: JAI Press, 67–115.
Olsen, J. P. (1983) *Organized democracy. Political institutions in a welfare state – The case of Norway*. Oslo: Universitetsforlaget.
Olson, M. (1965) *The logic of collective action. Public goods and the theory of groups*, Cambridge: Harvard University Press.
Pennings, P., Keman, H., and Kleinnijenhuis, J. (1999) *Doing research in political science. An introduction to comparative methods and statistics*, London: Sage.
Pestoff, V. (2000) 'Europeanization and globalization of business interest associations: exit provides two or more voices, but implies no loyalty', paper presented at the workshop on 'The impact of Europeanization and globalization on national patterns of interest intermediation', Florence: European University Institute.

Peters, B. G. (1992) 'Bureaucratic politics and the institutions of the European Community', in A. M. Sbragia (ed.) *Europolitics. Institutions and policymaking in the "new" European Community*, Washington, DC: Brookings, 75–122.

Peterson, J. (2003) 'Policy networks', *Discussion Paper*, Institute of Advanced Studies, Vienna (90).

Pfeffer, J. and Salancik, G. R. (2003 [1978]) *The external control of organizations. A resource dependence perspective*, Stanford, CT: Stanford University Press.

Pijnenburg, B. (1998) 'EU lobbying by ad hoc coalitions: an exploratory case study', *Journal of European Public Policy*, 5(2): 303–21.

Platzer, H.-W. (1984) *Unternehmensverbände in der EG – ihre nationale und transnationale Organisation und Politik. Dargestellt am Beispiel des Bundesverbandes der Deutschen Industrie, der Bundesvereinigung der Deutschen Arbeitgeberverbände, der deutschen industriellen Branchenverbände und deren EG-Verbandszusammenschlüsse*. Kehl: Engel.

Pollack, M. A. (1997) 'Representing diffuse interests in the European Union', *Journal of European Public Policy*, 4(4): 572–90.

Putnam, R. D. (ed.) (2001) *Gesellschaft und Gemeinsinn. Sozialkapital im internationalen Vergleich*, Gütersloh: Verlag Bertelsmann Stiftung.

Quittkat, C. (2002) 'Les organisations professionelles françaises: Européanisation de l'intermediation des interest?', *Politique Européenne*, 7: 66–95.

Radaelli, C. M. (2003) 'The Europeanization of public policy', in K. Featherstone and C. M. Radaelli (eds) *The politics of Europeanization*, Oxford: Oxford University Press, 27–56.

Rhodes, R. A. W. (1997) *Understanding governance. Policy networks, governance, reflexivity and accountability*, Buckingham: Open University Press.

Richardson, J. R. (1993) 'Interest group behaviour in Britain: continuity and change', in J. R. Richardson (ed.) *Pressure groups*, Oxford: Oxford University Press, 86–99.

Risse, T., Cowles, M. G., and Caporaso, J. (2001) 'Europeanization and domestic change: introduction', in M. G. Cowles, J. Caporaso, and T. Risse (eds) *Transforming Europe. Europeanization and domestic change*, Ithaca, NY: Cornell University Press, 1–20.

Rizutto, F. (1996) 'The French parliament and the EU: loosening the constitutional straitjacket', in P. Norton (ed.) *National parliament and the European Union*, London: Frank Cass, 46–59.

Rucht, D. (2002) 'The EU as a target of political mobilisation: is there a Europeanisation of conflict?', in R. Balme, D. Chabenet, and V. Wright (eds) *L'action collective en Europe/Collective action in Europe*, Paris: Presses de Science Po, 163–94.

Rueschemeyer, D. (2003) 'Can one or a few cases yield theoretical gains?', in J. Mahoney and D. Rueschemeyer (eds) *Comparative historical analysis in the social sciences*, Cambridge: Cambridge University Press, 305–36.

Rueschemeyer, D. and Evans, P. B. (1985) 'The state and economic transformation: toward an analysis of the conditions underlying effective intervention', in P. B. Evans, D. Rueschemeyer, and T. Skocpol (eds) *Bringing the state back in*, Cambridge: Cambridge University Press, 44–77.

Saalfeld, T. (1996) 'The German houses of parliament and European integration', in P. Norton (ed.) *National parliament and the European Union*, London: Frank Cass, 12–34.

Salisbury, R. H. (1984) 'Interest representation: the dominance of institutions', *American Political Science Review*, 78(1): 64–77.

Sandholtz, W. (1992) *High-tech Europe. The politics of international cooperation*, Berkeley: University of California Press.

Sandholtz, W. and Zysman, J. (1989) (1992) 'Recasting the European bargain', *World Politics*, 42(1): 95–128.
Sartori, G. (1976) *Parties and party systems. A framework for analysis*, Cambridge: Cambridge University Press.
—— (1984) 'Guidelines for concept analysis', in G. Sartori (ed.) *Social science concepts. A systematic analysis*, Beverley Hills, CA: Sage, 15–85.
Saurugger, S. (2008) 'Interest groups and democracy in the European Union', *West European Politics*, 31(6): 1274–91.
Scharpf, F. W. (1997) *Games real actors play. Actor-centered institutionalism in policy research*, Boulder, CO: Westview Press.
—— (2000) 'Notes toward a theory of multi-level governing in Europe', *Max-Planck-Institute for the Study of Societies Discussion Paper* 00/5.
Schattschneider, E. E. (1960) *The semi-sovereign people. A realist's view of democracy*, New York: Holt, Reinhart and Winston.
Schmidt, V. A. (1996) *From state to market? The transformation of French business and government*, Cambridge: Cambridge University Press.
—— (1999) 'National patterns of governance under siege: the impact of European integration', in B. Kohler-Koch and R. Eising (eds) *The transformation of governance in the European Union*, London: Routledge, 155–72.
—— (2002) *The futures of European capitalism*, Oxford: Oxford University Press.
—— (2006) *Democracy in Europe. The EU and national polities*, Oxford: Oxford University Press.
Schmitter, P. C. (1979) 'Still the century of corporatism?', in P. C. Schmitter and G. Lehmbruch (eds) *Trends toward corporatist intermediation*, Beverly Hills, CA: Sage, 7–52.
Schmitter, P. C. and J. R. Grote (1997) 'The corporatist sisyphus: past, present and future', *European University Institute Working Paper SPS* (97/4).
Schmitter, P. C. and Lehmbruch, G. (eds) (1979) *Trends toward corporatist intermediation*, Beverly Hills, CA: Sage.
Schmitter, P. C. and Streeck, W. (1981) 'The organization of business interests: a research design to study the associative action of business in the advanced industrial societies of Western Europe', Berlin: *Wissenschaftszentrum Berlin. Discussion Paper IIM/LMP 81/13*.
—— (1991) 'From national corporatism to trans-national pluralism: organized interests in the Single European Market', *Politics and society*, 19(2): 133–64.
Schneider, V. (1992) 'Organized interests in the European telecommunications sector', in J. Greenwood, J. Grote, and K. Ronit (eds) *Organized interests and the European Community*, London: Sage, 42–68.
—— (2001) 'Institutional reform in telecommunications: the European Union in transnational policy diffusion', in M. G. Cowles, J. A. Caporaso, and T. Risse (eds) *Transforming Europe. Europeanization and domestic change*, Ithaca, NY: Cornell University Press, 60–78.
Schwaiger, K. and Kirchner, E. (1981) *Die Rolle der europäischen Interessenverbände. Eine Bestandsaufnahme der Europäischen Verbandswirklichkeit*, Baden-Baden: Nomos.
Sebaldt, M. (1997) *Organisierter Pluralismus. Kräftefeld, Selbstverständnis und politische Arbeit deutscher Interessengruppen*, Opladen: Westdeutscher Verlag.
Secretary of State for the Home Department (1998) *The compact on relations between government and the voluntary and community sector in England*, London: Stationery Office Books.

Shonfield, A. (1965) *Modern capitalism. The changing balance of public and private power*, Oxford: Oxford University Press.

Siaroff, A. (1999) 'Corporatism in 24 industrial democracies: meaning and measurement', *European Journal of Political Research*, 36(2): 175–205.

Sidenius, N. C. (1998) 'A collective action problem? Danish interest associations and Euro groups', in J. Greenwood and M. Aspinwall (eds) *Collective action in the European Union. Interests and the new politics of associability*, London: Routledge, 81–107.

—— (1999) 'Business, governance structures, and the EU: the case of Denmark', in B. Kohler-Koch and R. Eising (eds) *The transformation of governance in the European Union*, London: Routledge, 173–88.

Steinmo, S., Thelen, K., and Longstreth, F. (eds) (1992) *Structuring politics. Historical institutionalism in comparative analysis*, Cambridge: Cambridge University Press.

Streeck, Wolfgang (1989) 'Interest heterogenity and organizing capacity: two class logics of collective action', Discussion Paper WZB-Berlin. Reprinted in: Wolfgang Streeck: *Korporatismus in Deutschland*, Frankfurt a.M.: Campus 1999, 251–79.

—— (1999) *Korporatismus in Deutschland. Zwischen Nationalstaat und Europäischer Union*, Frankfurt a.M.: Campus.

Streeck, W. and Schmitter, P. C. (1991) 'From national corporatism to transnational pluralism: organized interests in the Single European Market', *Politics and Society*, 19(2): 133–64.

Tömmel, I. (2005) *Das politische System der EU*, Munich: Oldenbourg.

Trade Association Forum (1999) *Report of the 1999 benchmarking study of trade associations*, London: Trade Association Forum.

Truman, D. B. (1951) *The governmental process. Political interests and public opinion*, New York: A.A. Knopf. Reprinted by the Institute of Governmental Studies, University of California, Berkeley, 1993.

van der Klaauw, J. (1994) 'Amnesty lobbies for refugees', in R. H. Pedler and M. P. C. M. van Schendelen (eds) *Lobbying the European Union. Companies, trade associations and issue groups*, Aldershot: Dartmouth, 259–83.

van Schendelen, R. (2002) *Machiavelli in Brussels. The art of lobbying the EU*, Amsterdam: Amsterdam University Press.

van Waarden, F. (1991) 'Two logics of collective action? Business associations as distinct from trade unions: the problems of associations of organization', in D. Sadowski and O. Jacobi (eds) *Employers' associations in Europe. Policy and organisation*, Baden-Baden: Nomos, 51–84.

—— (1992) 'Dimensions and types of policy networks', in *European Journal of Political Research*, 21(1): 29–52.

—— (1994) 'Is European law a threat to associational governance?', in V. Eichener and H. Voelzkow (eds) *Europäische Integration und verbandliche Interessenvermittlung*, Marburg: Metropolis, 217–62.

Voelzkow, H. (2000) 'Korporatismus in Deutschland: Chancen, Risiken und Perspektiven', in E. Holtmann and H. Voelzkow (eds) *Zwischen Wettbewerbs- und Verhandlungsdemokratie. Analysen zum Regierungssystem der Bundesrepublik Deutschland*, Wiesbaden: Westdeutscher Verlag, 185–212.

Vogel, D. (1986) *National styles of regulation. Environmental policy in Great Britain and the United States*, Ithaca, NY: Cornell University Press.

—— (1987) 'Political science and the study of corporate power: a dissent from the new conventional wisdom', *British Journal of Political Science*, 17(4): 385–409.

Walker, J. (1991) *Mobilizing interest groups in America. Patrons, professions, and social movements*, Ann Arbor: The University of Michigan Press.

Wallace, H. (1996) 'Relations between the European Union and the British administration', in Y. Mény, P. Muller, and J.-L. Quermone (eds) *Adjusting to Europe. The impact of the European Union on national institutions and policies*, London: Routledge, 61–72.
—— (2005) 'An institutional anatomy and five policy modes', in H. Wallace, W. Wallace, and M. Pollack (eds) *Policy-making in the European Union*, Oxford: Oxford University Press, 5th edition, 49–89.
Warleigh, A. (2000) 'The hustle: citizenship practice, NGOs and "policy coalitions" in the European Union – the cases of Auto Oil, drinking water and unit pricing', *Journal of European Public Policy*, 7(2): 229–43.
—— (2001) '"Europeanizing" civil society: NGOs as agents of political socialization', *Journal of Common Market Studies*, 39(4): 619–39.
Wartenberg, L. von (2000) 'Industrieller Wandel in Deutschland, Globalisierung und Europäisierung – Herausforderungen für den BDI', in W. Bührer and E. Grande (eds) *Unternehmerverbände und Staat in Deutschland*, Baden-Baden: Nomos, 157–63.
Webster, R. (1998) 'Environmental collective action: stable patterns of cooperation and issue alliances at the European level', in J. Greenwood and M. Aspinwall (eds) *Collective action in the European Union. Interests and the new politics of associability*, London: Routledge, 176–95.
Wessels, B. (2004) 'Contestation potential of interest groups in the EU: emergence, structure, and political alliances', in G. Marks and M. R. Steenbergen (eds) *European integration and political conflict*, Cambridge: Cambridge University Press, 195–215.
Wessels, W. (1992) 'Staat und (westeuropäische) Integration. Die Fusionsthese', in M. Kreile (ed.) *Die Integration Europas*, Opladen: Westdeutscher Verlag, PVS-Special issue 23, 36–61.
Wiesenthal, H. (1996) 'Organized business interests as outcomes and agents of socio-economic transformation in East and East Central Europe', *Forschungsberichte AG TRAP Max-Planck-Gesellschaft AG Transformationsprozesse in den neuen Bundesländern* (7).
Williamson, O. E. (1985) *The economic institutions of capitalism. Firms, markets, relational contracting*, New York: The Free Press.
Wilson, F. L. (1987) *Interest-group politics in France*, Cambridge: Cambridge University Press.
—— (1993) 'France: group politics in a strong state', in C. S. Thomas (ed.) *First World interest groups. A comparative perspective*, Westport, CT: Greenwood, 113–25.
Wilson, G. K. (1990) *Interest groups*, London: Basil Blackwell.
Wilson, J. Q. (1973) *Political organizations*, New York: Basic Books.
—— (1980) 'The politics of regulation', in J. Q. Wilson (ed.) *The politics of regulation*, New York: Basic Books, 357–94.
Windolf, P. (2002) *Corporate networks in Europe and the United States*, Oxford: Oxford University Press.
Woll, C. (2006) 'Lobbying in the European Union: from *sui generis* to a comparative perspective', *Journal of European Public Policy*, 13(3): 456–69.
Young, A. R. (1997) 'Consumption without representation? Consumers in the Single Market', in H. Wallace and A. R. Young (eds) *Participation and policy-making in the European Union*, Oxford: Clarendon Press, 206–34.
Zysman, J. (1978) 'The French state in the international economy', in P. J. Katzenstein (ed.) *Between power and plenty. Foreign economic policies of advanced industrial states*, Madison: The University of Wisconsin Press, 255–93.

Index

Aberbach, J.D. 22
Abromeit, H. 17
access 6–12, 19, 33, 68, 73, 90–1, 98, 109–10; definition of 131; empirical analysis of 146–53, 164–75; and influence 137–9; and organizational resources 119; politics of 131–46; towards a theory of 5, 157–64
accession countries 756
actors: collective actors 23–6, 118; corporate actors 23–6, 123, 137, 148; Eurogroups as 65–8; at EU level 68–73
ad hoc coalitions 72–3
adaptation: adaptational capacity 118–24; EU adaptational pressure 103–18; extent of adaptional pressure 105–8
Adshead, M. 118
agriculture associations 62–3, 64, 118
alliances 10, 22–7, 72–3, 87; *see also* coalitions
Almond, G.A. 139
American interest group system 73
Amnesty International 139
analysis of variance (ANOVA) 41, 45–6, 53, 55, 71, 133–4, 135–6, 146–7, 149, 205–6
Andersen, Sven S. 16, 62, 90
Ansell, C. 17, 88, 90, 106
Appleton, A. 40
Armstrong, K. 27
Aspinwall, M. 17, 72, 81–2, 105, 161
Assemblée Nationale 112
Association for the Monetary Union of Europe 143
associations: behavioural assumptions 22–3, 160, 182; organizational autonomy 44, 49, 66–7, 160; functions of 54–7, 65–8; *see also* business interest associations; domestic associations; Eurogroups
Atkinson, M.M. 11, 148, 156
Auel, K. 112
Austria, institutional order 33
autonomy 21, 23–4, 27, 44, 49, 66–7, 88, 110, 160
Averyt, W.F. 16

Bacher, J. 94
Balme, R. 3, 9, 16, 19, 70, 73, 162
Baltz, K. 16
Bartle, I. 74
Bartolini, St. 3, 4, 89
Baumgartner, F.R. 18, 19, 73, 77
Baumheier, U. 67
behavioural assumptions, businesses 22–3
Belgium: Eurogroup membership 78, 79–80; institutional order 34; social pact 29
Bennett, R.J. 36, 41, 98
Benz, A. 17, 18, 88, 90, 112
Bernhagen, P. 172
Beyers, J. 3, 4, 73, 129, 138, 158
Beyme, K. von 110
Bischoff, I. 75, 76, 77
Blank, O. 27, 74
Blank, St 35, 36
Block, F. 21
Boleat, M. 28, 41
book plan 12–13
Borragán, N. 11
Börzel, T.A. 16
bounded rationality 23, 160
Bouwen, P. 7, 19, 129, 130, 131, 145, 154, 156, 157, 168, 173
Brendle, U. 71

Brümmer, R. 16
budgets 53, 56–8, 123–4, 179; and access 161, 166, 169–71, 173–4; *see also* financial resources; revenue sources
Bulmer, S.J. 27
Bundesrat 110
Bundestag 112, 114
Burkhardt-Reich, B. 16
business consultation 116–17
business interest associations (BIAs): as actors 22–6; clusters in multilevel governance 93–9; Europeanization and governance capacities 118–24; form and exchange goods 142–6; functions of 51–7; importance in EU 71–2; integration into EU 87–99; in multilevel governance 91–3; organizational structures 160–1; relations with EU institutions 149–53; revenue sources 51–4; towards theory of EU access 157–64; *see also* domestic associations; Eurogroups
Butt-Philipp, A. 88

Camerra-Rowe, P.G. 21, 24
capitalism: varieties of 11, 23, 31–40, 182; and national interest group systems 43–51; and functions and roles of domestic interest groups 51–7; and adaptation of domestic groups to the EU 108, 117
Caporaso, J.A. 4, 15, 16, 65, 103, 104
case studies 7–11; versus comparative studies 19–20
Cawson, A. 156
centralized power: France 39–40; Germany 37; UK 35
Chabanet, D. 3, 9, 16, 19, 70, 73, 162
change, drivers of 26–30
chemical industry 143
Chi-tests 41–55, 96, 100, 115–16, 125, 150–1, 153, 205–7
Chief Executive Officers (CEOs) 39, 143
Christian Democratic Union, Germany 38
Clark, P.B. 81
cluster analysis 86–7, 91, 93–9, 101
cluster membership: and governance capacities 118–24; and negotiation capacities 120–3; and organizational resources 123–4
coalitions 184; ad hoc 72–3; political 66–7

Coen, D. 16, 19, 20, 69, 123, 129, 139, 142, 143, 144
Cohen, E. 109
Coleman, W.D. 11, 28, 29, 148, 156
collective action 17, 74
collective actors 23–6, 118
collective incentives 81–2
Collignon, St. 144
commercial lobbyists 24
Commission of the European Communities 70
Committee of Permanent Representatives (Coreper) 141, 146–53, 164–75
Committee of the Regions (CoR) 89, 142, 146–53
committee presence 133–7
committees, contact with 164–75
Common Agricultural Policy (CAP) 64
common foreign and security policy (CFSP) 139
comparative politics 15
comparative studies versus case studies 19–20
competition, interest group systems 46–51
compliance, enforcement of 105
CONECCS database 8, 61–3, 65, 74–6, 79
consensus formation 90
Conservative Party, UK 36
Constantelos, J. 90
contact patterns, domestic 109–13
cooperation: ad hoc 72–3; BIAs 48–9; domestic interest groups 116, 144; interest group systems 46–51, 184; large firms 68; lobbying 100
coordinated market economy 32, 34–5; Germany as 37–8
coordinating devices 35–6
corporate actors 23–6, 123, 137, 148
corporatism: and access 157–8, 165–72; and adaptational pressure 106–8, 115–16; and contact initiatives of EU institutions 181; effect on Eurogroup membership 77–8, 79–80; Germany 38; and negotiation capacities 120–2; overview 32–4
Council of Ministers 145, 146–53, 164–75
Council of the European Union: access to 140–1, 145–53; contacts with 147, 164–5; contacts by cluster 101–2; functions of 88–9, 140–1; importance of 90–3

countervailing interests, cooperation with 49
Cowles, M.G. 4, 16, 17, 19, 37, 69, 74, 103, 104, 106, 107, 108, 120, 123, 129, 141, 143, 144, 157, 158, 177
Cram, L. 66
Crombez, Ch. 7, 130, 131
cross-sectoral organizations 42–3, 44, 45–6
Cullen, P.P. 72
Culpepper, P.D. 39
Czada, R.M. 5, 32
Czech Republic, membership of Eurogroups 75

data 7–11
Davignon, Etienne 143
De Bièvre, D. 29
degree of fit 103–5, 158; implications for national interest intermediation 105–18
delegated legislation 139–40
democracy: EU democratic deficit 16–17, 132; and interest groups 3, 14, 16–17, 33–5, 159
Denmark: institutional order 33, 34; social pact 28
Department of Trade and Industry (DTI), UK 36
diffuse/various interests associations 62–3, 64, 70–2, 73, 183
DiMaggio, P. 48, 74
direct membership organizations 43–6, 49, 160–1
Directorates-General (DGs) 140, 141
dispute resolution 120–3
division of labour: functional 48–9, 122; territorial 97; traditional 68; under stress 72–3, unsatisfactory 91, 144
domestic associations: access patterns 146–53, 157–8, 165–75; cluster membership 95–9; collective action 74; contacts with EU institutions 93–5, 143–5; domestic contacts 87–91, 109–13; importance of 71–2; institutional context 157–8; interest representation strategies 133–7; negotiation capacities 120–3; overview 18–19; relevance of 91–3; role in EU 68–73; state relations 35–40
'domestic encompassing interest' 145, 147, 154, 157
Döring, H. 112

Dür, A. 20
Dyson, K. 4, 37, 38, 157, 172

Eastern Europe, membership of Eurogroups 75–6
Ebbinghaus, B. 28, 29, 64
Economic and Monetary Union (EMU) 29, 63–4
Economic and Social Committee (ESC) 89, 132, 142
economic globalization: effects of 186; as source of change 26–30
economic information 131–2, 145–6
economic prosperity, effect on membership 77, 79–80
economic weight 159, 166, 172–3
economy size, effect on membership 76–7, 79–80
Eder, K. 17
Eichener, V. 17, 18, 61
Eising, R. 3, 4, 17, 19, 33, 48, 49, 66, 68, 73, 74, 88, 90, 98, 105, 106, 138, 139, 152
electoral parties, contacts 111–12
electricity supply sector 74, 98, 138
Eliassen, Kjell A. 16, 62, 90
elite pluralism 129, 143
empirical analysis, access 146–53, 164–75
empirical scope 3–7
enlargement 18, 32
environmental interest groups 71–3
Eriksen, E.O. 17
EU–15; Eurogroup membership 75–6
Eurogroups: access patterns 146–53, 157, 165–75; in agriculture 62–4, 118; cluster membership 95–9; contacts with EU institutions 93–5, 143–5; of diffuse and various interests 62–4, 70–3, 183; evolution of 62–5; explaining membership in 73–83; functions and roles as actors, fora and instruments 65–8; importance of 71–2; industry 62–4; integration into EU 87–99; interest representation strategies 133–7; organizational incentives and membership decision 80–3; overview 18–19; professions 62–4, 142; in services 62–4
EUROLOB dataset 7–9, 41, 61, 69–70, 72, 80, 82, 130, 148, 163

European Association of the Chemical Industry (CEFIC) 143, 197
European Atomic Energy Community (EURATOM) 63–4
European Centre of Enterprises with Public Participation and of Enterprises of General Economic Interest (CEEP) 67
European Commission: access to 132, 139–40, 142–4, 145; contacts 147, 164–75; contacts by cluster 101–2; functions of 88–90; importance of 91–3; social regulation by 68–9; *see also* CONECCS database
European Community (EC): access to 139–42, 143, 146–53; enlargement 32; environmental action programme 71; importance of 93
European Community for Steel and Coal (ECSC) 18, 63, 64, 65
European Council: access to 138, 139–41, 145, 146; functions of 89; importance of 93
European Court of Justice (ECJ) 141–2, 89
European Economic Community (EEC) 63–4
European Environmental Bureau (EEB) 71–3
European Federation of Pharmaceutical Industries and Associations (EFPIA) 67
European Group of Energy Distribution Companies and Organizations (GEODE) 138
European Grouping of the Electricity Supply Industry (EURELECTRIC) 74, 138
European Industry Federation (EIF) 67
European Information, Communications and Consumer Electronics Technology Industry Association (EICTA) 74
European Monetary Union (EMU) 29, 143
European Parliament: access to 138, 139–40, 145–53; contacts with 147, 164–75; contacts by cluster 101–2; functions of 90; importance of 90–3
European People's Party 140
European Public Affairs Directory (EurActiv) 205
European Roundtable of Industrialists 141, 143
European Socialists 140

European Strategic Programme for Research and Development in Information Technology (ESPRIT) 143
European Trade Union Confederation (ETUC) 64, 67
European Union institutions: access patterns 157–64; contacts with 93–5, 101–2; importance of 87–93; openness of 185–6; politics of access 131–46; relations with BIAs 149–53; relevance of 158, 163
European Union players cluster 12, 86, 91–2, 94–100, 120–5; *see also* cluster membership
European Union: Directives 68, 104; firms/national associations/consultants in 68–73; institutional context 139–42, 157–8; interest mediation modes 105–8; membership duration and Eurogroup membership 78, 79–80; perceptions of political authority in 91–3; player clusters 94–9; political consultants in 69–70; politics of access 131–46; towards theory of access 157–64
Europeanization: concept 103–5; and governance capacities of BIAs 118–24; studies 17–19
'Eurosclerosis' 64, 143
Evans, P.B. 21
Everitt, B.S. 94
exchange goods 142–6, 158–9

Fairbrass, J. 109
Falkner, G. 3, 16, 17, 67, 89, 105, 156
Federation of Germany Industry (BDI) 107
federations: and access 161, 166, 173–4; cooperation in 49; domain size 43–4; and vertical integration of interest group systems 43–6
Feld, W.J. 68, 142
Fellowes, M. 75, 80
financial resources: and access 119, 161, 173–4; cross-national differences 51–4; Eurogroups 81; *see also* budgets; revenue sources
Finland: institutional order 33; social pact 28
firms: access patterns 146–53; adaptation capacity 120–4; cluster membership 95–9; cooperation with 48, 50–1; domestic contact patterns 109–13; domestic

relations 35–40; EU level interactions 87–91; importance of 71–2; political behaviour of 20–6; role in EU 68–73
fora, Eurogroups as 65–8
foreign trade ratio, effect on membership in EU groups 77, 79–80
fragmentation, interest group systems 41–6
France: access patterns 146–53, 168–72; adaptation capacity 118–24; case study criteria 10–11; contact density 108–9; domestic contact patterns 109–13; importance of BIAs 71–2; institutional order 32–5, 107, 108; interest group system 40–57; interest representation strategies 133–7; national/EU contacts 93–5; negotiation capacities 119; social pact 29; state institutions/capitalism/ state–business relations 38–40, 113–18; survey rates of return 9
functions: and clusters of interest groups 120–2; EU institutions 89; Eurogroups 1, 14–15, 65–8, 82; national associations 14–15, 54–7, 108, 183

Geddes, A. 17
geographical coverage, Eurogroups 75–6
Germany: access patterns 146–53, 168–72; adaptation capacity 118–24; case study criteria 10–11; contact density 108–9; domestic contact patterns 109–13; importance of BIAs 71–2; institutional order 32–5, 107, 108; interest group system 40–57; interest representation strategies 133–7; membership of Eurogroups 75; national/EU contacts 93–5; negotiation capacities 119; social pact 29; state institutions/capitalism/ state–business relations 113–18; survey rates of return 9
globalization 26–30
Goetz, K.H. 4
governance: capacities of BIAs 118–24; contribution of BIAs 16–17; multilevel governance approach 6–7, 17–18, 88–91
government departments: contacts 109–11; information from 114
Grande, E. 16, 37, 88, 98, 107, 138, 143
Granovetter, M. 90
Grant, W. 36, 50, 143–4
Gray, V. 5, 75, 80

Graziano, P. 4
Greece: institutional order 33; social pact 29
Greenwood, J. 16, 17, 37, 65, 66, 67, 68, 81–2, 83, 98, 118, 161
Gross Domestic Product (GDP), effect on membership 77, 79–80
Grote, J.R. 26, 27, 28, 68, 160
Grove, J.W. 36
Guéguen, D. 84

Haas, E.B. 15, 63, 65, 66, 74, 87
Hall, P.A. 5, 11, 31–2, 34, 35, 40
Hancké, B. 39
Hartlapp, M. 105
Harvey, B. 70
Hassel, A. 27, 28, 29
Haverland, M. 105
Hayes-Renshaw, F. 90
Hayward, J. 36, 68, 111, 143
Heinelt, H. 16, 17
Hellmann, K.U. 17
Helm, D. 28
Héritier, A. 98, 105
Herring, Pendleton 22
Hey, C. 71
higher order organizations 42–3, 49–50, 57
highly internationalized sectors 27–8
Hix, S. 4, 112, 140
Hoffmann, S. 15, 64
Honaker, J. 164
Hooghe, L. 17, 18, 88, 89, 90, 93, 118, 129
Höpner, M. 27
horizontal fragmentation 41–3
House of Commons 112
Howse, R. 18
Hueglin, T.O. 129

ideational effects 28–30
Imig, D. 9, 16, 19, 73, 118, 162
incentives: 11, 25, 51; adaptation 106–7; collective 81–3; EU contact 139–42; Eurogroups 80–3; material 61, 81–3; selective 56, 61, 81–3; social 71–2
industry associations 62–3, 64
influence, EU policy-making 137–9
information: and access 158–9; access to 113–14; flows 108–9, 131–3, markets 120–3; technical 132, 145–6

Inglehart, R. 77
insider strategy 133–7, 161–4, 166, 174–5, 186
institutional contexts: and access 157–8, 163, 165–72; EU level 139–42, 157–8; Eurogroups 73–80; national associations 157–8
institutional form, BIAs 142–6
institutional relevance 158, 163, 166, 172–3
institutional segmentation 16; effects of 185–6
institutional theory 5
instruments, Eurogroups as 65–8
integration theories 87–95; and BIA clusters 95–9
integration, interest group systems 41–6
inter-organizational networks: emergence of 22; Eurogroups 73; France 39; Germany 37; UK 36–7
inter-organizational cooperation 47–51
interaction modes, EU institutions 90
interest group: definition 4–5
interest group systems: cooperation and competition in 46–51; cross-national differences/similarities 183; evolution at EU level 62–5; fragmentation and integration in 41–6; resources and function of interest groups 51–7
interest intermediation 16; implications of integration theories 87–99; questionnaire 8–9, 188–202; typological analysis 106–8
interest intermediation modes 11, 23, 51, 120–3, 157–8; concept 31–5; and empirical interactions 108–18; and national interest group systems 41–57; national 36–40, 105–18
interest organization: definition 4–5
interest representation: BIAs 54–7; as core task 120–3; professionalism of 72–3; specialization 161, 166; strategies for 133–7, 161–4, 166, 173–4
intergovernmentalism: and Europeanization 86, 89, 91–3, 97; liberal 87–8; overview 15
intermediary institutions 36
internal differentiation of interest organizations 23–4, 47, 65, 160
Internal Market Programme (IMP) 63, 64, 68, 138, 141, 143

internationalization 27–8, 159, 166, 172–3
intra-organizational cooperation 47–51
investment power 21
Ireland: institutional order 34; social pact 28
isomorphism 74
Italy: institutional order 33; social pact 28

Jabko, N. 19, 66, 138
Jachtenfuchs, M. 17, 88
Jauß, C. 65
Jordan, G. 19, 61, 68, 74, 84, 110
Jörges, C. 17
Joseph, A. 164
Judge, D. 112

Kassim, H. 10
Katzenstein, P.J. 11, 31, 35, 38, 39, 77, 90, 114
Keohane, R.O. 64, 134
Kerremans, B. 73
Kerver, D. 105
Key, V.O. 87
Keynesianism 28
King, G. 164
Kirchner, E.15, 17, 67
Klein, A. & L. 17
Knill, C. 66, 74, 88, 98, 103, 104, 105
Knoke, D. 119, 160, 161
Kohler-Koch, B. 4, 15, 16, 17, 31, 33, 65, 68, 73, 88, 90, 92, 106, 114, 118, 139, 140, 152, 177
König, T. 16
Koopmans, R. 17
Kotzian, P. 67
Kratchowil, F.V. 32
Kreile, M. 38
Kriesi, H.-D. 27
Kurdelbusch, M. 27

Labour Party, UK 36–7
Lahusen, C. 17, 19, 65, 69
Länder 110, 118
Lane, C. 36, 38, 41
Lang, A. 26, 27, 160
large firms: adaptation capacity 120–4; autonomy of 23–4; cluster membership 95–9; EU access 142–4; influence on EU policy-making 68–9; membership costs 25–6; responses to globalization 27
Leech, B. 18, 19, 73, 77

legal information 131
Lehmbruch, G. 18, 22, 31, 33, 44, 66, 156, 172
Lehmkuhl, D. 19, 104, 105
Leiber, S. 105
Lenschow, A. 103
liberal intergovernmentalism 87–8
liberal market economy (LME) 32, 34–5; UK as 35–7
licenses, issuance of 120–3
Liefmann, R. 26, 38, 77
Lijphart, A. 8, 106
Lindberg, L.N. 63, 65, 70
Lindblom, C.E. 20, 21, 159
Lisbon Treaty 132, 186
lobbying activities 24; cooperation in 100; instruments for 133–7; professionalization of 69–70, 72–3; timing of 114–15
Longstreth, F. 5, 32
Lovecy, J. 27, 141–2
Lowery, D. 5, 75, 80, 133, 139
Lütz, S. 35, 37

Maastricht Treaty 63–4
McAdam, D. 86, 139
MacLaughlin, A. 19, 68
Mahoney, C. 129, 133
Majone, G. 21, 131, 133
Maloney, W. 3, 4, 19, 68, 110
Malta, membership of Eurogroups 75
March, J.G. 5, 32
market changes, responses to 26–30
market coordination: business associations 54–7; as core task 120–3
market information provision 120–3
market structure 67, 65–8
markets, globalization of 26–8
Marks, G. 17, 18, 73, 86, 88, 89, 90, 93, 139
Marsh, D. 20, 21
Martin, A. 64, 67, 89
material incentives 81–3
Mayntz, R. 3, 19, 22, 23, 88, 109–10
Mazey, S. 4, 16, 90, 131, 132, 139, 140, 141, 144, 150–1, 152, 159
media mobilization 133–7
Mediterranean market economy 32, 34; France as 38–40

Members of Parliament (MPs) 111–12, 117
Members of the European Parliament (MEPs) 140, 145–53, 164
Membership: and access 160–1; in BIAs 23, 25–6; density 43–6, 159, 166, 172–3; of Eurogroups 73–83; of national BIAs 42–3
Membership subscriptions 52–4; *see also* revenue sources
Mény, Y. 40
mergers 74
methodology 7–11
Meynaud, J. 15, 68, 129–30, 131, 138, 139, 143, 144, 146, 159
Michalowitz, I. 19, 69
Mitchell, N. 172
mixed membership organizations 43–6, 49, 161, 166, 173–4
Moe, T.M. 23, 24
Moravcsik, A. 15, 88, 110
multi-layered system, interest groups 183–4
multilevel governance (MLG) 86, 87–8; cluster membership 95–9; clusters of BIAs in 93–5; impact on EU-level interactions 88–91; BIAs in 91–3, 184–5
multilevel governance approach 6–7, 17–18, 88–91
multilevel players cluster 12, 86, 91–2, 94–100, 120–5, 185; *see also* cluster membership
Myrzik, B. 16

national capitalism: France 38–40; Germany 37–8; UK 35–7
national governments/parliaments, importance of 93
national institutional orders 28–30, 31–5
national interest intermediation modes 105–18
national membership, Eurogroups 74–6
national modes, interest intermediation 105–18
national players cluster 12, 86, 91–2, 94–100, 120–2, 124, 185; *see also* cluster membership
national state–business relations 113–18
national trade/umbrella organizations, cooperation with 48

national-level interactions, numbers of 87–91
nationalistic strategy 133–7, 161–4, 174, 179
negotiation capacities 118–19; and cluster membership 120–3
neofunctionalism 15; and Europeanization 86, 87–8, 89, 91–3, 97
neoliberalism as source of change 26–30
Netherlands: institutional order 33, 34; social pact 27
network governance 106
Neyer, J. 17
NGOs: cooperation with 48–9; importance of 71–2
niche organizations cluster 12, 86, 94–100, 120–4; *see also* cluster membership
Nicolaïdis, K. 18
non-membership, opportunity costs 26
non-occupational groups 62–3, 64, 70–3, 183

occasional players cluster 12, 86, 94–100, 120–4; *see also* cluster membership
Offe, C. 9, 24, 26, 73
Olsen, J.P. 5, 9, 32, 182
Olson, M. 17, 23, 45, 47, 56, 61, 70, 76, 81, 82, 161
opportunity structures 27, 86, 106, 139, 142, 163
opportunity costs 26
ordered regression models 164–5
Organization for Economic Cooperation and Development (OECD), Economic Indicators 79
Organization for European Economic Cooperation (OEEC) 64, 74
organizational characteristics 5; and EU access 142–6; Eurogroups 66–7
organizational domain 23, 160–1; cross-sectoral 42–3, 44; of Eurogroups 63–7; sectoral 42–3, 44, 166, 173–4; size 42–3, 44; sub-sectoral 42, 44
organizational factors and access 173–4
organizational rationalization 27–8
organizational resources 118–19; and cluster membership 123–4

organizational segmentation 106
organizational structure, and access 160–1, 166, 173–4
organizational types 43–6, 49, 160–1
outsider strategy 133–7, 161–4, 166, 174–5, 186

parliamentary committees: contacts 111–12, 164; information from 114
parliamentary debates 117
parliamentary parties 140; contacts 111–12; information from 114
personal contacts 133–7
Pestoff, V. 27
Peters, B.G. 10, 139
Peterson, J. 16, 88, 106
Pfeffer, J. 5, 158
pharmaceutical industry 67
Pijnenburg, B. 72
Platzer, H.-W. 16, 66
pluralism: and access 157–8, 165–72; and adaptational pressure 106–8, 115–16; and contact intiatives of EU institutions 181; definitions of 107–8; UK 37; and negotiation capacities 102–2; overview 32–4
police and judicial cooperation 139
policy implementation: of EU law 98–9, 106; role of national associations 32–3, 108–9; *see also* policy-making cycle
policy information 108–9; and access 158–9; and resource dependency 131–3
policy networks, widening of 184
policy-making cycle, lobbying during 101–2, 114–15; *see also* cluster analysis
policy-making: EU process 107–8; influence on 137–9; and interest intermediation mode 33–4; role of Eurogroups 65–8; role of government departments 110; role of national associations 68–73, 108–9; role of national parliaments 112
political authority, EU 91–3
political behaviour, firms 22–6
political coalitions 24–5
political competencies, delegation of 66–7
political consultants 24; cooperation with 48; importance of 71–2; role in EU 68–73

political exchange 20–2; exchange goods 142–6, 158–9
political initiatives 115–18
political integration: effects of 184–5; interest group systems 41–6; theories of 87–99
political leadership, contacts 110–11, 164–75
political structures/practices, effect on membership 77–8
politics of access 131–46
Pollack, M.A. 17, 25, 49, 70, 126, 139
population size, effect on membership 75–6, 79–80
Portugal: membership of Eurogroups 75; social pact 29
position papers, tabling of 133–7
Powell, W.W. 48, 74
powers, Eurogroups 66–7
pragmatic bargaining 65
preliminary ruling procedure 141–2
professional associations 62–3
professional services liberalization 141–2
public administration, contacts 109–11
public affairs activities, professionalization of 143–4
public funding 52–4; *see also* revenue sources
public mobilization 133–7
Putnam, R.D. 22

questionnaires 8–9, 188–202
Quittkat, C. 4

rational choice 22–6, 160, 182
rationality 10, 49, 148, 175, 177; bounded rationality 23, 160, 182
Raunio, T. 112
refugee/asylum policy 139
regional associations 62–3
regional political authorities, importance of 93
regression analysis 78–80
regulation, interest intermediation 132
regulatory and standardization authorities 93
Rehder, B. 27
research agenda 186–7

resource dependency: and access 130–2, 158–9, 163, 166, 172–3; and policy information 131–3; and political exchange 20–2; theory 5
resources 51–7 and access 173–4; and cluster membership 123–4; organizational 118–19
revenue sources, BIAs 51–4
Rhodes, R.A.W. 22
Richardson, J.R. 4, 16, 37, 90, 92, 131, 132, 139, 140, 141, 144, 150–1, 152, 159
Risse, T. 4, 103, 104
Rizzutto, F. 111, 112
Rockman, B.A. 22
Ronit, K. 16, 67, 68
Ross, G. 64, 67, 89
Rucht, D. 9, 17
Rueschemeyer, D. 19, 21

Saalfeld, T. 112
Salancik, G.R. 5, 158
Salisbury, R.H. 23, 24, 25
Sandholtz, W. 15, 143
Sartori, G. 19, 41
Scharpf, F.W. 3, 23, 24–5, 88, 90, 109–10
Schattschneider, E.E. 32, 129
Scheve, K. 164
Schmidt, T. 17
Schmidt, V. 4, 16, 19, 31, 33, 37, 40, 41, 50, 107–8, 114, 120, 156, 157, 158, 177
Schmitter, P.C. 16, 20, 25, 26, 27, 28, 33, 41, 42, 44, 66, 118, 156, 160, 161
Schneider, G. 27
Schneider, V. 16, 17, 74
Schumann, W. 16
Schwaiger, K. 15, 17, 67
Schwarzer, D. 144
scientific evidence, tabling of 133–7
scientific institutes, cooperation with 48
sectoral domains 42–3, 44, 160, 166, 173–4
selective incentives 81–3
self-interest 22–3
service associations 62–3, 64
service provision 54–7; as core task 120–3; specialization in 161
services revenue 52–4
Shonfield, A. 22, 156

Siaroff, A. 33, 37, 41, 78
Sidenius, N.C. 19, 82
Sidjanski, D. 15, 68, 129–30, 131, 138, 139, 143, 144, 146, 159
Singh, N. 164
Single European Act (SEA) 91
small and medium-sized enterprises (SMEs): membership costs 25–6; reliance on BIAs 142; response to globalization 27–8; versus large firms 23
Social Dialogue 67, 89
social incentives 71–2
Social Market Economy, Germany 38
social pacts 28–9
social regulation 21, 68–9
socio-economic structures, Eurogroups 73–80
Soskice, D. 11, 31–2, 34, 35
Spain, social pact 29
specialization of services 161
state autonomy 21
state institutions: domestic contacts 105–18; France 38–40; Germany 37–8; UK 35–7; resource dependency 20–3
statism 32, 33, 106, 107, 108, 115–16; and access 165–72; and contact iniatives of EU institutions 181; France 40; Germany 38; and negotiation capacities 102–2; UK 37
Steenbergen, M. 73
Steinmo, S. 5, 32
strategic choices 133–7; and access 161–4, 166, 174–5; *see also* nationalistic strategy; insider strategy; outsider strategy
Streeck, W. 11, 16, 20, 25, 26, 27, 33, 42, 43, 44, 45, 47, 118, 156, 158, 160, 161
sub-sectoral organizations 42, 44
Sweden: institutional order 33; social pact 29

Tarrow, S. 9, 16, 19, 73, 118, 162
Taylor, R.C.R. 5, 32
technical factors, Eurogroup membership 73–4
technical information 132, 145–6
technologies, globalization of 26–8
telecommunications sector 74
territorial competencies, EU institutions 89
Thelen, K. 5, 32
theoretical scope 3–7
Tömmel, I. 18
Trade Association Forum (TAF), UK 36
trade unions: cooperation with 48–9; in ETUC 64; importance of 71–2
Transatlantic Business Dialogue (TABD) 107
Trenz, H.-J. 17
Trieb, O. 105
Truman, D.B. 26, 61, 73, 77, 119, 160

UK: access patterns 146–53, 168–72; adaptation capacity 118–24; case study criteria 10–11; contact density 108–9; domestic contact patterns 109–13; importance of BIAs 71–2; institutional order 32–5, 107, 108; interest group system 40–57; interest representation strategies 133–7; national/EU contacts 93–5; negotiation capacities 119; state institutions/capitalism/state–business relations 35–7, 113–18; survey rates of return 9; unilateral state action 29
unilateral action of firms 22
Union Internationale des Producteurs et Distributeurs d'Energie Electrique (UNIPEDE) 74
Union of Industrial and Employers' Confederations of Europe (UNICE) 66, 67, 74, 143
units of analysis/observation 104, 106–7

van der Klaauw, J. 139
van Waarden, F. 3, 28, 42, 44, 45, 55, 156
variance-seeking methods 41
vertical integration of interest group systems 43–6
veto power 159
Vink, M. 4
Visser, J. 64
Voelzkow, H. 11, 17, 18, 61
Vogel, D. 21, 159

Walker, J. 131, 133, 160, 184
Wallace, H. 90, 112, 140, 141

Warleigh, A. 17, 72
Wartenberg, L. von 28
Webster, R. 17, 65, 66, 98, 118
welfare state 21, 28–9, 36
Wessels, B. 18, 75, 76
Wiesenthal, H. 9, 11, 24, 26, 73
Wilson, F. 39, 114
Wilson, G. 11, 22, 36, 41, 111
Wilson, J. 21, 23, 25, 51, 52, 90, 119, 131, 133, 156, 157, 160, 161, 162, 184
Wilson, J.Q. 81
Windolf, P. 35, 36, 37, 39
working level contacts: domestic 110–11; EU level 141, 146–53, 164–75
Works Councils 68–9, 143
Wright, V. 9, 10, 16, 19, 70, 162

Young, A.R. 70

Zysman, J. 15, 39

eBooks – at www.eBookstore.tandf.co.uk

A library at your fingertips!

eBooks are electronic versions of printed books. You can store them on your PC/laptop or browse them online.

They have advantages for anyone needing rapid access to a wide variety of published, copyright information.

eBooks can help your research by enabling you to bookmark chapters, annotate text and use instant searches to find specific words or phrases. Several eBook files would fit on even a small laptop or PDA.

NEW: Save money by eSubscribing: cheap, online access to any eBook for as long as you need it.

Annual subscription packages

We now offer special low-cost bulk subscriptions to packages of eBooks in certain subject areas. These are available to libraries or to individuals.

For more information please contact webmaster.ebooks@tandf.co.uk

We're continually developing the eBook concept, so keep up to date by visiting the website.

www.eBookstore.tandf.co.uk